BLOODY DELICIOUS!

BLOODY DELICIOUS!

A LIFE WITH FOOD

JOAN CAMPBELL

WITH
CATHERINE HANGER

A Sue Hines Book
Allen & Unwin

First published in 1997

A Sue Hines Book
Allen & Unwin Pty Ltd
9 Atchison Street
St Leonards, NSW 2065 Australia
Phone: (61 2) 9901 4088
Fax: (61 2) 9906 2218
E-mail: frontdesk@allen-unwin.com.au
URL: http://www.allen-unwin.com.au

National Library of Australia
Cataloguing-in-Publication entry:
Campbell, Joan.
Bloody delicious! : a life with food.

Includes index.
ISBN 1 86448 349 0.

1. Campbell, Joan. 2. Food writers – Australia – Biography.
3. Cookery. I. Title.
641.092

Designed by Cheryl Collins
Typeset by J&M Typesetting
Produced in Australia by the Australian Book Connection
Bound by M&M Binders

10 9 8 7 6 5 4 3 2 1

Disclaimer:
The recipes in this book were collected over a long period of time.
Every effort has been made to contact copyright holders: the author and publisher
would be grateful to be notified of any omissions.

vi   ACKNOWLEDGEMENTS

vii   AUTHOR'S NOTE

ix   PREFACE BY LEO SCHOFIELD

1   EARLY MEMORIES

31   ON THE BEACH

49   COUNTRY LIFE

97   COOKING CLASSES

123   CATERING DAYS

163   MAGAZINES

197   POSTCARDS

239   CONVERSIONS

240   GENERAL INDEX

242   INDEX OF RECIPES

ACKNOWLEDGEMENTS

Thank you, James Woolhouse, for your help in
organising the business side of all things to
do with the book. I simply could not
have done this without you.

My Editor on *Vogue Entertaining* and now
a Director of Condé Nast Australia,
Sharyn Storrier Lyneham, became so sick and
tired of hearing my description of food as being
'bloody delicious!' that she suggested it would be
a good title for a book! Thank you, Sharyn, for
suggesting this book should be written and
for organising all things that made it happen.

AUTHOR'S NOTE

If you live long enough, you get well
known, let's face it.

The way I keep in touch with a lot of my
history is through food. I remember the events
and the people and parties and places
through the dishes I've prepared or eaten.

I've called myself a bush cook, and I've frequently
said that I admire simplicity, but apart from that
I don't think I have a style at all. I just move with the
times, or do what my editor asks me to do. I don't
really have a favourite food or way of doing things;
the most important thing to me is just to cook
a good dish or a good meal and have everyone
say it's delicious.

It's been hard work, but I've enjoyed it.

This book gives you a bit of my history and
some of the recipes I've especially liked
eating or cooking.

Joan Campbell

PREFACE

Sydney 1977. The 'more-food-than-plate' movement is in full juggernaut mode and the two words on the lips of the city's foodies, this writer included, are '*nouvelle*' and '*cuisine*'.

Imagine, then, the shock of going to a party and discovering not nano-nibbles, filaments of finger food, but an old-fashioned buffet, a table bowed by the weight of a glazed ham, whacking great platters of chook, tubs of salad, upon which the guests, malnourished on things 'nouvelle', descended like Goth and Vandal. It was a rare case of truth triumphing over fashion.

The twin begetters of this splendid feast were Joan Campbell and her partner in a catering business, Consuelo Guinness. It was on this occasion that I asked (and I have never been allowed to forget it) 'Who's Joan Campbell?'.

Over the intervening two decades, I have grown to know Joan well and to love her dearly. Her food is a metaphor for her personality, defiantly true, embarrassingly generous.

Her sway at *Vogue* placed her in a unique position to promote the sort of food and the chefs she really believed in. And her position of power, never abused, allowed her to pronounce without fear or favour. She would describe anonymous chicken in some hazy cream sauce as 'chicken sick'. Some dishes were dismissed as 'muck'. This was preferable to 'filth'. Her frankness was, and is, simultaneously disarming and charming.

I once described her as the mother of all foodies. She is truly that, and there are few in the food game in Australia who are not, in some way or another, in her debt.

Leo Schofield

EARLY MEMORIES

I was born in Brisbane and I had a very strict Presbyterian upbringing. My mother was from Elgin, of Scottish parents called Grigor who had come to Sydney, Australia, when she was a small child. My grandfather, her father, was what they called then a shipping chemist, which really meant he imported chemicals and sold them wholesale. My uncle, my mother's brother, William Ernest Grigor, was a Macquarie Street specialist who obtained his degree at Edinburgh University and was decorated during World War I for finding a cure for venereal disease. He was a Lieutenant-Colonel, officer commanding the Australian Hospital at Bulford on the Salisbury Plains in England. I always found him a charming and amusing person.

My father was third-generation Australian, born in Brisbane, where he ran the family ironmongery business, housed in Brisbane's tallest building – eight storeys – in Albert Street, called Perry House and now a building of smart apartments. My father used to tell me the building was insured for one million pounds! I was very close to his mother, my grandmother Leila Perry. She was very proud of the fact that I, her granddaughter, was a descendant of Alice Keppel, the Hon. Mrs George Keppel, who was King Edward VII's 'favourite'. My grandmother (they were her side of the family) vowed I resembled Mrs Keppel strongly, and strangely enough, I think I did. Apparently my grandmother was famous for the glamorous dinner parties she gave and I have a newspaper cutting that says, 'Mrs Herbert Perry's Literary Ball'.

ANGELS ON HORSEBACK

These were served at my great-grandmother's and grandmother's dinner parties as a first course. Other first courses included Turtle Soup (obviously made from a tin), Braised Sweetbreads and Chicken Paté. I still have the menu with these dishes from my grandmother's Silver Wedding.

fresh oysters
very thinly sliced bacon rashers, rinds removed and
    bacon cut in small pieces
cayenne pepper
butter

To serve
hot toast

Place one or two oysters on each slice of bacon. Sprinkle with a little cayenne, then roll up and skewer with a toothpick. Heat a little butter in a frying pan and fry the rolls until the bacon is cooked.

To serve
Carefully remove the toothpicks and serve three or four rolls on hot toast.

ANGELS' FOOD

Served at early dinner parties as a dessert, probably with passionfruit, which grew in profusion on every fence.

(Serves 6 to 8)

2 tablespoons gelatine, dissolved in a little warm water
1.25 litres milk
$\frac{1}{2}$ cup sugar
3 to 4 egg yolks, beaten
juice of 1 to 2 lemons
3 to 4 egg whites, beaten until stiff
vanilla extract
sherry

To serve
whipped cream
chopped and sweetened strawberries or passionfruit

Add the gelatine to a third of the milk and stir until combined. Bring the rest of the milk to the boil, add the gelatine mixture and the sugar and cook, stirring, until the sugar is dissolved. Remove from the heat and pour a little of the hot milk onto the egg yolks, whisking to mix. Gradually stir the egg mixture back into the milk, taking care that it does not curdle.

Pour the mixture into a bowl, add the lemon juice to taste and set aside to cool, stirring occasionally until the mixture begins to set. Fold in the beaten egg whites, adding vanilla and sherry to taste.

Transfer the mixture to a suitable mould that has been rinsed in cold water. Cover and chill in the refrigerator for 2 hours or until set.

To serve

Turn out onto a platter and serve with a spoonful of whipped cream and either strawberries or passionfruit.

GRANDMOTHER PERRY'S BAKED CARAMEL CUSTARD

*This was made by the cooks in my grandmother's kitchen in an attempt to rectify the damage done by Nanny Vine with her lumpy egg custard. I **still** do not like eggs!*

(Serves 6)

100 g sugar
60 g butter
3 cups lukewarm milk
4 eggs, beaten

Preheat the oven to 180°C. In a large saucepan, make a caramel with the sugar and butter. Remove from the stove and pour on the milk. The mixture will bubble and rise to the top of the pot. Stir until the caramel is melted.

Add the mixture to the beaten eggs and mix well. Pour into an oven dish and cook in a bain-marie in the preheated oven for 30 to 35 minutes or until the custard is set.

Grandmother Perry died while I was very young, from complications following an operation, and I think it affected me deeply because I was very attached to her. My mother was away a lot, and I have letters that I wrote to my mother as a little girl, just missing her. My grandmother was very sweet to me. The house she and my grandfather lived in, Miegunyah in Jordan Terrace at Bowen Hills, was built on the hill and another house for my great-aunt and her family was built across the road. At the bottom of the road was the cow paddock, now a bowling club and called Perry Park. Miegunyah is now a National Trust property and one can go through it and still see my grandmother's name cut into the glass in her bedroom window with a diamond. We lived there with her while my brother was being born, and when my father was away at the war. I can actually remember him going off to France as a Lieutenant, it made such an impact on me. I have an image of us careering along in an open-topped car chasing the train. I was about two, and sitting on my mother's knee. My father's brother, Uncle Herbert, was at the wheel.

The Perry great-grandparents also lived in a house which still exists and now belongs to the National Trust. It is Newstead Park, at Breakfast Creek. However, during the great floods of the late 1800s Great-grandfather Perry decided it was too dangerous to live there any more, so, accompanied by the Aborigines who lived around the house and garden, they moved up to the top of the nearest hill and bought another house and lived there. It was called Folkestone. I never saw this house on the hill because, just before I arrived in the world, one of the cousins played with matches and the house was burned to the ground. All that remained was broken glass and china and a beautiful Italian garden fountain which had been acquired on one of their many trips overseas.

My parents met next to the Blowhole at Kiama, south of Sydney. My father drove his mother down for a holiday – he was the first person to drive his car over the Blue Mountains down to Sydney from Brisbane, it was reported in all the papers – and my mother was in Kiama holidaying there with her mother. They were introduced, right next to the Blowhole, by a mutual friend, and that was that. My mother was always slightly embarrassed by the story.

I only discovered after my mother died that she was a year older than my father. She was the most beautiful thing you've ever seen in your life.

My mother called me Johnny, because she wanted a boy. I was actually christened Joan: Joan Constance Harcourt Perry. I was the first-born and 'Harcourt' was a family name.

When I was a child we had servants to do the cooking and nannying and everything else. My mother did cook, but only on the cook's day off or when we went to the family house on the beach at Surfers Paradise. My mother cooked very well, mostly braises and grills and marvellous cakes and biscuits. I adored her curried rabbit and she cooked delicious oxtail, and liver and bacon, and cutlets baked in the oven instead of frying them. I remember her making many cakes and puddings such as baked roly poly, flummery, and Cape gooseberry jelly from the wild fruit growing on the patch of ground next to the house, then in Palm Avenue, Ascot, Brisbane. She also liked to make pickles and chutneys.

My mother's mother, Grandmother Grigor, introduced me to haddock and oatcakes. She would come to Brisbane and stay with us sometimes when my mother was on one of her many holidays in Sydney, but I never did learn how she made this dish.

BARLEY BROTH
(Serves 4 to 6)

Stock
3 litres cold water
2 kg lamb bones
2 carrots, cut in chunks
2 onions, peeled and cut in chunks
stick of celery, sliced
1 parsnip, cut in chunks
salt and pepper to taste

Soup
1 carrot, peeled and diced
1 onion, peeled and diced
stick of celery, diced
1 parsnip, peeled and diced
$\frac{1}{2}$ cup barley
a little chopped parsley

To make the stock
Fill a large pot with cold water and bring to the boil with the lamb bones, carrots, onions, celery, parsnip and salt and pepper. Simmer gently until the meat has fallen from the bones and the stock has plenty of flavour, about 2 to 3 hours.

Strain the stock into a large bowl and discard the bones, meat and vegetables. Allow the stock to cool, then cover and place in the refrigerator. When the fat has set, remove it and transfer the stock to a pot. You should have 2 litres of stock.

To make the soup
Bring the stock to the boil, add the diced vegetables and barley, cover and simmer until the barley is cooked. Taste for salt and pepper, before serving. Serve the soup in hot bowls, sprinkled with a little chopped parsley.

DEVILLED STEAK

A recipe we loved during our school days. It would be served with a salad or a green vegetable and lots of mashed potatoes.

a large porterhouse or rump steak 2.5 cm thick
juice of 1 lemon

Marinade
2 tablespoons brown sugar
2 teaspoons any dark jam
1 tablespoon Worcestershire sauce
2 tablespoons tomato sauce
2 tablespoons vinegar
salt and pepper to taste

To finish
a little butter

Lightly score both sides of the steak. Squeeze the lemon juice on both sides, then place in a dish.

Mix all the marinade ingredients together, then pour over the steak in the dish, pressing the marinade well into each side of the meat with a wooden spoon. Marinate for 2 hours, turning a few times. Drain the steak and keep the marinade.

Grill the steak on both sides. When it is cooked, heat the remaining marinade, adding a little butter. Pour over the steak and serve at once.

BABY CHEESE SCONES
2 cups self-raising flour
¼ teaspoon mustard powder
pinch of salt
generous pinch of cayenne pepper
30 g butter
75 g grated sharp cheese
1 beaten egg
½ cup milk

Preheat the oven to 200°C. Sift together the flour, mustard, salt and cayenne. Rub in the butter so the mixture resembles breadcrumbs. Add the cheese, then moisten the mixture with the egg and milk beaten together. Be careful that the dough is neither too dry nor too wet. It may be necessary to add a little more milk. Roll the dough out on a floured surface and cut with a bite-sized round biscuit cutter.

Brush the tops of the scones with a little milk and place on a greased biscuit tray. Bake on the centre shelf of the preheated oven for 10 minutes. Allow to cool on the tray and when completely cool, pack away in an airtight container.

Before serving, carefully reheat the scones in a 150°C oven, then split and butter generously. Serve from a warm platter.

BAKED ROLY POLY WITH BOILED CUSTARD
This was a very popular winter pudding for the family. To flavour the custard, you can use the pure vanilla extract that we are able to get today, instead of the vanilla bean. The extract should be added to the custard after it is cooked.

(Serves 4)

Boiled custard
500 ml milk
1 vanilla bean
6 egg yolks
½ cup sugar

Roly poly
1½ cups self-raising flour
pinch of salt
125 g butter
1½ tablespoons iced water
apricot jam

Syrup
1 cup water
½ cup sugar

To serve
cream

To make the custard
Bring the milk to the boil with the vanilla bean. Remove from the heat and allow to stand for at least 1 hour.

Beat the yolks and sugar together well. Bring the milk to the boil again and remove the vanilla bean. Pour a little milk on the yolk mixture and whisk well. Return the mixture to the hot milk and cook over low heat, stirring with a wooden spoon, until the mixture coats the back of the spoon. Strain at once into a bowl, allow to cool, then chill.

To make the roly poly
Preheat the oven to 190°C. Mix the flour, salt and butter with your fingers or in a food processor until the mixture resembles fine breadcrumbs. Add the iced water and mix to a stiff dough. Roll out to a long rectangle about 5 mm thick. Spread liberally with apricot jam and roll up. Place the roll in a deep casserole dish.

Bring the water and sugar to the boil and pour the boiling syrup over the roll. Bake on the centre shelf of the preheated oven for 45 minutes. The roll will spread and some sauce will form at the sides. Serve sliced, with custard and cream.

SAGO PLUM PUDDING
(Serves 6)

4 tablespoons sago
1¾ cups milk
1 cup fresh breadcrumbs
½ cup raisins
½ cup sultanas
¼ cup mixed peel
20 g butter
1 cup sugar
1 teaspoon mixed spice
1 teaspoon bicarbonate of soda

To serve
cream and boiled custard

Soak the sago in ³⁄₄ cup milk in a basin for 2 hours. Add the breadcrumbs, raisins, sultanas, mixed peel, butter, sugar and spice. Dissolve the bicarbonate of soda in the remaining milk and add to the sago mixture. Pour into a greased pudding bowl. Cover the bowl, place in a steamer and steam, covered, for 4 hours.

To serve
Turn the pudding out onto a serving plate and serve hot with cream and boiled custard.

QUEEN'S SOUFFLÉ

A special dinner party pudding. This soufflé is made a good eight hours before the dinner.

(Serves 8)

Soufflé
butter and castor sugar to line the mould
8 egg whites
good pinch of salt
185 g castor sugar

Custard
1 litre milk
8 egg yolks, beaten
3 tablespoons sugar
¹⁄₂ teaspoon vanilla extract

Caramel
1 cup sugar
1¹⁄₂ tablespoons water

To serve
6 ripe passionfruit sweetened with a little sugar

To make the soufflé
Butter and sugar a 2-litre charlotte mould or a straight-sided metal basin and preheat the oven to 180°C. Beat the egg whites with salt until they form soft peaks. Gradually add the sugar and continue beating until the mixture holds stiff peaks. Spoon the mixture carefully into the mould and smooth the top lightly with the back of a spoon.

Place the mould containing the soufflé mixture in a baking tin, add boiling water to the tin, and bake on the bottom shelf of the preheated oven for 40 minutes. Remove the mould from the water and allow the soufflé to cool: it will probably shrink a little. Refrigerate, uncovered.

To make the custard

Bring the milk to the boil. Beat the egg yolks with the sugar. Pour a little boiling milk onto the yolks, and whisk. Pour the mixture back into the saucepan and stir over low heat with a wooden spoon until the custard coats the back of the spoon. Strain into a bowl and beat in the vanilla extract. Allow to cool, then cover and refrigerate. One to two hours before serving, turn the soufflé out onto a deep dish and pour the custard around.

To make the caramel

Bring the sugar and water to the boil, stirring just until the sugar is dissolved. Boil slowly until the caramel is a light brown. Pour the caramel immediately over the top of the soufflé. Return the soufflé to the refrigerator and chill for 1 to 2 hours.

To serve

Just before serving, remove the soufflé from the refrigerator and spoon the pulp from the passionfruit over the soufflé.

To serve, crack the toffeed caramel and cut the soufflé into slices. Spoon the custard into individual shallow bowls and place on it a slice of soufflé with some of the toffee and passionfruit.

BREAD AND BUTTER PUDDING

These days they make this pudding with various toppings. Anton Mosimann in London is famous for his pudding with a brioche top.

(Serves 6)

5 eggs
4 tablespoons sugar
1 litre milk, warmed but not boiled
1 teaspoon vanilla extract
3 tablespoons raisins
3 or 4 slices white bread
soft butter
castor sugar
ground cinnamon

Preheat the oven to 190°C. Beat the eggs with the sugar until pale and frothy. Add the milk and vanilla. Pour into an oven dish and sprinkle in the raisins. Butter the bread and cover the top of the custard (the bread will probably sink).

Place the dish in a baking tin filled 2.5 cm deep with boiling water and bake in the preheated oven. When the bread forms a crust on top of the pudding, sprinkle with castor sugar and cinnamon and continue cooking until the custard is set and the top is golden. Serve lukewarm or cold.

CREAMY RICE PUDDING
(Serves 6)

3 tablespoons rice
4 tablespoons sugar
$1/2$ teaspoon ground nutmeg
1 litre milk
1 tablespoon butter

Preheat the oven to 160°C. Place the rice in a baking dish with the sugar and nutmeg. Pour in the milk and stir until the sugar is dissolved. Add the butter.

Bake in the preheated oven, stirring a few times until the butter melts and a skin forms on the milk. Cook for $1^{1}/2$ hours, until the pudding is creamy and the top is golden. Serve warm.

CARAMEL BANANAS
(Serves 6)

6 large bananas
1 cup brown sugar
3 tablespoons cream
40 g butter
$1/2$ teaspoon vanilla extract

To serve
300 ml thickened cream
vanilla extract

Peel the bananas and slice in halves lengthwise. Place, cut side down, in a china or glass serving dish. Place the brown sugar, cream and the butter in a saucepan and cook over low heat for about 5 minutes, or until the mixture thickens slightly. Remove from the heat, stir in the vanilla and pour the mixture over the bananas. Allow to cool, and refrigerate for at least 2 to 3 hours.

To serve
Whip the cream with a little vanilla to taste and spoon it over the bananas. This can be refrigerated for a further 2 to 3 hours before serving.

PICKLED PEACHES
Good to eat with baked ham.

1.5 kg small peaches
$1^{1}/2$ cups vinegar
3 cups sugar
1 stick cinnamon
$1/2$ teaspoon whole cloves

Blanch the peaches in boiling water and, when cool enough to handle, peel off the skins. Put the vinegar, sugar, cinnamon stick and cloves in a saucepan and boil for 10 minutes. Drop in the peaches, a few at a time, and cook until tender.

Transfer the peaches, as they are cooked, to warm, clean jars. Fill the jars with the hot syrup and seal immediately. Store for a week before using.

MANGO CHUTNEY

We would always have this in cold lamb sandwiches and with curry. In those days, curry was always made to use up left-over meat, with raisins added. We thought it very tasty!

12 green mangoes
250 g raisins
250 g stoned dates, chopped
250 g preserved ginger, chopped
500 g white sugar
500 g brown sugar
1 x 750 ml bottle vinegar
60 g garlic, peeled and chopped finely
2 teaspoons salt
1/8 cup red chillies

Peel the mangoes, cut the flesh into small pieces and place in a large bowl. Cut the remaining fruit into small pieces and add to the mangoes. Sprinkle with the white sugar, cover and leave overnight.

The next day put the brown sugar and half the vinegar in a large preserving pan and bring to the boil. Add the fruit mixture, garlic and salt to the hot syrup. Slice some of the chillies, tie the remainder in a piece of muslin and add to the pan. (My mother suggested tying the chillies in mosquito net!) Cook, stirring occasionally, until the mixture begins to thicken, then add the rest of the vinegar by degrees, as the mixture thickens. Simmer, stirring more frequently, until the mixture is thick and the fruit tender. Remove the chillies in muslin, and bottle the mixture, just before it cools, in clean jars.

ROSELLA JAM

Rosellas grew wild on the same land as the Cape gooseberries.

Remove the red fleshy leaf-like sepals from the rosella calyxes (the hard part in the centre) and set aside. Place the remaining calyxes in a saucepan with enough water to cover and bring to the boil. Cook until they are soft. (This is where the jelly comes from.)

Strain the juice and discard the solids. Measure the juice and return it to the saucepan. For each 600 ml of juice, add 500 g sugar. Weigh the reserved sepals and measure out an equal amount of sugar. Set the sugar aside and add the sepals to the saucepan.

Bring the mixture to the boil and cook for 30 minutes, or until the sepals are well cooked. Add the reserved sugar and boil until a teaspoon of the syrup gels when placed on a cold plate. Allow the jam to cool a little, then pour into clean, warm jars and seal.

GRAPEFRUIT JAM

Weigh the grapefruit, then cut into very fine slices. For every 500 g fruit, add 2 litres of water. Let stand overnight, then bring to the boil. As soon as the fruit boils, take out 5 cups of the water and add 5 cups of fresh water (this helps to reduce the bitterness). Continue to cook and, when the fruit is soft, weigh the pulp and add 500 g sugar for each 500 g grapefruit. Return the mixture to the boil and cook until a teaspoon of the syrup gels when placed on a cold plate. Allow to cool a little, then pour into clean, warm jars and seal.

There are only a few of us left, I suppose, who can remember 'When Mabel Laid the Table' (the title of my friend Warren Fahey's book). My mother had a housemaid, a Mabel who laid and waited on the table, but her name was Katie. She arrived by ship from Scotland with hair as black as coal, cheeks like shining red apples and a broad Scottish accent. Katie seemed to be with us for a great deal of our childhood. I would watch her making jams, jellies and pickles and such delights as tripe and onions, pig's head brawn, boiled mutton and caper sauce, and the best bread sauce to go with roasted stuffed chicken.

MISS AMY SCHAUER'S GOOD PIG'S CHEEK AND VEAL OR BEEF BRAWN

'Miss' Schauer, as she was called, was a great name in food in Brisbane for as long as I can remember and, if I do remember, she cooked biscuits and cakes for people. I also remember the trotters and pig's cheek and sheep's tongues were pink, so they must have been 'corned'.

3 pig's trotters, cut in half
1/2 fresh pig's cheek
1 knuckle of veal
750 g shin of beef
3 sheep's tongues
1 tablespoon salt
1/4 teaspoon cayenne pepper
1 blade mace
2 bay leaves
2 cloves
6 allspice berries
12 peppercorns

Wash the pig's trotters and soak in cold water for 30 minutes. Thoroughly wash the pig's cheek. Drain the trotters, wash well under cold running water and put into a large saucepan with the pig's cheek, veal knuckle, shin of beef, sheep's tongues, salt and cayenne. Tie the remaining spices in a small piece of muslin and add to the pan. Add just enough cold water to cover, and place the lid tightly on the saucepan. Bring to the boil and simmer for 3 to 4 hours or until the meat is tender.

Transfer the meats to a large dish. Skin the tongues. Remove all the meat remaining on the bones and discard the bones. Quickly cut all the meat into cubes. Put the meats into a large basin, season to taste with salt and cayenne.

Boil the liquor in the saucepan over high heat for 10 minutes. Take $1/2$ cup of the boiling liquor and pour over the meat in the basin. Pack the mixture tightly into wet moulds, cover and place weights on top, and refrigerate overnight. Turn out onto a platter to serve.

BOILED LEG OF LAMB AND CAPER SAUCE
(Serves 4 to 6)

1 leg of lamb, weighing about 1.5 kg (ask the butcher to
    leave the shank attached)
2 large onions, peeled and quartered
stick of celery
2 carrots, peeled and cut in chunks
1 clove of garlic
salt and pepper

Caper sauce
175 g butter
3 tablespoons plain flour
salt and pepper to taste
$2^1/2$ cups boiling milk
4 tablespoons capers, rinsed, drained and coarsely
    chopped

To serve
boiled potatoes and a green vegetable

Put the lamb leg in a large boiler and add the onion, celery, carrots and garlic with plenty of salt and a grind of pepper. Add water to cover the leg and put on the lid. Bring to the boil and simmer gently for $1^1/2$ hours or until the meat is cooked. While the meat is cooking, make the sauce.

To make caper sauce
Melt the butter and add the flour, salt and pepper. Cook the mixture a little, then remove from the stove and, beating with a whisk, add the milk all at once. Return the saucepan to the stove and, still beating, bring the sauce to the boil and simmer for a few minutes. Add the capers and taste for salt and pepper.

To serve

Carve the meat in slices, ladle the caper sauce over each individual serving and serve with a green vegetable and boiled potatoes.

SUNDAY ROAST CHICKEN WITH BREAD SAUCE AND GRAVY

(Serves 4)

Stuffing

125 g butter
1 onion, peeled and chopped finely
2 tablespoons chopped parsley
small pinch of dried herbs
2 cups firmly packed, fresh white breadcrumbs
salt and pepper

Chicken

1 onion, peeled and chopped
1 x No.16 chicken
250 g butter, melted
salt and pepper

Gravy

1 tablespoon plain flour
$1^1/2$ cups chicken stock (a little more if necessary)
salt and pepper

To serve

bread sauce (recipe follows)
roasted potatoes and a green vegetable

To make the stuffing

Melt the butter in a frying pan and gently cook the onion until it softens. Remove from the stove and add the parsley, herbs, breadcrumbs, and salt and pepper to taste.

To prepare and cook the chicken

Preheat the oven to 190°C. Put the chopped onion in the centre of a baking tin. Remove and discard the fat from the inside of the chicken and dry cavity with paper towels. Fill the cavity with the stuffing and secure with poultry pins. Pin the neck flap back and tie the legs together with string. Place the chicken on the bed of onion and pour over the melted butter. (Besides giving flavour to the chicken, the onion browns and gives colour to the chicken and the gravy.) Sprinkle the chicken skin with salt and pepper.

Roast the chicken on the centre shelf of the oven, basting from time to time, for 1 to $1^1/4$ hours, or until cooked. If the chicken is browning too quickly, put a small piece of foil loosely over the top. When the chicken is cooked, turn off the oven, stand the chicken on a platter and keep warm in the turned-off oven while you make the gravy. Pour off the fat and remove any burnt bits of onion from the baking tin, leaving the juices from the chicken.

To make the gravy

Mix the flour with the pan juices and add the chicken stock. Place the baking tin over medium heat on the stove top and cook the gravy, whisking well as the liquid boils and thickens. Taste for seasoning.

To serve

Carve the chicken and serve with the stuffing, gravy, bread sauce, some roasted potatoes and a green vegetable.

BREAD SAUCE

100 g white bread (crusts removed), cut into cubes
5 cloves
1 onion, peeled
250 ml milk (a little more if necessary)
60 g butter
good pinch of ground nutmeg
salt and white pepper to taste

Put the bread cubes in a heavy saucepan. Poke the cloves into the onion and push the onion well down into the bread. Pour in the milk and add the butter, nutmeg, salt and pepper.

Simmer very slowly, being careful not to let the sauce burn. (If you have a simmer pad, put it under the saucepan.) As the bread swells it may be necessary to add a little more milk. Taste, and when the sauce has plenty of flavour, remove the onion and cloves and beat the sauce. Correct the seasoning and add a little more milk and butter if the sauce is too thick. Serve hot with the chicken.

My mother said she really learnt to cook during the Depression, although before that she used to give strict instructions to the cooks on how to prepare food. She was just a natural, she taught herself. Like me: I never actually learnt to cook. Like her, I just did it. I remember my father telling a story about my mother making him a first cup of tea. When she poured it out, a long piece of straw came out as well because she hadn't known to rinse the new teapot.

I remember we had a sort of food safe which is where my mother put the Sunday puddings when they were made. One day, when I was a very little girl, I took to swinging on the door of the safe and it fell over, depositing me and the puddings in a dreadful mess. I was in big trouble for that.

These are the sort of puddings that would have fallen out of the tipped-over safe.

PINEAPPLE FLUMMERY

(Serves 6)

skin and core of 1 large pineapple, chopped
2 cups water
$\frac{1}{2}$ cup sugar
1 tablespoon gelatine
juice of 1 lemon
1 tablespoon plain flour, mixed with a little water

Place the pineapple skin and core in a saucepan with the water and sugar, and simmer gently for 25 to 30 minutes.

Strain and discard the solids and return the syrup to the saucepan. Add the gelatine to the hot pineapple syrup and dissolve. Add the lemon juice and the flour mixture. Return the saucepan to the heat, boil the mixture for 3 minutes, then set aside and allow to cool.

Beat the mixture until it is white and foamy. Pour into a clean bowl, cover and chill. This is good served with pouring cream.

CAPE GOOSEBERRY JELLY

(Serves 6)

2 cups water
1 cup castor sugar
2 cups Cape gooseberries, after the husks are removed
2 tablespoons gelatine, dissolved in $\frac{1}{4}$ cup hot water
vegetable oil for the moulds

Bring the water and castor sugar to the boil, then turn the heat to low and add the Cape gooseberries. Cook over low heat until the berries are just cooked. (A few of them will burst, but the seeds look pretty in the jelly.) Add the dissolved gelatine and stir gently to mix.

Lightly oil six one-cup moulds with the vegetable oil and ladle in equal amounts of the mixture. Allow to cool and refrigerate for 5 to 6 hours, or until the jelly is firmly set.

To serve, unmould on individual plates and serve with pouring cream.

LEMON MOUSSE

We used to eat this with slices of fresh mango.

(Serves 6)

6 eggs, separated
$^1/_2$ cup sugar
juice of 2 lemons
finely grated rind of $1^1/_2$ lemons
1 tablespoon gelatine, dissolved in 4 tablespoons water
2 tablespoons white Curaçao
pinch of cream of tartar
150 ml cream, whipped

Beat the egg yolks with the sugar. Add the lemon juice and rind, and cook in a saucepan over medium heat, stirring constantly, until the mixture starts to thicken and coats the back of a spoon.

Add the gelatine and Curaçao. Pour into a bowl and leave to cool but not set. Beat the egg whites with the cream of tartar until stiff peaks form. Add the whipped cream to the lemon mixture, then fold in the egg whites, using a metal spoon. Cover and refrigerate until set.

My father always had a plentiful garden that furnished the household with fruit and vegetables including chokoes, which we only ever ate tiny and whole like baby squash. There were tomatoes, including egg and cherry tomatoes; pawpaws and custard apples; lemons, grapefruit and mangoes and persimmons; and the then-rather-exotic mignonette lettuce, grown from seeds given to us by our American neighbours, the Dobells. I remember those lettuces had hard hearts. My mother would cut them into quarters and just before serving would pour a dressing over them which was probably made of something like condensed milk! In those days we had not yet heard of tossed salad with oil and vinegar. I remember a man used to come with the milk container to deliver the milk, and people came to the back door to sell prawns – they were as small as your little finger and I learnt to peel prawns at a very young age, because they weren't peeled and I loved eating them – and buckets of tiny pineapples and large passionfruit. The only way you could buy chooks was to order them from these back-door providores. They always gave us the cleaned heart, liver, gizzards and feet. We had giblet soup made from these pieces, which were also chopped up into the soup.

Our diet was never very varied, but it was very wholesome and delicious: meats prepared in all the old-fashioned ways, roast chook, and always beautifully prepared vegetables. My mother taught me to cook vegetables and I continue to cook them in this fashion to this day: never overcooked, and always in boiling salted water, not steamed. I never steam a vegetable. I think they're the most tasteless, awful things. And they're tough and not properly cooked. I've always put them in boiling salted water. If they're properly cooked like that, they're tasty and they keep their nutrition.

One of my other important early memories of food is attached to my mother's great friend, our neighbour Gladys (Glad) Dobell. Mrs Dobell was American, and I used to walk across the street to watch her cooking things like Glad's Yum Yum Cake (a boiled chocolate cake with raisins, which later became one of my important catering cakes), Southern Fried Chicken with Milk Gravy, and a Baked Ham – a dish that she taught me and that has become my own – made in those days with sliced, cooked pineapple, brown sugar, pineapple juice and a dash of sherry. Mrs Dobell also taught me how to cut up a chicken to make Southern Fried Chicken, and how to make Angel Food Cake iced with chocolate or strawberry icing, and Devil's Food Cake.

I think it is due to Mrs Dobell's early input that, when I started cooking, it had a slightly American influence. I was only about eight or nine when I encountered Mrs Dobell. I remember she introduced me to avocado, a strange fruit she brought back with her on the ship from America, and I thought it was absolutely disgusting. I like avocados now, but I like them with a bit of texture, not too soft.

MRS DOBELL'S SOUTHERN FRIED CHICKEN WITH MILK GRAVY AND CORN CAKES
(Serves 4)

2 x No.12 chickens
1 cup flour
1 teaspoon salt
$\frac{1}{2}$ teaspoon freshly ground pepper
100 g butter, melted
100 ml vegetable oil

Milk gravy
flour left from coating the chicken pieces
500 ml milk
salt and freshly ground pepper

Corn cakes
1 cup fresh corn kernels
2 eggs, beaten
$^1/_3$ cup self-raising flour
$^1/_2$ teaspoon salt
pinch of ground nutmeg
butter for frying

Cut the wing tips from the chickens. Cut off the wings and legs and divide the legs into 2 pieces (drumsticks and thighs). Cut the breasts, with their bones, from the carcasses and cut each breast into 2 pieces. (Reserve the carcasses for making stock on another occasion or, for people who like to 'pick their bones', cut the carcass into 4 large pieces, dust with flour and fry in the pan.)

Place the prepared chicken pieces in a colander and sprinkle with a little cold water. Just before cooking the chicken, combine the flour, salt and pepper and coat each piece of chicken. Reserve any remaining flour mixture to make the milk gravy.

Heat the butter and the oil in a large frying pan and add the chicken in a single layer, skin-side down. Fry until golden brown, turning the chicken only once, then cover the pan. The breasts will be cooked first, so remove them from the pan and set aside in a warm place. The wings will be ready next, followed by the legs, then the thighs. Drain the pieces on kitchen paper and set aside with the breasts.

To make the milk gravy
Pour off the excess fat from the pan, leaving about 1 tablespoon for the gravy. Add 2 tablespoons of the reserved seasoned flour, and mix well. Whisk in 3/4 of the milk and cook over medium heat, stirring with a wooden spoon until you have a good creamy gravy. If it is too thick, add more milk and taste for salt and pepper. Traditionally, you do not strain this sauce.

To make the corn cakes
Combine the corn with the eggs, then stir in the flour, salt and nutmeg. Stir well to eliminate any lumps. Heat the butter in a frying pan and fry spoonfuls of the mixture, turning once, until the cakes are golden on both sides. Serve at once with the fried chicken and milk gravy.

A green salad served with this makes a really delicious meal.

BAKED HAM

This makes a really good Sunday lunch served to hungry people with a large bowl of green salad and hot baby potatoes tossed with melted butter and chopped parsley.

(Serves 12)

1 cooked leg ham
1 x 440 g can pineapple juice
$1/4$ cup sherry
500 g brown sugar
prepared mustard
powdered cloves

Preheat the oven to 150°C. Put the pineapple juice, sherry and brown sugar in a saucepan and cook to a syrup.

Carefully remove the skin from the ham and rub in the prepared mustard to colour the fat a pale yellow. Dust with powdered cloves.

Place the ham in a large baking tin and pour the syrup around the ham, not over the top. Cook on the bottom shelf of the oven for 30 minutes, then basting frequently with the syrup, cook for a further 60 minutes. Serve hot or cold.

ANGEL FOOD CAKE

whites of 8 x 60 g eggs
pinch of salt
1 teaspoon cream of tartar
$1^{1}/4$ cups castor sugar
$3/4$ teaspoon vanilla extract
$1/4$ teaspoon almond essence
1 cup plain flour (after sifting)

Strawberry icing

5 to 6 strawberries, well mashed
350 g icing sugar, sifted
40 g soft butter
pinch of salt

Preheat the oven to 170°C. Beat the egg whites with salt and cream of tartar until they hold stiff peaks. (Do not overbeat or the mixture will be too dry.) Gradually fold in the sugar with a large metal spoon, about 2 tablespoons at a time. Fold in the vanilla extract and almond essence. Carefully fold in the flour, sifting $1/4$ cup at a time over the surface.

Spoon the mixture into an ungreased angel-food cake tin and bake in the centre shelf of the oven for 45 minutes. Remove from the oven, invert the can and balance it on an upturned jar for about 1 hour or until the cake is cold (this will make it easier to remove the cake from the tin).

To make the icing
Put the strawberries, icing sugar, butter and salt in a bowl and beat with an electric beater. Add a little milk if necessary (the strawberries will moisten the icing as it stands). Ice the cake on a serving platter as it is soft and may crack when moved.

MRS DOBELL'S LEMON MERINGUE PIE
(Serves 6 to 8)

Pastry
1½ cups plain flour
2 tablespoons icing sugar
pinch of salt
125 g hard, unsalted butter, cut in dice
1 small egg, beaten

Filling
1 cup sugar
½ cup cornflour
⅛ teaspoon salt
2 cups water
4 egg yolks, beaten
60 g butter
⅓ cup lemon juice
3 tablespoons grated lemon rind

Meringue
4 egg whites
pinch of cream of tartar
120 g castor sugar
¼ teaspoon vanilla extract

To make the pastry
Preheat the oven to 190°C. Place all the dry ingredients and the butter in a food processor and process until the mixture resembles breadcrumbs. Add the egg and process until the mixture forms a mass. Wrap the dough in plastic wrap and refrigerate for 1 hour. Roll out the dough on a floured board and line a 23-cm round pie dish.

Prick the pie shell well with a fork and cook on the centre shelf of the preheated oven for 25 to 30 minutes until brown and crisp. Place the pie dish on a cake rack to allow the pastry to cool.

To make the filling
Mix together the sugar, cornflour and salt in a saucepan. Gradually add the water and whisk until the cornflour is dissolved. Bring the mixture to the boil, stirring occasionally, and simmer for 10 minutes. Pour a little of the hot mixture onto the egg yolks, mix well, then pour the mixture back into the saucepan. Cook, stirring constantly, for 5 minutes.

Remove the pan from the heat and beat in the butter, lemon juice and rind. Pour the mixture into a bowl and allow to cool to lukewarm, stirring occasionally to prevent a skin forming. Pour the filling into the cold pie shell.

To make the meringue

Preheat the oven to 180°C. Beat the egg whites with the cream of tartar until they hold soft peaks. Gradually add the sugar and beat until the mixture holds stiff peaks. Beat in the vanilla extract. Pile the meringue on top of the lemon filling, spreading well over the pastry to seal and prevent the meringue shrinking from the edges. Cook in the preheated oven for about 10 minutes to brown the surface.

Allow to cool, then cut in slices to serve with vanilla ice-cream or thick cream.

GLAD'S YUM YUM CAKE
(Makes 8 to 10 slices)

$1^1/_2$ cups water
1 cup raisins
250 g butter
1 cup sugar
$^1/_2$ teaspoon ground cinnamon
$^1/_2$ teaspoon ground cloves
3 heaped tablespoons good cocoa
$^1/_4$ teaspoon salt
1 teaspoon bicarbonate of soda
1 teaspoon vanilla extract
2 cups plain flour

Chocolate icing
150 g good-quality dark chocolate
150 ml cream
30 g butter

Preheat the oven to 180°C. Put all the ingredients, except the bicarbonate of soda, vanilla and flour, in a large saucepan and bring to the boil. Cook for 5 minutes, then set aside to cool.

Dissolve the bicarbonate of soda in a little warm water and add to the cooked mixture with the vanilla. Sift in the flour and beat the mixture together with a wooden spoon until well amalgamated. Pour the mixture into a ring tin, well greased with vegetable oil, and cook in the oven for 45 minutes. Turn out onto a cake rack to cool.

To ice the cake

Melt the ingredients together in a saucepan over low heat until the chocolate is melted. Mix together until smooth, then allow to cool a little. Pour the chocolate mixture over the cake and spread with a knife.

MRS DOBELL'S PINEAPPLE UPSIDE-DOWN CAKE
(Serves 8)

125 g butter
2 cups brown sugar
1 x 825 g can pineapple rings
walnut halves

Butter sponge
125 g butter
1 cup castor sugar
2 eggs
$1^{1}/_{2}$ cups sifted self-raising flour
$^{1}/_{4}$ cup juice from the canned pineapple

To serve
whipped cream or thick cream

Melt the butter in a 25 cm short-handled, cast-iron pan that will fit in the oven. Remove from the heat. Sprinkle evenly with the brown sugar. Drain the pineapple rings and reserve the juice. Arrange the pineapple rings on the brown sugar and fill the spaces with walnuts.

To make the butter sponge
Preheat the oven to 190°C. Beat the butter and sugar to a cream, then beat in the eggs, one at a time, until the mixture is thick and fluffy. Fold in the sifted flour alternately with the pineapple juice. Pour the sponge mixture over the pineapple rings and bake on the centre shelf of the preheated oven for about 1 hour. Set aside to cool.

To serve
Turn the cake out onto a platter and serve with whipped or thick cream as a special pudding. This is also good on a buffet table.

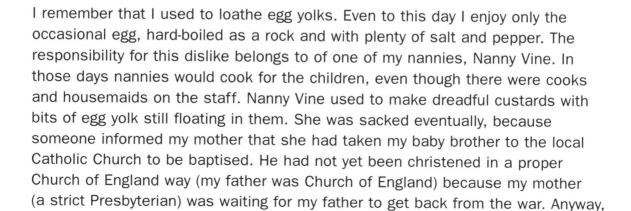

I remember that I used to loathe egg yolks. Even to this day I enjoy only the occasional egg, hard-boiled as a rock and with plenty of salt and pepper. The responsibility for this dislike belongs to of one of my nannies, Nanny Vine. In those days nannies would cook for the children, even though there were cooks and housemaids on the staff. Nanny Vine used to make dreadful custards with bits of egg yolk still floating in them. She was sacked eventually, because someone informed my mother that she had taken my baby brother to the local Catholic Church to be baptised. He had not yet been christened in a proper Church of England way (my father was Church of England) because my mother (a strict Presbyterian) was waiting for my father to get back from the war. Anyway, my mother was appalled and that was the end of Nanny Vine. I think she was already under a cloud because I told on her about meeting a *boy* in the park. She must have been a curious sort of woman because I remember she also took us to the local Chinese joss-house on one of our excursions, to see what it was like. I was very pleased when she went because it meant that I no longer had to eat the dreadful custards.

My parents were very fussy about manners and etiquette. We used to sit at table for all meals, even when we were very small. We had to use table napkins and, of course, were not allowed to call them 'serviettes'. My mother once told me a story about etiquette. At the ripe age of eighteen she was dining at the German Consulate in Sydney and was seated at the right hand of the Consul himself. All proceeded well until dessert. She helped herself to one dessert and then along came dessert number two. So she took a small spoonful of this also. To her eternal horror, no one else at the table had both desserts. It ruined her evening and, she swore, her life. Apparently she was in love with a German at that dinner, who, she would tell, completely lost interest in her because of her *greed*. Later, I heard that this man went back to Germany where he supposedly became the Red Baron, famous for shooting down British and Australian airmen!

I remember my family entertained a lot, and my mother played endless bridge and golf. There seemed to be many cocktail parties and dinner parties. Of course, at their cocktail parties they served genuine cocktails, well shaken and presented in cocktail glasses graced either with a cherry or an olive. I learnt the things I later did for drinks parties in my catering days from the sort of food my mother served then. She taught me to make really good sandwiches, for example and, in those days, endless bits on toothpicks.

I went to boarding school in Toowoomba in my teenage years, returning home for the holidays. The school was called Glennie Memorial. I went back there about six or seven years ago for a visit and they couldn't even find me in the records, although I was there for three years and I was a pro-prefect and got to be quite respectable. I was not a great scholar, but I did win a prize for baking a cake. I can't remember what it was, that cake, probably a simple butter cake from my mother's recipe. The other things I loved were sport, particularly tennis and swimming (I got my certificate for lifesaving), and I had a great passion for acting. I took the lead in all the school plays. I have an early photograph of myself as the lead role in *The Prince Who Was a Piper*. Otherwise, I spent much of my time staring out of the windows at boys in trains going back to university in Sydney.

MY MOTHER'S PLAIN BUTTER SPONGE

My mother made this as her basic cake, and so did I. It is also the cake we used for a trifle. Buttered, sprinkled with cinnamon and castor sugar, it makes a fresh plain cake. Add grated orange peel and ice with orange icing. Add sultanas and candied peel, dust with flour, and it becomes a light fruit cake. Cut into small blocks, iced with chocolate and rolled in coconut, it is a lamington.

Make it round, square, oblong or in a ring tin. It will be your basic cake, too.

125 g butter
1 cup sugar
2 eggs
1½ cups sifted self-raising flour
pinch of salt
½ cup milk

Preheat the oven to 190°C. Beat the butter and sugar together until light and fluffy. Add the eggs, one at a time, then fold in the sifted flour and salt alternately with the milk, beating with a wooden spoon.

Spoon the mixture into a buttered and floured 23 cm cake tin and bake in the preheated oven for 30 to 35 minutes. Turn out onto a cake rack to cool.

At school we had absolutely no cooking classes of any kind. Apart from my moment of glory with the cake, the only food memories I have of school are of morning and afternoon teas, which were served to us with Cocky's Joy – bread soaked in golden syrup. It was disgusting, but we all loved it. I still love golden syrup.

I left school at seventeen. We weren't really allowed to do anything, except 'come out' as a debutante. I used to do a fair amount of tapestry and sewing, hand-sewing that is. My mother was an exquisite seamstress, fine as fine, and I used to watch her doing it and that's how I learnt. Later, I did lots of smocking and fine stitching for my children's clothes. I also learnt to ride a horse and had dancing lessons, useful for all the balls and parties I was attending.

I went out to the country to stay with a school friend and met a young man called Charles Wilson. He was my first love. But, sadly, he was hit on the head by the crank handle of a tractor and was killed.

David McNicoll wrote about Charles in his book, *Luck's a Fortune*. Charles' brother, Hamley, was David's great friend and they had all attended Scotch College in Melbourne. David wrote of Charles' death in his book and said, 'Charles was a Scotch College hero. He had stroked the Scotch crew to victory.'

When I married Henry White, Mr Wilson, Charles' father, came up to Brisbane from Melbourne for my wedding.

My personal ambition was to be an actress. Let's face it, I was an actress, I should have been an actress. In fact, Madge Elliott and Cyril Richards, a famous acting couple of the day, asked me to join them and go back to London. This proposal was met with a frosty reception from my parents. I was forbidden to go. Instead, I went along to the local radio station – Station 4BH – and they gave me a job: an hour a day acting in plays and reading the news and weather and, unfortunately, race results. My mother, who had been away on a long holiday and did not know that I was *employed*, came back and heard me reading the race results and nearly had a fit. All this went against her strict, Scottish Presbyterian values and, as they used to say in those days, NOCD – Not Our Class, Dear! So she sent my father to come and get me from the station. He, being quite a powerful and wealthy member of the community, told them to give me the sack. Which they did.

So I was rather unhappy and bored. I was invited to go and stay with my father's cousin, Sheila Arnott, on her property at Coolah. There I met Henry White, who took one look at me and decided he wanted to marry me. He was about ten years older than me, and had been madly in love with another girl who married someone else. I was supposed to look quite like her. I knew him for three weeks before we got engaged. When he asked me to marry him, I thought, 'It's not a bad life here, I quite like this polo, the life suits me down to the ground'. So I said yes. We were married three months later and I was only allowed to see him once in that time, when he came to Brisbane to meet my parents. So we didn't know each other all that well.

In the time between my engagement and my marriage I remember spending time copying out some of my mother's recipes, particularly the biscuit recipes. When I returned on visits to Brisbane, I would sometimes copy out other recipes from her handwritten books, but unfortunately the books were lost before I could really go through them thoroughly. However, I was to discover that I have a very good memory for taste and the lucky ability to reproduce it in dishes, a talent that has obviously served me very well. My childhood memories of flavours and food have never left me and remain at the base of my approach to cooking.

After I began writing this book my sister-in-law, Leah Perry from Brisbane, found one of my mother's cook books and sent it to me.

SAND CAKE

250 g butter
250 g castor sugar
4 eggs, beaten
250 g arrowroot, sifted 3 times
2 teaspoons baking powder

Lemon icing
125 g butter
375 g icing sugar
finely grated rind of 1 lemon
lemon juice

Preheat the oven to 180°C. Beat the butter and sugar to a cream, gradually add the eggs and continue beating until the mixture is pale and fluffy. Carefully fold in the sifted arrowroot and beat for 15 minutes, adding the baking powder at the end.

Butter and flour a ring cake tin, spoon in the mixture and cook on the centre shelf of the oven for 50 to 60 minutes. Test with a fine poultry pin or cake tester. When the cake is cooked, turn it out onto a cake rack and allow to cool before icing.

To make the icing
Beat together the butter, icing sugar, lemon rind and enough lemon juice to moisten the icing. When fluffy, spread on the cake.

ALMOND CAKE WITH CHOCOLATE ICING

I remember this being served for my mother's bridge afternoon teas.

2 eggs
125 g sugar
125 g ground almonds
3 heaped tablespoons fine, soft white breadcrumbs made
    from three-day-old bread
pinch of salt

Chocolate icing
75 g pure bitter-sweet cooking chocolate, cut in small
    pieces
3 tablespoons icing sugar
60 g butter

Preheat the oven to 180°C. Beat the eggs with an electric beater and gradually add the sugar until the mixture looks like a good sponge-cake mixture. Carefully fold in the ground almonds and breadcrumbs with a pinch of salt.

Butter a shallow, oblong bar tin, fill with the mixture and bake on the centre shelf of the oven for 40 minutes. Turn out onto a cake rack to cool.

To make the icing

Melt the chocolate in a bowl over warm water. Stir in the icing sugar, then the butter. Mix well and spread immediately over the cake.

BELGIAN SHORTBREAD

This was a favourite when we got home from school.

1 cup sugar
2 cups self-raising flour
pinch of salt
250 g butter
1 egg
raspberry jam
dates, stones removed
shelled raw peanuts
castor sugar

Preheat the oven to 150°C. Mix the sugar, flour and salt in a bowl and rub in the butter until the mixture resembles breadcrumbs. Mix in the egg. Form the dough into a ball and cut in halves.

Press one half of the mixture into a buttered baking dish approximately 30 cm x 20 cm. Spread raspberry jam over the surface and cover generously with dates.

Roll out the remaining dough to fit and place over the dates. Press peanuts over the biscuit top and sprinkle with castor sugar. Bake in the preheated oven for 1 hour. Allow to cool then cut into fingers to serve. Store in an airtight container.

CHOCOLATE WALNUT BISCUITS

125 g butter
1 cup brown sugar
1 egg
1 level teaspoon bicarbonate of soda
$\frac{1}{2}$ cup sour milk
$1\frac{1}{2}$ cups plain flour
4 tablespoons cocoa
$\frac{3}{4}$ cup chopped walnuts

Preheat the oven to 190°C. Butter and flour one or two biscuit trays, depending on the size. Beat the butter and brown sugar together, then add the egg and beat until pale and creamy. Dissolve the bicarbonate of soda in the milk. Mix the flour and cocoa together and add alternately with the milk mixture, beating with a wooden spoon. Stir in the walnuts.

Place heaped teaspoonfuls of the mixture on the prepared trays and bake on the centre shelf of the preheated oven for 15 to 20 minutes. Remove from the trays with a spatula and cool on a cake cooler. Store in an airtight container.

COCONUT BISCUITS
50 g butter
3 tablespoons sugar
1 egg
5 tablespoons self-raising flour
desiccated coconut

Preheat the oven to 190°C. Beat the butter and sugar to a cream, then beat in the egg. Add the flour and mix until smooth. Take small spoonfuls of the mixture and roll in desiccated coconut. Place on a buttered and floured biscuit tray and bake on the centre shelf of the preheated oven for 15 to 20 minutes. Remove from the tray with a spatula and cool on a cake cooler. Store in an airtight container.

MRS BAXTER'S BISCUITS
125 g butter
90 g castor sugar
1 egg
185 g plain flour
1 teaspoon baking powder
60 g mixture of sultanas and chopped candied peel

Preheat the oven to 190°C. Butter and flour one or two biscuit trays, depending on the size. Beat the butter and castor sugar together, then add the egg and beat until pale and creamy. Sift the flour and baking powder together and beat into the mixture with a wooden spoon. Stir in the sultanas and candied peel.

Place spoonfuls of the mixture on the prepared trays and bake on the centre shelf of the oven for 15 to 20 minutes. Remove from the trays with a spatula and cool on a cake cooler. Store in an airtight container.

CLIFFORD BISCUITS
250 g butter
2 cups brown sugar
2 eggs
3½ cups plain flour
1 teaspoon bicarbonate of soda
½ teaspoon salt
1 cup chopped walnuts

Preheat the oven to 190°C. Butter and flour one or two biscuit trays, depending on the size. Cream the butter and brown sugar together, then add the eggs and continue to beat. Sift the flour, soda and salt together and beat into the mixture with a wooden spoon. Stir in the chopped nuts.

Place spoonfuls of the mixture on the prepared trays and bake on the centre shelf of the oven for 15 to 20 minutes. Remove from the trays with a spatula and cool on a cake cooler. Store in an airtight container.

BURNT ALMOND BISCUITS

125 g butter
125 g sugar
155 g self-raising flour
1 small egg
blanched almonds

Preheat the oven to 150°C. Melt the butter and let it burn to a light brown colour. Pour the butter into a bowl and allow to cool. Beat in the sugar until creamy, then add the egg and beat again. Add the flour and mix to a smooth dough. Roll the dough into small balls and place on a buttered biscuit tray. Place an almond on top of each ball and press down. Bake in the oven until golden and cooked.

MY MOTHER'S ROSE, GINGER, PEPPERMINT AND COFFEE FONDANTS

Basic fondant

2 cups sugar
1/2 cup water
pinch of cream of tartar
pinch of salt
1 tablespoon liquid glucose

Put all the ingredients in a saucepan and boil until the mixture reaches 118°C on a candy thermometer. Allow to cool, but not to get cold. Beat with a wooden spoon until the mixture thickens, starts to look milky and loses its stickiness.

Quickly pour out on a flat surface and knead with your hands until you have a smooth, creamy-textured fondant. Break off a small piece and flavour and colour as you wish. Cover the rest with a slightly damp tea-towel to prevent a crust from forming.

Peppermint fondants

Add peppermint essence and a drop of green colouring, and roll into balls.

Rose fondants

Add rosewater and a little rose colouring, roll into balls and stick a crystallised rose petal on top of each fondant.

Ginger fondants

Add vanilla and very finely chopped crystallised ginger to the basic mixture and roll into balls or form into a roll shape.

Coffee fondants

Add coffee essence, cut in squares and press a chocolate-coated coffee bean on top of each fondant.

THE BEACH

My parents always had a beach house. In the beginning, we had a house at Southport and then, after the bridge was built, the next one was at Surfers Paradise. It was never a very swish home, particularly the first one, but we always had a marvellous time. We went frequently on weekends and during school holidays, especially in the summer.

My father was a great fisherman and when we had the house at Labrador Beach in Southport he would catch fish from the beach with 'set' lines. The lines would be 'set' overnight with two or three hooks, a practice not allowed any more. In the morning he would appear with two enormous fish, perhaps a flathead and a snapper. My mother would cook them in our big, blue enamel steamer and make a rich white sauce, perhaps with a bit of chopped egg in it. Or she sometimes baked the fish with lots of butter and white wine and onion rings. Any fish I ever had as a child, apart from the prawns delivered to the door in Brisbane, were caught by my father and prepared by my mother at our beach house.

BAKED FISH

My father used to catch these fish with a set line. In Western Australia you can substitute dhufish for pearl perch.

1 large white fish such as snapper, pearl perch, flathead
　　or parrotfish, scaled, cleaned and gills removed
salt and pepper to taste
2 small onions, peeled and cut in fine rings
125 g butter
1 x 750 ml bottle white wine

Preheat the oven to 200°C. Put the fish in a baking tin. Sprinkle the salt and pepper inside and outside the fish. Place some of the onion rings in the cavity and scatter the remainder over and around the fish. Add some of the butter to the cavity and dot the rest over the surface of the fish. Pour over the white wine.

　　Put the baking dish on the second top shelf of the oven and bake the fish, basting two or three times, until the flesh near the head flakes when tested with a fork.

　　Serve the fish with the onion rings and spoon over some of the sauce.

POACHED FISH WITH EGG SAUCE

My mother had a fish kettle which would hold large fish like those that we baked. Prepare the fish in the same way as for Baked Fish. Place the fish on the rack in the kettle, salt and pepper well inside and out, and pour in enough water to reach the rack. Cover the kettle and poach the fish over medium heat until cooked: the flesh near the head will flake easily when tested with a fork.

　　This fish was served with the following egg sauce, which is a simple white sauce with chopped hard-boiled eggs added.

Egg sauce
600 ml milk
1 onion, peeled and chopped
2 bay leaves
6 peppercorns
60 g butter
60 g plain flour
salt to taste
4 hard-boiled eggs, peeled and chopped finely

Put the milk, onion, bay leaves and peppercorns in a saucepan and bring slowly to the boil. In another saucepan melt the butter, add the flour and cook, stirring, until the mixture is smooth. Strain on the boiling milk and beat with a whisk until the sauce returns to the boil and is thick and smooth. Simmer for 2 to 3 minutes. Add the chopped hard-boiled eggs, bring back to the boil and taste for salt and pepper. Serve with the poached fish.

FISH PIE

Sometimes we used the left-over baked or poached fish to make this pie.

Preheat the oven to 190°C. Remove the skin and bones, then break up the cooked fish into flakes and mix with the same white sauce that you used to make the Egg Sauce. (If you wish, you can put the chopped egg in the sauce.) Flavour the sauce to taste with nutmeg and lemon juice. Pour the mixture into a lightly buttered ovenproof dish. Sprinkle over fresh white breadcrumbs, season with salt and pepper and dot with butter.

Bake in the preheated oven until the sauce is bubbling and the crumbs have browned.

FRIED FISH

The fish my mother used for frying were whiting, bream, parrotfish and garfish, or anything my father caught. These fish were captured in nets in the still water at Narrow Neck and Southport and pulled onto the beach. They were scaled and well cleaned by my father and sometimes filleted or sometimes the small ones were left whole.

My mother put the fish in flour with salt and pepper, then dipped it in beaten egg and then floured it again. She would fry it in a mixture of lard and butter, but today you can substitute olive oil or peanut oil.

No chips were served, but quarters of lemon were served on the plates to squeeze over the fish.

The preparation of fish was always fairly plain, but we didn't have any of the ingredients in those days that are available now. Even cheese was just a great lump of rat-trap cheddar.

People have said that seafood is one thing I do well, and I really like to eat it. I have also always enjoyed cooking and creating with seafood and I would say my favourite recipe is one that I made up, which I call Australian Fish Stew. I had in mind a bouillabaisse (although Australian fish varieties are different to those used in the traditional forms of the dish) with rouille and aïoli. I had read about it and heard about it, but never eaten it. I can hear about a dish or read about it, then imagine it. I throw things in until I think it tastes right, and then I have my basic recipe. I have always been able to do this pretty effortlessly with all sorts of food – except Asian food, which is quite different although I have even come up with some successful Asian-style recipes by reading and tasting and experimenting.

Anyway, for my fish stew I use fish stock, although in the traditional Mediterranean version they don't do so. I like to prepare it for about six or eight people at a time, as it needs huge pots. I cook the fish in one pot and the shellfish in another, then I put them together to serve. This method of separating the ingredients is not conventional, but I find that if you cook it all together it cooks the fish too much. And, of course, mussels are very salty, so be careful of this in the mix.

I first experimented with this dish for my seafood cooking classes and they absolutely loved it. I served it in huge bowls with rouille, aïoli and croutons to add as they wish.

FISH STOCK
(Makes 2 litres)

3 kg fish heads and bones (use only white, non-oily fish:
    snapper, bream, whiting, pearl perch and flathead are
    suitable, but snapper is best)
2 sticks of celery, chopped
2 large carrots, chopped
2 large onions, peeled and chopped
2 litres cold water
500 ml white wine
a little pepper

Remove the gills from the fish heads as well as any blood or guts still in the fish. (Removing the gills from the fish is very important: the stock seems to be bitter when they are left in.) Wash the fish well under running water. Put all the ingredients in a large pot and cover with a lid. Bring to the boil and simmer for no more than 1 hour (too much boiling will also make the stock bitter). Strain through a fine strainer.

There should be approximately 2 litres of fish stock. If there is more, put the stock into a clean saucepan and reduce. Transfer the stock to a bowl and refrigerate. It should set to a light jelly and there will be some fat to skim.

If the stock is for making sauces, reduce to 1 litre as this will make a richer concentrate to add to the sauce. No salt is added until the soup or sauce is made as usually fish stock or glaze is well flavoured. The rich or sticky look and thickness you see in a good soup or sauce is the stock or 'essence'.

AUSTRALIAN FISH STEW
(Serves 8)

2 onions, peeled and chopped
1/2 cup olive oil
4 cloves garlic, peeled and chopped
sprig of thyme or oregano
2 bulbs fennel, tender centre part only, chopped
6 tomatoes, peeled, seeded and chopped (or 1 x 810 g tin
    peeled tomatoes, chopped)
2 sticks of celery, chopped finely
1 large leek, washed well and sliced finely
1 bay leaf
zest of 1 orange
1 bottle white wine
2 litres fish stock (see recipe on p. 34)
1/2 teaspoon saffron threads
salt and pepper
a selection of: mussels, scrubbed and beards removed;
    calamari tubes, sliced in rings; 2 or 3 small lobsters,
    heads removed and cut in two; 2 or 3 small crabs,
    broken up and cleaned; 1 kg green prawns, shelled
    and cleaned
2 kg fresh white fish fillets with firm flesh and, if
    possible, no bones

To serve
croutons made from French bread
rouille and aïoli (recipes follow)

Cook the onions in the olive oil in a large boiler, until soft and translucent. Add the garlic, thyme or oregano, fennel, tomatoes, celery, leek, bay leaf and orange zest. Reserve a little of the wine to cook the mussels, then add the remaining wine, the fish stock and lastly the saffron, and simmer together for 30 minutes. Add salt and pepper to taste.

Have all the fish prepared and standing by. Cook the mussels separately in a saucepan in the reserved wine until they just open, then remove them to a warm place, reserving the salty wine to flavour the soup. Divide the stock between two large pots, bring to the boil and cook the calamari and white fish in one and the lobsters, crabs and prawns in the other.

To serve
Have ready and heated two very large serving bowls. Put half the crab, lobster, prawns and mussels in each bowl. Add the fish and calamari. Quickly mix the two pots of stock together and add the reserved mussel stock to taste (you will get the salt flavour from this stock). Add the combined stock to the two serving bowls and serve at once with the croutons and with bowls of rouille and aïoli to spoon into the soup.

ROUILLE

3 large cloves garlic, peeled
2 small red chillies (or 1 large), seeds removed
2 very thick crustless slices of white bread, soaked
    in a little fish stock
2 large egg yolks
¾ cup good olive oil

Place all the ingredients, except the olive oil, in a food processor and process to a purée. With the motor running, gradually add the oil in a thin stream and continue to process until the rouille thickens. Transfer to a bowl to serve.

AÏOLI

4 egg yolks
4 cloves garlic, peeled
½ teaspoon Dijon mustard
2 tablespoons lemon juice
salt and pepper
750 ml olive oil

Place the egg yolks, garlic, mustard and lemon juice in a food processor and process until the garlic is puréed. With the motor running, gradually add the oil in a thin stream and continue to process until the aïoli thickens. Transfer to a bowl to serve.

PRAWN SOUP

This is another fish dish I came up with for my cooking class.

(Serves 6 to 8)

1 kg cooked prawns, shells removed and reserved,
    digestive tracts removed and discarded, and flesh
    chopped finely
a good lump of butter
1 onion, peeled and chopped
2 leeks, white part only, washed and chopped
1 carrot, peeled and chopped
600 ml fish stock (see recipe on p. 34)
500 ml white wine
2 large ripe tomatoes, peeled, seeded and chopped
1 thick slice Italian-style bread, broken in pieces
100 g rice
300 ml cream
salt and pepper to taste

Fry the prawn shells in melted butter and add the onion, leeks and carrot. Cook until the onion is tender but not browned, then add the fish stock and white wine. Add the tomatoes, bread and rice and boil until the rice is cooked. Purée in a food processor, then strain, discarding the solids.

Just before serving, bring the strained stock mixture to the boil, add the cream and reserved chopped prawns, and simmer until heated through. Taste for salt and pepper and serve at once.

From an early age I have always loved crab. We ate a lot of them at Southport, stopping off on the drive down to buy live mud crabs at the side of the road, and then boiling them up in seawater in a kerosene tin over a rough fire my father would make. My mother wouldn't allow them to be cooked on the electric stove as a 'boil-over' would blow up the stove. Later, when we built the house at Narrow Neck (it was the last house on the Neck before the crossing to the Surfers Paradise side, and still stands) and my father caught his own crabs by setting pots in the creek off the jetty, we would still always cook them by the same method. I think it is the best way to cook a crab. My father would kill them just before boiling by skewering them through the head; otherwise they tend to shed their claws.

We could only buy prawns from the fishermen who called at the kitchen door. Caught in the Brisbane River, they were the smallest prawns I have ever seen and it took a long time to remove the shells. Now, of course, we can buy many varieties of prawns at our markets – where some of them come from, I hate to think, but they are fresh and full of flavour.

PRAWN BISQUE
(Serves 4)

750 g cooked prawns, shelled and cleaned
90 g butter
2 tablespoons grated onion
3 cups warm milk
1 cup cream
salt and pepper
paprika
grated nutmeg
3 tablespoons sherry
finely chopped parsley or chives

Put the prawns in a food processor and process until smooth. Set aside.

Melt the butter in saucepan and cook the onion until it is soft and translucent. Add the prawns and milk, stir to mix and bring to the boil. Turn down the heat and gradually stir in the cream, but do not let it boil. Add salt, pepper, paprika and nutmeg to taste. Stir in the sherry. Mix in the parsley or chives and serve at once.

THAI PRAWN SALAD

This is a recipe I learned as an adult. It uses flavours that we were not aware of in my childhood.

(Serves 6 to 8)

Dressing
2 tablespoons lemon juice
2 tablespoons tamarind water (made with tamarind
    concentrate)
2 tablespoons fish sauce
3 teaspoons palm sugar

Salad
1.5 kg cooked prawns, shelled and cleaned
12 spring onions, chopped finely
4 stalks lemon grass, tender part only, sliced finely
2 large red chillies, seeds removed, sliced finely
2 tablespoons julienne of fresh ginger
2 tablespoons finely sliced kaffir lime leaves
roots and bottom parts of stems from 2 bunches
    of coriander, chopped finely

Put the lemon juice, tamarind water, fish sauce and sugar into a small saucepan. Bring to the boil, stirring occasionally. Remove from the heat and set aside.

In a bowl mix together the prawns, spring onions, lemon grass, chillies, ginger, lime leaves and coriander. Pour the cooled dressing over the salad and stir well. Allow to stand, covered, in the refrigerator for 1 to 2 hours before serving.

GINGERED PINK PRAWNS

(Serves 20)

3 kg green medium-sized green prawns
3 to 4 teaspoons bicarbonate of soda
250 g butter
1 bunch spring onions, sliced finely (white part and some
  of the green)
2 tablespoons well-drained, sliced Japanese pink ginger
  (you may have to chop the ginger into smaller pieces)
salt and freshly ground pepper
2 cups gin

Peel the prawns and remove the digestive tracts. Soak the prawns for 30 minutes in cold water to which you have added the bicarbonate of soda, then drain well. Melt half the butter in each of two large frying pans. Add half the spring onions to each pan and sauté for a few seconds. Quickly place half the prawns and ginger in each pan. Season well with salt and pepper.

Cook over high heat until the prawns are just cooked; this will only take a few minutes. Pour half the gin over each pan of prawns and tip the pan. The gin will flame up, so be careful. Cook for a few seconds until the flames die. Serve at once.

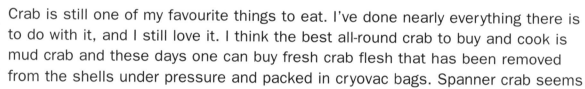

Crab is still one of my favourite things to eat. I've done nearly everything there is to do with it, and I still love it. I think the best all-round crab to buy and cook is mud crab and these days one can buy fresh crab flesh that has been removed from the shells under pressure and packed in cryovac bags. Spanner crab seems to be the number one favourite in this method of packaging.

HOW MY FATHER COOKED MUD CRABS

My father used to catch mud crabs in a crab pot amongst the mangrove trees in the creek at the back of the house. To cook them, he would kill them quickly with a knife before dropping them into boiling seawater. When the water returned to the boil he would continue to cook them briefly until the colour of the crab changed to bright red and he decided they were cooked.

The crabs would be removed from the cooking pot and allowed to cool, then he would remove and crack the claws. The body shell would be removed, the lungs and odd bits discarded and the body rinsed in lightly salted water and cut in four. The crab would be eaten at once.

AMERICAN CRAB CAKES

2 slices white bread made into fine breadcrumbs
1 tablespoon olive oil
3 teaspoons cream
1 teaspoon dry mustard
$1/2$ teaspoon paprika
$1/2$ teaspoon Tabasco sauce
1 teaspoon cracked black pepper
250 g fresh crab meat (available from specialty
  fish shops)
2 egg yolks
2 teaspoons grated horseradish
$2/3$ cup béchamel sauce (see recipe on p. 44)
juice of $1/2$ lemon
salt to taste
2 egg whites
butter for frying

To serve
tomato rémoulade (recipe follows)

Soak the breadcrumbs in the olive oil and cream in a bowl. Mix together the mustard, paprika, Tabasco and pepper and combine with the breadcrumb mixture. Stir in the remaining ingredients except the egg whites and the butter. Beat the egg whites until they hold soft peaks and fold into the crab mixture.

Melt the butter over medium heat in a heavy-based frying pan and fry spoonfuls of the crab cake mixture until golden brown on both sides. Serve with the tomato rémoulade.

TOMATO RÉMOULADE

1 cup home-made mayonnaise
2 tablespoons Dijon mustard
1 tablespoon freshly grated horseradish
1 tablespoon lemon juice
$1/4$ cup finely chopped celery
$1/4$ cup chopped chives
$1/2$ teaspoon cayenne pepper
1 clove garlic, peeled and crushed
$1/2$ cup peeled, seeded and diced tomatoes, drained well

Combine all the ingredients in a bowl and refrigerate for several hours before serving.

THAI STEAMED SEAFOOD CURRY
(Serves 4)

Spice paste
6 eschalots, peeled and chopped
3 garlic cloves, peeled and chopped
2 tablespoons peeled and shredded fresh galangal
2 tablespoons thinly sliced tender part of lemon grass
1 teaspoon thinly sliced kaffir lime rind
2 tablespoons chopped coriander roots and stems
5 peppercorns
$1/2$ teaspoon salt
1 teaspoon shrimp paste
$1/2$ cup coconut cream

Curry
2 cups coconut cream
200 g shelled and cleaned green prawns
100 g cleaned squid, cut in pieces
200 g sea perch fillets
2 teaspoons Thai fish sauce (nam pla), or to taste
4 cups shredded Chinese cabbage
2 cups sweet basil leaves
3 to 4 Thai chillies, seeded and sliced finely
2 tablespoons very finely sliced kaffir lime leaves
150 g cooked fresh crab meat

To make the paste
Grind the paste ingredients, including the coconut cream, in a mortar until smooth, or purée in a blender.

To cook the curry
Add the spice paste to $1^1/2$ cups of the coconut cream, stirring until well mixed. Add the prawns, squid and fish, and stir carefully to mix well. Add the fish sauce to taste.

Place the cabbage and basil leaves in a large shallow bowl and toss to mix. Spoon the seafood mixture on top. Pour over the remaining $1/2$ cup of coconut cream and sprinkle with the chillies and kaffir lime leaves.

Place the bowl in a steamer over rapidly boiling water. Cover the steamer and steam over high heat for 15 minutes, adding the crab meat to the top a few minutes before the end to heat through.

The rocks behind the house at Narrow Neck held another treat – oysters. My father would collect and open the oysters, and now and then pop one straight into my mouth. Needless to say, this remains my favourite way of eating them, although my mother used to prepare them with cocktail sauce or on toast.

MY MOTHER'S OYSTER COCKTAIL SAUCE

300 ml tomato sauce
2 tablespoons Worcestershire sauce
juice of 1 lemon

Mix thoroughly and set aside for at least an hour before using. Mix with oysters 15 minutes before serving. (Sometimes my mother would add a little cream to the sauce.)

OYSTER SOUP

(Serves 6)

2 litres fish stock (see recipe on p. 34)
500 ml hot milk
150 ml cream
plenty of freshly grated nutmeg
salt and pepper to taste
1 to 2 tablespoons lemon juice
3 dozen fresh oysters, removed from the shells

Bring the fish stock to the boil and simmer until reduced by about half. Add the hot milk and cream and reheat, but do not let the mixture boil. Season with nutmeg, salt, pepper and lemon juice to taste. Put six oysters on the bottom of each heated soup plate, pour over the hot soup and serve at once.

GAR'S BUTTERED OYSTERS ON TOAST

These were my mother's specialty simply because she didn't like raw oysters. My children always called her Gar.

(Serves 4)

4 slices country-style bread, toasted and buttered
75 g butter
4 to 5 dozen freshly opened oysters
freshly ground pepper

Prepare the slices of toast and place on four warm plates.

Melt the butter in a frying pan, toss in the oysters and grind over some pepper. Quickly heat the oysters in the butter and remove from the heat as soon as they are warm. They should not be overcooked or they will become tough.

Spoon the oysters over the slices of toast on each plate and serve at once.

I should not forget the pipis we picked up on the beach at Surfers Paradise and at Broadbeach. To collect them, we would bury our feet in sand at the edge of the surf and swivel our bodies so that our feet were firmly anchored. Then, as the surf rolled back, we would dash about collecting the pipis in its wake. We would take them home and wash them: you could *never* get all the sand out of them, but well strained through a cloth the stock made the most delicious soup.

PIPI SOUP
(Serves 4 to 6)

First, catch your pipis! Wash several times in buckets of salted water to remove as much sand as possible: you won't be able to get it all out.

30 g butter
2 onions, peeled and chopped
2 kg pipis in their shells
3 litres water
thin cream
freshly ground pepper to taste

Melt the butter in a large pot and sauté the onion until soft. Throw in the pipis and add the water and freshly ground pepper. (There is no need to add salt as pipis are very salty.)

Bring the liquid to the boil and simmer for 20 minutes, then strain through a sieve lined with a clean, wet tea-towel to remove all the sand. Discard the solids and return the liquid to a clean pan. Bring to the boil and add a little cream and pepper to taste. Serve at once.

This soup is also delicious poured over oysters, as in the recipe for Oyster Soup (see p. 42).

In those days, people often worked on Saturday mornings, so our weekend drive to Southport would begin at about midday and we would eat our lunch on the way. One vivid memory I have of the drive was stopping off for provisions at Guerns (I am no longer sure of the spelling), which was an early sort of delicatessen run by Germans of the same name. They made the most extraordinary pickled cucumbers – whole, crunchy and vaguely sweet – and even though I was a child I adored the taste: I remember pulling them out of the large, fragrant wooden vats. We would also buy sliced leg ham and some strange bread, and eat in the car as we drove.

Even after I married Henry White and moved to the country, I always spent time at the beach. I had my own beach house at Terrigal, overlooking the water.

Generally I would go down there straight after Christmas with the children and stay for the whole summer holiday, and I would also visit at other times too. After Christmas and New Year, we were part of a glamorous and quite exclusive beach fraternity, the holidaying rural community, all with their own beach houses. I remember that there was a party almost every night: the women would dress up in fashionable beach gear, the men would gamble and drink at all-night card games; they would win or lose up to two or three grand a night – and that was in pounds, in those days. There were no pubs there to distract them then. Mostly they were graziers and polo players: Bragg, Mackay, Thompson, Moses, Munroe and, of course, White are some of the names I remember.

Later, when I was married to Lindsay Campbell, we had our own house at Pearl Beach on the central coast of New South Wales. It was my second home and I adored it. When we were there we did precisely nothing. This was where we went on the weekends when I wasn't catering. The children used to come down for visits. I used to just wander along the beach – it was so unspoilt then (the first years of the seventies) – and there were still the most remarkable bits of shell to discover. One of the special, ritual things we made was what came to be called Pearl Beach Pâté; it is the most unusual recipe and really delicious.

JULIE COX'S PEARL BEACH PÂTÉ
(Serves 18 to 20)

850 g young lamb's liver pieces, skinned and trimmed
500 g rindless bacon
10 fillets tinned anchovies
2 cloves garlic, peeled and crushed
freshly ground pepper to taste

Béchamel sauce
500 ml milk
2 onions, chopped
1/4 teaspoon mace
2 bay leaves
8 peppercorns
90 g butter
3 tablespoons plain flour

To assemble the pâté
very thinly sliced bacon rashers, rinds removed,
    to line two terrines

Mince the lamb's liver, bacon and anchovies very finely. Add the garlic and ground pepper. (Alternatively, this can be done in small batches in a food processor.)

To make the béchamel sauce

Put the milk, onions, mace, bay leaves and peppercorns in a saucepan and bring slowly to the boil. In another saucepan melt the butter, add the flour and cook a little. Strain on the boiling liquid and beat with a whisk until the sauce is thick and smooth and returns to the boil. Taste for salt and pepper. Add the sauce to the liver mixture.

To assemble and cook the pâté

Preheat the oven to 175°C. Line the terrines with the bacon rashers and pour in the liver mixture. Place the terrines in a baking dish of boiling water and cook in the oven for 1 hour. Allow to cool and refrigerate for 24 hours.

To serve

Turn the terrines out onto a flat platter and decorate with watercress sprigs or fresh herbs. Serve with unleavened bread, split and baked in the oven until crisp, or with French bread.

Years later we learnt to cook varieties of fish and shellfish with Asian tastes and to make Swedish gravlax with its sauce. I learnt how to make gravlax from Mrs Thumbergier. I catered for her daughter's wedding and she asked me to make this dish from fresh salmon. I thought it sounded quite frightful, but made it exactly as she had instructed me. It was to be served with a dill sauce and hot baby potatoes. At that time the only salmon we could buy came, headless and frozen stiff, from Canada. Mrs Thumbergier's gravlax turned out to be quite remarkably delicious and I cannot tell you how many times I have made the dish since, with fresh salmon from Tasmania. In fact, today, John Wilson from Mohr Foods uses this recipe for his gravlax.

MRS THUMBERGIER'S GRAVLAX
(Serves 8 to 10)

1 whole Atlantic salmon (or ocean trout)
120 g sugar
120 g salt
1 tablespoon cracked white pepper

Sauce
2 tablespoons sugar
2 tablespoons white vinegar
2 tablespoons finely chopped dill
2 tablespoons Dijon mustard
1 teaspoon salt
2/3 cup vegetable oil

To serve

boiled baby potatoes with butter, salt and freshly ground pepper

Remove the fillets from the salmon or trout and cut off the fins, all fat and bones. Use tweezers to pull out any tiny bones.

Mix the sugar, salt and cracked pepper together. Cover the underside of one fillet with a quarter of the sugar mixture. Place the fillet in a large dish on a bed of dill and sprinkle the top with another quarter of the sugar mixture. Cover with more dill. Sprinkle the other fillet with a quarter of the sugar mixture and place, skin side up, on top of the first fillet. Sprinkle with the remaining sugar mixture and cover with the remaining dill.

Wrap the dish well in aluminium foil and leave in the refrigerator for at least 24 hours, turning the fish two or three times so that the marinade is well distributed.

To make the sauce

Place the sugar, vinegar, dill, mustard and salt in a bowl and beat the ingredients together well. While still beating, gradually add the oil and beat until it is amalgamated and the mixture resembles a light mayonnaise.

To serve

Unwrap the fish, remove the dill and scrape off any excess pepper. Slice the fish off the skin at an angle in very thin slices, as if you were slicing smoked salmon. Place the slices on a plate and serve with the sauce and hot, buttered, new baby potatoes.

CONSUELO'S CEVICHE

My friend Consuelo Guinness taught me to make ceviche and escabeche of snapper. She used to make these dishes for special catering parties.

(Serves 8)

16 small whiting fillets
juice of 6 to 8 limes
1 cup very finely sliced baby white onions
2 to 3 fresh red chillies, chopped finely
salt and white pepper

To serve

1 bunch fresh coriander
lime slices

Remove the skin and all the bones from the whiting fillets and cut the flesh into four to six pieces. Place in one layer in a glass or ceramic dish. Pour the lime juice over the fish, and scatter over the onion rings and chopped chillies. Cover and place in the refrigerator and, after 2 hours, season with salt and pepper. Leave for another 2 hours or overnight. The fish will be white and have a cooked appearance.

To serve

Chop about half the bunch of coriander, including some of the stems and add to the fish mixture. Place in a glass serving dish and decorate with slices of lime and sprigs of coriander. Serve as a first course.

CONSUELO'S ESCABECHE OF SNAPPER
(Serves 8)

Beer batter
250 g self-raising flour
$^1/_2$ cup beer
1 cup cold water

Snapper
8 small snapper fillets
plain flour
olive oil for deep-frying
1 cup white wine vinegar
1 cup dry white wine
1 cup olive oil
peppercorns and salt to taste
2 white onions, peeled and sliced finely
olives
sour gherkins
capers
assorted pickles (Italian giardiniera-style)

To make the batter

Put the flour in a food processor. With the motor running, gradually add the beer and water and process until the mixture is smooth. Pour the batter into a bowl and set aside for 1 hour. The batter should have the consistency of pouring cream, so if it has thickened too much after standing, beat in a little extra water.

To cook the snapper

Skin the snapper fillets and pat dry with paper towels. Cut into large pieces, dust lightly with flour and dip into the prepared batter. Deep-fry lightly in the olive oil and drain on paper towels, then transfer to a china or glass serving dish.

Bring the vinegar, white wine, 1 cup of olive oil, peppercorns and salt to the boil. Cool a little and pour over the fish. Add the finely sliced onions, and olives, gherkins, capers and a little of the assorted pickles to taste. Store covered in the refrigerator until ready to serve. The escabeche will keep in the refrigerator for two to three days. Serve as a first course.

COUNTRY LIFE

My wedding to Henry White in St John's Cathedral in Brisbane on 10 November 1937 was a grand affair. After the ceremony, we held an afternoon tea party in a marquee in the gardens of my great-uncle George and great-aunt Cordelia Perry's house in Brisbane. I carried a bunch of water lilies and wore a short veil: very chic and slightly way-out in those days! The men wore morning suits and spats – white cotton fittings to cover the shoelaces and socks. We went to Melbourne for our honeymoon and stayed at the Windsor Hotel. I was pregnant straight away with my first child: a son, Michael. After the honeymoon we went to Talbragar to live on Henry's property at Coolah, near Mudgee, and I lived the life of a grazier's wife. I subsequently had two daughters, Sue and Carolyn. I went to Sydney to have Michael, but the two girls were born in the local hospital in the nearby village of Cassilis, with Dr Bray in attendance. It is frightening how one can multiply: I now have three children, seven grandchildren and two great-grandchildren.

We were also involved in the racing world. Henry's father, Hunter White, was on the Australian Jockey Club (AJC) Committee. Henry himself owned a great racehorse named Rogilla, which unfortunately broke down in the pastern while racing in the Caulfield Cup in Melbourne and spent the rest of his life grazing on the green pastures at Talbragar. There was a stud of thoroughbreds on the White family property, Havilah in Mudgee, which necessitated visits to the yearling sales held in Sydney each year. We had delicious lunches in the AJC Committee Rooms, and I remember lunching with Margaret and Gough Whitlam on the day that the Petrov couple were pulled off a plane. The Russian Secret Service men were trying to push them up the steps onto a plane bound for Russia, and our Secret Service men managed to get them off so that they could spend the rest of their lives in Australia.

At Talbragar we had servants to run the household. I remember going to visit Henry's parents in Sydney soon after we were married and being severely reprimanded for doing the washing. Henry had reported, with pride, to his formidable mother that I had been marvellous enough to do the washing: she called me into her bedroom and said to me imperiously, over her breakfast tray, that she never wanted to hear of me doing such a thing again! I used to think of this interview with some amusement later in life when I was catering full-time and lugging heavy boxes here and there.

TAPIOCA CREAM
This was Henry White's favourite pudding and was served at St Brigid's – the town residence of Mr and Mrs Hunter White – at my first dinner with the family on our return from our honeymoon. (It was usually served with poached fruit and cream.)

(Serves 6 to 8)

4 tablespoons tapioca
4 cups milk
4 egg yolks
vanilla extract to taste
6 tablespoons sugar
8 egg whites

Soak the tapioca in water overnight, then drain and set aside. Bring the milk to the boil and stir in the tapioca. Boil slowly until the tapioca is clear, stirring from time to time to prevent burning.

When the tapioca is cooked, beat the egg yolks with the vanilla and 4 tablespoons of the sugar. Add the egg mixture to the tapioca and milk, mixing well with a wooden spoon. Remove from the heat.

Beat the egg whites with the remaining sugar until stiff and fold into the tapioca mixture. Taste for sweetness. Pour the mixture into a bowl, cover and chill.

I couldn't spend too much time in the kitchen at Talbragar because the staff didn't like the interference. Florence Bateman was the cook: she had come from England to cook for Henry, and really resented my arrival. So, when I arrived, Henry built me a small kitchen by the meat-house and put in it a kerosene stove (like a big, upright gas stove). I set up a production line of Fowlers jars and did all the preserves and pickles and chutneys from the abundant produce of the property. We would eat them with meat and pies and puddings and baked custards.

I made lots of tomato sauce, tomato jam and green tomato chutney. I understood that tomatoes were extremely dangerous to bottle unless they were boiled twice in the Fowler preserving kit, because tomatoes are the first fruit to get botulism. I also made quince jelly and fig jam, bottled peaches, plums and apricots, and I pickled anything I could find.

TOMATO RELISH
2 kg tomatoes, peeled, seeded and chopped
500 g sugar
125 g sultanas
300 g fresh ginger, peeled and grated
300 g garlic, peeled and chopped finely
1¾ cups white vinegar
2 tablespoons salt
3 or 4 chillies, seeds removed and the flesh chopped
2 tablespoons plain flour, mixed with a little water

Place all the ingredients except the flour in a large preserving pan and bring to the boil, stirring constantly. Continue to cook over low heat, stirring frequently for 30 minutes. Stir in the prepared flour and continue to cook until the relish has thickened. The mixture should be bright red.

Pour the relish into clean, warm jars while still hot, and seal.

GREEN TOMATO CHUTNEY
3.5 kg green tomatoes, sliced
500 g green apples, peeled, cored and chopped
500 g onions, peeled and chopped finely
500 g sultanas
12 small chillies, seeds removed, sliced finely
2 tablespoons peeled and finely chopped fresh ginger
750 ml vinegar
500 g brown sugar
1 tablespoon salt

Place all the ingredients in a large preserving pan and bring slowly to the boil, stirring until the sugar dissolves. Boil for 1 hour until thick, stirring freqently. Allow to cool and bottle when cold in clean jars.

TOMATO JAM
2 kg very firm red tomatoes
butter
sugar
juice and finely grated rind of 2 lemons
pinch of salt

Place the tomatoes in a basin and pour over boiling water. Allow to stand for 2 to 3 minutes, then drain and peel off the skins. Weigh the tomatoes, then cut in thick slices and place in a lightly buttered preserving pan and add an equal weight of sugar.

Bring slowly to the boil, stirring until the sugar dissolves. Add the lemon juice and rind and boil rapidly. The jam is ready when a teaspoonful sets after being placed on a cold saucer. Pour the jam into warm, clean jars and seal.

GREEN TOMATO JAM
2 kg sugar
500 ml water
a large piece of fresh ginger, peeled and crushed
1 stick of cinnamon
10 cloves
3 kg green tomatoes, just starting to colour
juice of 2 lemons

Put the sugar and water in a large preserving pan and bring to the boil. Tie the ginger, cinnamon stick and cloves in a clean piece of cloth and add it to the syrup. Boil the spices for about 10 minutes. Prick the tomatoes well with a skewer and add them to the syrup with the lemon juice. Simmer for $2^1/2$ to 3 hours, stirring from time to time. It is a good idea to use a simmering pad under the pan.

Pour the jam into warm, clean jars and seal.

APRICOT CHUTNEY
2 kg apricots, cut in halves and stones removed before
   weighing
2.5 kg sugar
500 g seeded raisins
60 g garlic, peeled and sliced finely
125 g ginger, peeled and shredded
3 teaspoons cayenne pepper
salt to taste
2 cups vinegar

Put the apricots and sugar in a large preserving pan and bring to the boil. Add the raisins, garlic, ginger and cayenne, and cook until the mixture resembles jam, stirring from time to time. Slowly add the vinegar, stirring until mixed and cook again until the chutney thickens. Add salt to taste, then bottle in clean screw-top jars and leave at least 1 week before eating.

FIG JAM
1 kg slightly unripe figs
1 kg sugar
juice of 4 lemons

Cut off and discard the stalks of the figs and slice fruit in half lengthwise. Place the sliced figs in layers in a basin and using 500 g of the sugar, sprinkle a little over each layer. Cover and set aside for 12 hours.

Transfer the sugared figs to a preserving pan, add the lemon juice and cook over medium heat, stirring until the mixture boils. Turn down the heat and boil slowly for 30 minutes, stirring from time to time, then add the remaining 500 g of sugar and stir until it dissolves. Increase the heat and boil quickly until the mixture thickens to a jam consistency. Pour the jam into warm, clean jars and seal.

LEMON SYRUP
We used to drink large quantities of this in the very hot summer – the children especially.

4 cups water
4 cups sugar
1 tablespoon tartaric acid
1 tablespoon lemon essence

Put the water and sugar in a large saucepan and bring to the boil, stirring until the sugar dissolves. Add the tartaric acid and lemon essence and stir well. Allow the syrup to cool and when cold store in clean, dry bottles.

To serve, put 1 or 2 tablespoons of the syrup into a tall glass and add iced water or soda water.

At Talbragar I liked to make the butter myself, because I was very thorough about removing all the whey and consequently it didn't sour so quickly. I had a churn in my private little kitchen and would take over once the boy who was specially employed to milk the cows and separate the milk had done his job. I also made a sort of curd cheese strained through double gauze.

When I first arrived on the property, all the ladies of the district announced their visits with calling cards. I well remember that when old Mrs J. M. Arnott was about to 'call' I made a Blowaway Ginger Sponge, which was something my mother used to make for such occasions. It required whipped cream and it didn't take me long to learn that freshly separated cream needed a couple of days' rest before it could be whipped – no cream topping on my Blowaway Sponge that day! It was at this point that I decided to send Florence down to the relations at Havilah and engaged my own cook.

BLOWAWAY GINGER SPONGE
3 eggs
$1/2$ cup sugar
1 teaspoon golden syrup
1 tablespoon plain flour
$1/2$ cup arrowroot
1 teaspoon cream of tartar
$1/2$ teaspoon bicarbonate of soda
2 teaspoons ground ginger
1 teaspoon cocoa
$1/2$ teaspoon ground cinnamon

To serve
300 g thickened cream, whipped with vanilla extract
    to taste
finely sliced glacé ginger

Preheat the oven to 200°C. Beat the eggs for 5 minutes with the sugar, then add the golden syrup and beat for a further 10 minutes. Mix together the plain flour, arrowroot, cream of tartar, bicarbonate of soda, ground ginger, cocoa and cinnamon. Sift over the beaten egg mixture and fold in quickly. Spoon the mixture into buttered and floured sandwich tins and bake on the centre shelf of the oven for 10 minutes or until a skewer inserted in the centre comes out clean. Turn the cakes out onto a rack to cool.

To serve
Sandwich the cakes together with vanilla-flavoured whipped cream, cover the top with another layer of the whipped cream and sprinkle over the glacé ginger.

As for cook books, I had few of them during my early married life. I had the *Country Women's Coronation Cook Book* and *Oh, For a French Wife!* and *Oh For a Man Who Cooks* and, of course, Escoffier. These few books became terribly important to me later on in my catering and teaching days, but I didn't realise then how influential they were to be. I didn't get my main recipes from them, because I was still cooking from the ones I had collected from my mother and Glad Dobell.

At Talbragar, we had no electricity laid on from the town supply (Coolah was twelve and a half miles from the property) but we had 32-volt electricity from a generator. Great for lighting, but one couldn't run appliances from it. We used old flat irons heated on the stove to iron the clothes and linen sheets; I found this a bit problematic, having come from the city where we had rather sophisticated electric irons. Mostly, the cooks used a wood stove and hot-water boiler, and we heated the house with wood fires. Much later we had an Aga stove, which was fuelled by coke.

I got into trouble over the Aga, too, which I ordered without the permission of my father-in-law. He subsequently disinherited Henry of 9000 acres on another property as a punishment. My son Michael has inherited the Aga, and he and his wife Jill still cook on it, insisting that it makes marvellous meals. My daughter Carolyn can remember me bending over it, making a slow-cooked brisket and baked quinces. I took over a lot more of the cooking after the war, when it became very difficult to attract good staff.

SLOW-COOKED BRISKET

This is one of Lee Bailey's recipes I learned subsequently, which I think is an improvement on the one I cooked at that time.

(Serves 6 to 8)

2 kg beef brisket
2 large cloves garlic, peeled and crushed
1 teaspoon paprika
$\frac{1}{2}$ teaspoon ground cumin
$\frac{1}{2}$ teaspoon dried oregano
$\frac{1}{4}$ teaspoon black pepper
1 teaspoon salt
$\frac{1}{2}$ teaspoon sugar

To serve
fiery sauce (recipe follows)

Preheat the oven to 110°C. Rub the surface of the meat with the crushed garlic. Mix the remaining ingredients together and pat well into the beef. Wrap the seasoned beef securely in two sheets of heavy-duty aluminium foil, making sure there are no air holes and that the foil is sealed at the top of the parcel so the liquid does not escape. Place in a roasting dish and bake until tender, approximately 7 hours.

To serve
Slice the beef and spoon the cooking juices over. Top each serving with the fiery sauce.

FIERY SAUCE
(Makes about 2 cups)

40 g butter
1 large onion, peeled and chopped finely
2 large cloves garlic, peeled and chopped finely
$1/2$ teaspoon powdered ginger
$1/4$ teaspoon ground cumin
$1/2$ teaspoon paprika
1 teaspoon black pepper
$1/2$ teaspoon salt
3 generous tablespoons dark-brown sugar
1 teaspoon English mustard
1 tablespoon grainy Dijon mustard
$1/2$ teaspoon Tabasco sauce, or to taste
3 tablespoons cider vinegar
4 tablespoons Worcestershire sauce
4 tablespoons lemon juice
1 cup beef consommé, or more if necessary

Heat the butter in a medium frying pan and add the onion and garlic. Cook over low heat until browned but not burnt. Add the dry ingredients and stir until mixed. Stir in the liquid ingredients and simmer the mixture over very low heat for about 20 minutes. When ready to serve, reheat and, if the sauce is too thick, add a few tablespoons of the cooking juices from the meat.

When I first arrived at Talbragar we had the most extraordinary refrigerator-cum-ice-chest, which was like an old-fashioned icebox. It had to be heated with a lamp every night and it made exactly six little blocks of ice. Luckily it wasn't long before we got kerosene refrigerators and I discovered that if I turned them up high enough and the weather wasn't too hot, it was possible to freeze meat in them – hence, we had two refrigerators. Sometimes we were able to get a block or two of ice from Mudgee, with which I was able to make the great luxury of ice-cream. I had an ice-cream churn, which involved putting the cold mixture into the container, packing ice and coarse salt around it, and hand-churning until the ice-cream was made. I still like home-made ice-cream, but these days it's a lot easier to make.

VANILLA BEAN ICE-CREAM
(Serves 20)

2 litres cream
2 vanilla beans, split lengthwise
20 yolks from 60 g eggs
1½ cups castor sugar

Bring the cream and vanilla beans to the boil. Remove from the heat and set aside until the cream is cold. Remove the split beans and scrape out all the seeds and flesh. Place the cream with the vanilla seeds and flesh in a clean saucepan and return to the boil.

Beat the egg yolks with the castor sugar. Pour a little of the hot cream onto the beaten yolks, and whisk. Return the cream and egg mixture to the saucepan and cook over low heat, stirring constantly with a wooden spoon, until the mixture just starts to coat the back of the spoon.

Pour the mixture into a bowl and allow to cool. Cover and refrigerate overnight, then freeze in an ice-cream machine as instructed by the manufacturer.

Talbragar was a sizeable property: 9,400 acres. We ran a Corriedale sheep stud and Devon cattle. Shearing was a big event once a year, but I didn't know very much about it – they definitely didn't want women around the yards. I played tennis madly: there was no tennis court on the property, but friends would ask us for tennis parties and the women played bridge as well, so we had a lot of bridge lunches during the week. We sat down for a properly cooked meal at the property for both lunch and dinner. The housemaid waited on the table and we dressed in something suitable. All that stopped abruptly with World War II.

EASY STEAK AND KIDNEY PIE
(Serves 6 to 8)

Pastry:
1½ cups plain flour
pinch of salt
125 g hard butter, cut in cubes
1½ teaspoons iced water
1 egg, beaten with 1 teaspoon water

Steak and kidney

1 kg trimmed chuck steak, cut in cubes
750 g veal kidneys, trimmed of all fat and membranes,
    and cut in cubes
plain flour
salt and freshly ground pepper to taste
ground nutmeg to taste
3 onions, peeled and sliced
125 g butter
1 x 420 g can of beef consommé
420 ml water

To make the pastry

Place the flour, salt and butter in a food processor and process until the mixture resembles breadcrumbs. Add the water and process until the mixture forms a dough. Wrap in plastic wrap and refrigerate for 1 hour.

Preheat the oven to 190°C. Roll out the pastry on a floured board and cut into large leaf shapes. Place on a buttered biscuit tray and paint with the egg and water wash.

Bake the pastry on the centre shelf of the oven for 12 to 15 minutes or until the pastry is light-brown and crisp. Store in an airtight container.

To cook the steak and kidney

Toss the steak and kidney cubes in a mixture of the flour, salt, pepper and nutmeg. Fry the onions in half the butter in a frying pan, until lightly coloured. Using a slotted spoon, transfer the onions to a large saucepan. Add the remaining butter to the frying pan and gently brown the meat and kidneys. Add to the onions in the saucepan and pour in the consommé and water. Cover and simmer for 1 hour. Taste for salt, pepper and nutmeg, and stir frequently to prevent the meat from sticking to the pan.

To serve:

Reheat the pastry leaves. Spoon the hot steak and kidney onto individual serving plates and arrange the pastry leaves on top. Serve with vegetables of your choice.

BURGUNDIAN OXTAIL

Serve this dish with a large bowl of mashed potatoes.

(Serves 10)

60 g butter
6 onions, peeled and sliced
250 g smoked pork speck, rind removed and speck
   cut in small pieces
plain flour
salt and freshly ground pepper
4 kg oxtail, trimmed of all fat and cut into pieces
   at the joints
vegetable oil
1 bottle red wine
500 ml light stock or water
2 sticks of celery, each broken into 3 pieces
3 carrots, peeled and cut in half
$^{1}/_{2}$ teaspoon dried mixed herbs
4 bay leaves

To serve
500 g small onions
80 g butter
salt and pepper
200 g tiny button mushrooms

Preheat the oven to 150°C. Melt the butter in a large, heavy-based pan and fry the onions over low heat until they are soft and brown. Transfer the onions to a large heavy casserole.

Fry the speck in the frying pan until it is golden, remove from the pan with a slotted spoon and drain on paper towels. Add the speck to the onions.

Mix the flour with the salt and pepper, and coat the pieces of oxtail. Fry the oxtail pieces, a few at a time, in the fat from the speck until they are browned on all sides, adding oil to the pan if necessary. Add the oxtail to the casserole.

Discard all the fat and oil from the frying pan and pour in the wine and stock to deglaze the pan. When the wine and stock are boiling, pour into the casserole. Add the celery, carrots, mixed herbs, bay leaves and salt and pepper to taste. Mix well and bring the casserole to the boil on top of the stove. Cover and cook in the oven for $2^{1}/_{2}$ to 3 hours, or until the meat is well cooked.

Remove the casserole from the oven, allow it to cool, and refrigerate overnight. It is necessary to do this as there will be a lot of fat that must be skimmed from the surface when cold.

To serve

Remove the celery and carrots and bring the casserole to the boil on top of the stove. Fry the spring onions in half the butter in a small frying pan with salt and pepper to taste, until they have coloured and softened slightly.

Sauté the mushrooms in another frying pan in the remaining butter with salt and pepper until cooked.

Stir the onions and mushrooms into the casserole and cook for a further 5 to 10 minutes before serving.

NAVARIN OF LAMB
(Serves 8)

2 kg lamb from the leg (after trimming), cut in cubes
olive oil
2 onions, peeled and chopped
250 g eschalots, peeled
2 garlic cloves, peeled and chopped
6 tomatoes, seeds and skins removed, and flesh cut in
    pieces
3 cups chicken stock
salt and freshly ground pepper
6 to 8 small carrots, peeled and cut in lengths
250 g freshly cooked, or frozen, peas
2 x 240 g cans white Italian haricot beans, drained

Garlic toast
1 head of garlic
6 tablespoons virgin olive oil
salt
slices of French bread

Fry the lamb pieces, a few at a time, in olive oil in a frying pan over high heat until brown, then transfer to a large heavy pot.

Fry the onions and eschalots in the same frying pan until golden. Add the garlic and fry for a few seconds. Transfer the mixture to the pot and add the chicken stock with salt and pepper to taste. Cover and simmer for about 45 minutes. Add the carrots and cook for 15 minutes more. Add the peas and beans, cover and simmer for a further 10 to 15 minutes.

Remove the pot from the stove and transfer the contents to a bowl. Allow to cool, then refrigerate and remove any fat that has set.

To make the garlic toast

Preheat the oven to 200°C. Bake the garlic head in the oven for 25 to 30 minutes, or until soft. Remove from the oven and squeeze the garlic flesh into a small bowl. Add the oil with a little salt and mash the mixture to a paste.

Place the bread under the griller and toast one side only. Remove from the griller and spread the untoasted side with the garlic paste. Return the bread to the griller and toast until crisp and golden.

To serve

Reheat the lamb, taste for salt and pepper and serve in bowls with the garlic toast.

CHICKEN PIE

This is adapted from a recipe by the late Jane Grigson.

(Serves 8)

Pastry
3 cups plain flour
pinch of salt
250 g cold butter, cut in cubes
3 to 4 tablespoons iced water

Filling
2 chickens, about 3 kg weight in total, jointed
plain flour, seasoned with salt and pepper
90 g butter
2 onions, peeled and chopped finely
2 bunches parsley, chopped finely
150 ml milk
500 ml cream
salt and freshly ground pepper

To make the pastry

Place the flour, salt and butter in a food processor and process until the mixture resembles coarse breadcrumbs. Add the iced water and process until the mixture forms a ball. Then form the pastry into a flat cake, wrap in plastic wrap and refrigerate for at least 1 hour.

To make the filling

Preheat the oven to 220°C. Coat the chicken pieces in the seasoned flour. Melt half the butter in a frying pan and cook the onions until translucent. Set aside. Add the remaining butter to the pan and fry the chicken pieces, a few at a time, until golden.

Spoon half the onion into a large, deep pie dish and arrange half the chicken on top. Cover with the remaining onion and chicken.

Simmer the parsley in the milk and half the cream for 2 minutes and pour over the chicken. Season well.

Roll out the pastry. Cut a strip 2 cm wide and long enough to go around the rim of the pie dish. Paint the rim of the dish with milk and cover with the pastry strip. Paint the rim of the pastry lid with a little milk and cover the pie, pressing the edges together.

Make a hole in the centre of the pastry, insert a small roll of white card or foil to keep it open and wind a strip of pastry around it to decorate the centre of the pie. Brush the pastry with milk and cook in the preheated oven for 15 minutes. Reduce the heat to 180°C and continue to cook for 1 hour.

Heat the remaining cream and pour it into the pie through the central hole. Remove the roll of card or foil and serve the pie at once.

The mailman, Percy Soles, came twice a week to Talbragar with papers and mail to put in the box at the entrance to the property, which was about two and a half miles from the house. Bread came in automatically, on order from the baker. If we needed extra groceries or fruit we would order from Haynes the Grocer, who kept an adequate amount of groceries, or Fardouleys, who kept a reasonable range of fruit and vegetables.

We were largely self-sufficient in fruit and vegetables, having an extensive garden. We always had a gardener, of course, and the one I remember best was a man called Ivan Svetcoff. 'I haf shust come from Poland' he announced, which was about the only English he knew when he arrived. He taught me some extraordinary things, including adding feta cheese and vinegar to vegetable soup. He brought a pocketful of capsicum seeds, in brilliant colours, with him from his homeland, quite illegally of course. However, we planted them and saw for the first time all those years ago the amazing colours that we are able to buy in shops today.

He taught me to pull out the tomato plants and tie them upside-down in an empty stable when the first frost of winter was imminent. In this way, we could pick ripe tomatoes for the greater part of the winter. We grew very exotic vegetables like Jerusalem artichokes, and we had two huge and prolific asparagus beds that would be top-dressed with sheep manure. In the spring we had hundreds of succulent asparagus shoots that had to be picked every day. We had olive trees, which took a long time to fruit, but we got olives eventually and preserved them. Chillies weren't very popular in those days, but we grew a few. We had beds of strawberries and boysenberries, and we grew all the root vegetables, including beetroot. One delicious thing I learned was to thin the lines of beetroot when the vegetable was about as big as a cherry, then wash it, leaves and all, cook it in salted water, strain and chop it, add salt, pepper and butter and eat it straight away. It is still one of the best vegetables I have eaten.

I also had three acres of wonderful flower garden, with a huge variety of roses and iris and exquisite wisteria vines. This garden was at its peak at Melbourne Cup time, which was good because in those days I invited the neighbours to lunch for the great event, which we listened to on the wireless.

PROVENÇALE-STYLE JERUSALEM ARTICHOKES
(Serves 8)

1 kg Jerusalem artichokes
2 cups chicken stock
80 g butter
3 tomatoes, peeled and seeded
2 cloves garlic, peeled and crushed
1 onion, peeled and chopped finely
salt and pepper
$\frac{1}{2}$ teaspoon chopped fresh oregano
1 tablespoon chopped parsley

Peel and dice the artichokes and cook in the chicken stock for 8 minutes or until tender, then drain. Discard the stock.

Melt the butter in a frying pan, add the tomatoes, garlic and onion, and sauté fairly quickly. Add the artichokes and oregano to the pan, mix thoroughly and cook until heated through. Taste for salt and pepper.

Serve sprinkled with parsley.

ASPARAGUS WITH HARD-BOILED EGG SAUCE
fresh green asparagus spears

Sauce (for each serving)
1 small hard-boiled egg
35 g butter
freshly grated nutmeg
salt and freshly ground pepper

Fill a large saucepan with water and bring to the boil. Add a liberal amount of salt.

With a sharp knife cut off the hard ends of the asparagus. Drop about 12 pieces of asparagus at a time into the water. Do not cover the pan. Cook for 5 to 6 minutes, or until you can just pierce the stem with a poultry pin or small knife. Drain and serve with the sauce.

To make the sauce
Shell and mash the egg. Melt the butter in a pan and add the mashed egg, nutmeg, salt and freshly ground pepper to taste. Heat well and spoon over the asparagus.

SUE'S BAKED TOMATOES
(Serves 8)

1 cup olive oil
5 tablespoons balsamic vinegar
16 medium tomatoes, peeled but with cores intact
sea salt
freshly ground black pepper to taste
sugar
1 onion, peeled and chopped finely
4 cloves garlic, peeled and chopped finely
6 eschalots, peeled and chopped finely

To serve
fresh Italian bread

Preheat the oven to 160°C. Combine the olive oil with 4 tablespoons of the balsamic vinegar and pour into a shallow baking dish. Lay the tomatoes in the dish, core ends down. Sprinkle with sea salt, pepper, a little sugar and the onions, garlic and eschalots. Place the dish on the centre shelf of the oven and cook for 50 minutes, basting occasionally.

   Remove from the oven, sprinkle each hot tomato with a little extra balsamic vinegar and allow to cool to room temperature.

To serve
Place two tomatoes on each plate and spoon the juices around them. Serve with Italian bread as a first course.

FENNEL NIÇOISE
(Serves 4)

4 bulbs of fennel
40 g butter
2 medium onions, peeled and sliced
2 cloves garlic, peeled and crushed
4 tablespoons olive oil
450 g red tomatoes, peeled, seeded and
   cut in chunks
150 ml white wine
$\frac{1}{2}$ teaspoon finely chopped thyme leaves
   or a pinch of dried thyme
salt and ground pepper

To serve
black olives

Trim the fennel and cut off the stems. Cut the bulbs in quarters and sauté in butter until just soft. In another pan, sauté the onions and garlic in olive oil until soft. Add the tomatoes, white wine, thyme, and salt and pepper to taste. Cover the pan and simmer until the liquid has reduced.

Add the fennel with its cooking juices to the tomato mixture and cook for a few minutes.

To serve
Serve the fennel hot or cold, decorated with black olives.

VEAL WITH CHERRIES
(Serves 4)

1 kg shoulder or neck of veal, cubed
2 onions, peeled and chopped finely
40 g butter
1 tablespoon plain flour
½ cup chicken stock
½ cup port
salt and pepper to taste
1 cup cooked, drained cherries
1 tablespoon lemon juice
½ cup sour cream

To serve
crusty bread
salad of mignonette lettuce leaves and flat-leafed parsley,
    dressed with a walnut oil and lemon juice vinaigrette

Lightly brown the veal and onions in the butter. Sprinkle the flour over and cook a little longer, stirring from time to time. Add the stock and port. Cook, stirring, until the mixture boils. Add salt and pepper, lower the heat and simmer for 20 minutes.

Add the cherries and lemon juice and cook until the meat is tender. Stir in the sour cream just before serving and correct the salt, pepper and lemon juice.

To serve
Serve with a basket of crusty bread and with the mignonette salad.

CARAMELISED FIGS

(Serves 8)

16 ripe figs
3/4 cup brown sugar
a little water
powdered cloves
150 g unsalted butter
1/4 cup white sugar
3/4 cup Orange Curaçao
whipped cream or vanilla ice-cream

Preheat the oven to 150°C. Prick the skin of the figs 2 or 3 times with a fork. Place in a baking dish and sprinkle with the brown sugar. Add a little water to the dish.

Bake on the centre shelf of the preheated oven for about 30 minutes. Baste from time to time with the syrup. Remove with a slotted spoon, dust with the powdered cloves and set aside.

Melt the butter in a large frying pan, add the white sugar and cook until lightly caramelised. Place the figs in the pan to caramelise a little. Warm the Curaçao and pour it over the figs to flame. Serve with whipped cream or vanilla ice-cream.

CHERRIES JUBILEE

This and the following selection of country puddings were very popular with the family.

(Serves 6)

500 g red cherries
1/2 cup water
60 g castor sugar
1 cinnamon stick
grated rind and juice of 1/2 orange
1 teaspoon cornflour

To serve
2 tablespoons Cognac
3 tablespoons cherry brandy
vanilla ice-cream

Remove the stems and place the cherries in a saucepan with the water. Bring to the boil and cook for 8 minutes. Strain, set the cherries aside and return the juices to the saucepan. Add the castor sugar, cinnamon stick, orange rind and juice and the cornflour. Cook rapidly until the liquid is a thick syrup. Remove the cinnamon stick, return the cherries to the syrup and bring back to the boil.

To serve
Put the Cognac and cherry brandy in a small pan and warm slightly. Ignite and pour over the cherries. Shake the pan to mix well, then serve with vanilla ice-cream.

APPLE CRUMBLE
(Serves 6)

8 apples, peeled, cored and sliced
1 cup sugar
a little water

Topping
2 cups brown sugar
1 cup self-raising flour
125 g butter

Cook the apples in a saucepan with the sugar and water until mushy. Spoon into a baking dish.

To make the topping
Preheat the oven to 180°C. Mix the brown sugar and flour together in a bowl with the tips of your fingers and rub in the butter until the mixture resembles coarse breadcrumbs. Sprinkle the topping over the hot apples. Cook in the preheated oven for 30 minutes, or until the top is brown. Serve hot or cold with custard or cream.

CURRANT TART
(Serves 6)

Pastry
1½ cups plain flour
2 tablespoons icing sugar
pinch of salt
125 g hard unsalted butter, cut in dice
1 small egg, beaten

Filling
1 egg
1 cup sugar
1½ cups currants
1 teaspoon mixed spice
1 teaspoon vanilla extract
2 teaspoons vinegar
2 tablespoons melted butter

To serve
boiled custard
cream

To make the pastry

Place all the dry ingredients and the butter in a food processor and process until the mixture resembles breadcrumbs. Add the egg and process until the mixture forms a mass. Wrap the dough in plastic wrap and refrigerate for 1 hour. Roll out the dough on a floured board and line a 23-cm tart can.

To make the filling and cook the tart

Preheat the oven to 190°C. In a bowl, mix together all the filling ingredients and pour the mixture into the pastry case. Bake on the centre shelf of the oven for 30 to 35 minutes, until the pastry is golden and the filling is set.

To serve

Serve the tart warm or cold with custard and cream.

APPLE CHARLOTTE

(Serves 8)

8 large Granny Smith apples
1 cup sugar
a little water
225 g butter, melted
1 loaf white sandwich bread sliced thinly

To serve

boiled custard (see recipe pp. 6–7)

Preheat the oven to 150°C. Peel, core and slice the apples (reserving some of the peelings) and cook with the sugar and a little water until tender. Melt the butter. Cut the crusts off the bread and dip the slices in the melted butter.

Line an ovenproof dish with the buttered bread, leaving enough to cover the top. Pour in the hot apples and place on the remaining buttered bread. Cover the top with the reserved apple peelings. (This is an old-fashioned way of preventing the top from browning too much before the charlotte is cooked.)

Bake in the preheated oven for $2^1/2$ hours, then remove the apple peelings and continue baking for another hour. The charlotte is cooked when the bread is golden and crisp and the apples pink. The juice from the apples will run into the buttery bread and become slightly caramelised. Serve warm with custard.

STEAMED GOLDEN SYRUP PUDDING

(Serves 6)

Pudding
50 g butter
125 g sugar
2 eggs
175 g self-raising flour, sifted
pinch of salt
3 tablespoons milk
vanilla extract to taste
very cold golden syrup

To serve
thickened cream

To make the pudding
Beat together the butter and sugar until well mixed. Add the eggs, one at a time, and beat until the mixture is pale and fluffy. Add the flour and salt gradually, alternating with the milk and vanilla extract.

Line a pudding bowl with a thick layer of golden syrup. Spoon the batter into the bowl and cover tightly with aluminium foil or a lid. Place the bowl in a large pot of simmering water (the water should come three-quarters of the way up the bowl). Cover the pot and simmer the pudding for $1^1/2$ hours.

To serve
Turn the pudding out onto a flat plate. Cut in slices like a cake and serve with thickened cream.

CRÈME BRÛLÉE

(Serves 6)

3 cups cream
6 egg yolks
90 g sugar
1 teaspoon vanilla extract
$^3/_4$ cup brown sugar

To serve
fresh peaches or strawberries

Heat the cream until it reaches boiling point. Beat the egg yolks with the sugar. Stir a little cream into the beaten yolks and pour the mixture back into the saucepan. Cook over low heat, stirring constantly, until the mixture thickens, taking care not to boil the custard. Add the vanilla and pour the custard into an ovenproof dish, cover and refrigerate overnight.

Just before serving, sprinkle the brown sugar evenly over the top and place under a hot griller to caramelise the sugar.

To serve
Serve the crème brûlée with fresh peaches or strawberries. This dessert is very rich and you will only need small helpings.

CHOCOLATE RICE PUDDING
(Serves 4 to 6)

2 cups milk
$1/4$ cup rice
$1/2$ teaspoon salt
20 g butter
$1/2$ cup sugar
$2^1/2$ tablespoons cocoa
$1/2$ cup raisins
$1/2$ cup chopped blanched almonds
1 teaspoon vanilla extract
2 egg whites
2 cups cream, lightly whipped

To serve
cream

Bring the milk to the boil in a heavy saucepan. Add the rice and salt, and cook until the rice is tender. Add the butter, sugar, cocoa, raisins, almonds and vanilla essence.

Preheat the oven to 190°C. Beat the egg whites until they hold stiff peaks and fold into the rice mixture with the cream. Pour into a buttered ovenproof dish and bake in the oven for 20 to 30 minutes until the pudding has set.

To serve
Serve the pudding cold with pouring cream.

PEACH DUMPLING
(Serves 4 to 6)

5 ripe peaches
4 tablespoons sugar
3 tablespoons water
$1^1/2$ cups plain flour
2 teaspoons baking powder
pinch of salt
60 g butter
$1/4$ cup milk, or a little more if needed

To serve

butter and sugar to spread on the crust
    when the dumpling is cooked
cream

Preheat the oven to 190°C. Peel and slice the peaches and spread over the bottom of a buttered oven-proof dish. Sprinkle the sugar over the peaches, then sprinkle with the water.

Put the flour, baking powder, salt and butter in a food processor and process until the mixture resembles coarse breadcrumbs. Mix in the milk with a fork (the dough should be quite soft and sticky). Spread the dough over the peaches.

Bake in the preheated oven, one shelf above the centre, for 30 minutes, or until the dumpling is cooked.

To serve

When cooked, spread liberally with butter and sprinkle with sugar. Serve warm with pouring cream.

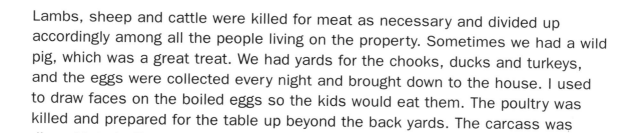

Lambs, sheep and cattle were killed for meat as necessary and divided up accordingly among all the people living on the property. Sometimes we had a wild pig, which was a great treat. We had yards for the chooks, ducks and turkeys, and the eggs were collected every night and brought down to the house. I used to draw faces on the boiled eggs so the kids would eat them. The poultry was killed and prepared for the table up beyond the back yards. The carcass was dipped into boiling water in a kerosene tin and the feathers plucked. Of course, we kept the feet, neck, hearts, livers and gizzards and used them too.

Sometimes we 'corned' beef in the meat-house, where we had a large barrel of brine that was replenished from time to time. At Christmas we bought a huge ham, uncooked, which was first boiled in the copper in the laundry and then baked following Mrs Dobell's recipe. Washing was done in the same copper (no electricity or washing machine), put through the wringer and hung out to dry. Typically, we would also have a turkey and a plum pudding for Christmas dinner.

CHRISTMAS TURKEY WITH WALNUT AND RAISIN STUFFING

Stuffing
2 onions, peeled and chopped finely
250 g butter
2 loaves of stale white bread, made into
    soft breadcrumbs
300 g walnut pieces
250 g raisins
salt and pepper

Turkey
1 x 5.8 kg turkey
heavy-duty aluminium foil
salt and pepper
250 g butter, melted

To prepare the stuffing
Place the onion and butter in a frying pan and sauté gently until the onion starts to soften. Place the breadcrumbs, walnuts and raisins in a large bowl. Add the cooked onion and butter, with salt and pepper to taste. Toss well so that the crumbs absorb the butter.

To cook the turkey
Preheat the oven to 170°C. Remove the giblets and neck and clean the bird. Wipe well with paper towels. Fill the neck with the stuffing, fold back the skin and seal with poultry pins. Sew up the opening above the 'parson's nose' with double thread and a darning needle. Stuff the remaining mixture into the body cavity, sew up the opening and tie the turkey legs together with string.

Place a double sheet of heavy-duty aluminium foil in a large baking dish, covering the bottom and sides. Put the turkey on top, being careful not to pierce the foil. Salt and pepper the bird and pour over the melted butter. Place another piece of double foil over the bird and seal the edges until you have a tight parcel. Cook the turkey on the second bottom shelf of the preheated oven for 2 hours.

Remove the dish from the oven, unwrap the turkey and remove all the foil from the baking dish. Baste the turkey thoroughly with the pan juices, return it to the oven and cook for up to another hour, basting several times during this final cooking.

Allow the turkey to stand in a warm place for 20 to 30 minutes before serving.

SWEET POTATO SOUFFLÉ
This soufflé can be made one or two days before being served and can be reheated just before eating.

1.75 kg sweet potatoes
225 g castor sugar
finely grated rind of 1 lemon
½ cup brandy
1 teaspoon ground nutmeg
1 teaspoon ground allspice
1 teaspoon ground cinnamon
good pinch of salt
350 g butter, melted
6 egg yolks, well beaten
425 ml cream
6 egg whites

Cook the sweet potatoes in boiling, salted water, then remove the peel and purée finely. Add the sugar, lemon rind, brandy, spices, salt, melted butter, egg yolks and cream.

Preheat the oven to 180°C. Butter a large ovenproof dish. Beat the egg whites until they hold soft peaks and fold into the sweet potatoes. Pour into the buttered oven dish and bake in the oven for 1 hour.

PLUM PUDDING
225 g butter
225 g sugar
4 eggs
50 g plain flour
$\frac{1}{2}$ teaspoon mixed spice
$\frac{1}{4}$ teaspoon ground nutmeg
$\frac{1}{2}$ teaspoon salt
225 g fresh breadcrumbs, made from three-day-old bread
225 g raisins
225 g sultanas
225 g currants
125 g crystallised cherries, cut in half
250 g mixed candied peel
125 g preserved figs, chopped
125 g preserved ginger, chopped
1 carrot, peeled and grated
grated rind of 2 oranges
grated rind of 1 lemon
125 g whole blanched almonds
75 ml beer
75 ml brandy

To serve
hard sauce (recipe follows)

Beat the butter with the sugar to a creamy consistency. Add the eggs, one at a time, and beat well. Add the flour, mixed spice, nutmeg, salt and breadcrumbs and mix well. Add the fruits and almonds and, lastly, the beer and brandy.

Place a small circle of buttered greaseproof paper in the bottom of a large buttered pudding bowl. Pour in the pudding mixture, cover the bowl with a double layer of heavy-duty aluminium foil and tie it firmly under the rim with kitchen string, sealing the sides well so that water will not get into the pudding as it cooks. Bring the string over the top to make a handle.

Trim the edges of the foil, place the pudding bowl in a large boiler with a lid and pour in hot water to come three-quarters of the way up the side of the bowl. Cover the boiler, bring the water to the boil and simmer the pudding for 4 hours. Watch that the water does not boil dry and burn the pudding; add a little more hot water from time to time as necessary.

Remove the pudding bowl from the water, allow to cool, then store in a cool place until Christmas morning. Before serving, simmer the pudding for 2 hours in exactly the same way as before.

To serve

Turn out the pudding on a large platter and serve with hard sauce.

HARD SAUCE

This sauce can be made two or three days before serving.

300 g butter
500 g pure icing sugar
1/2 cup brandy

Beat all the ingredients together with an electric beater until the mixture is white and creamy. Spoon into a glass bowl, cover and refrigerate until the pudding is served.

CHRISTMAS CAKE

(Makes 1 x 25 cm square cake)

500 g currants
500 g sultanas
750 g seeded raisins
250 g crystallised ginger, cut in small pieces
250 g dried figs, cut in small pieces
250 g glacé cherries
250 g chopped, mixed candied peel
grated rind of 1 orange
250 g blanched almonds, cut in half
100 g brazil nuts, cut in half
1/2 cup rum
1/2 cup brandy
500 g butter
500 g sugar
10 eggs
1 tablespoon coffee essence
1 tablespoon lemon essence
625 g plain flour
1 teaspoon mixed spice
1 teaspoon ground nutmeg
1 teaspoon ground ginger
1/2 teaspoon powdered cloves
1 teaspoon baking powder
1 tablespoon cocoa
whole blanched almonds
1/2 cup brandy (optional)

Put all the fruits and nuts in a large bowl, mix together and pour the rum and brandy over. Cover and leave overnight.

Beat the butter and sugar together and add the eggs one at a time, beating between each addition. Add the coffee and lemon essences.

Mix all the dry ingredients together. Add a quarter of the dry ingredients to the fruit mixture. Mix the rest of the dry ingredients with the butter mixture. Add this butter and flour mixture to the fruit and mix together well. (You will probably have to use your hand for this.)

Preheat the oven to 135°C. Line the bottom and sides of the cake tin with at least two layers of buttered baking paper. Spoon the mixture into the prepared tin, smooth the top and decorate the surface with whole blanched almonds.

Cook the cake on the bottom shelf of the oven for 5$\frac{1}{2}$ hours. When the cake is cooked, remove it from the oven and set the tin aside on a cake rack. Spoon over the extra brandy, if used, and allow the cake to cool in the tin.

My daughter Sue remembers me teaching the station-hands the finer points of cutting up a killed sheep. She says I am the only foodie in Australia who understands the vagaries of butchering – how to clean tripe, prepare offal from scratch and get the brains out of a sheep's head without mashing them! This wonderful brain pâté recipe has become a favourite.

ELLIE SAW'S BRAIN PÂTÉ
(Serves 6)

4 sets lamb's brains
1 onion, peeled and chopped finely
$\frac{1}{2}$ cup vegetable oil
small glass of white wine
2 eggs, beaten
$\frac{1}{2}$ cup shelled pistachio nuts
$\frac{1}{4}$ cup chopped tarragon

To serve
fresh breadcrumbs
butter
1 small clove garlic, peeled and crushed

Soak the brains in salted water for 1 hour. Drain and remove the membranes.

Preheat the oven to 180°C. Cook the onion in the oil until soft and translucent, then add the brains and wine and cook over high heat until all the liquid has evaporated. Allow to cool a little, then mash the brains with a fork. Add the eggs, pistachio nuts, tarragon, and salt and pepper to taste, and mix well.

Pour the mixture into an oiled loaf can and bake in the preheated oven for 25 minutes, or until set. Allow to stand for 10 minutes before turning out onto a serving platter. Refrigerate for at least 2 hours before serving.

To serve
Fry the breadcrumbs in butter with the garlic until crisp. Cut the pâté into twelve slices and serve on individual plates sprinkled with the fried breadcrumbs.

CRUMBED BRAINS
(Serves 2 to 3)

6 sets lamb's brains
salt to taste
1 teaspoon vinegar

To fry the brains
plain flour
2 eggs, beaten with 2 tablespoons milk
fine breadcrumbs
salt and pepper to taste
olive oil or vegetable oil

To serve
grilled bacon rashers

Soak the brains in cold water for 1 hour. Drain, and remove any membranes as well as you can. Poach the brains in water with the salt and vinegar for 5 to 8 minutes, then drain and set aside to cool.

To fry the brains
Separate each set of brains into 2 pieces. Dust lightly with flour, dip in the egg and milk mixture, then coat well with breadcrumbs and salt and pepper. Heat the oil in a large frying pan. Place the brains in the pan, rounded side down, and fry until golden-brown (about 4 minutes). Turn and cook the other side.

To serve
Transfer to warm serving plates and serve with grilled bacon rashers.

TRIPPA ALLA ROMANA
(Serves 6)

2 kg tripe
3 onions, peeled and cut in quarters
2 sticks of celery
2 carrots, peeled and cut in chunks
salt

Tomato sauce
2 onions, peeled and chopped finely
200 ml olive oil
1 x 440 g can tomato purée
1 x 900 g can peeled tomatoes
3 tablespoons tomato paste
1 sprig rosemary
1 sprig oregano
1 sprig mint
2 garlic cloves, peeled and crushed
1 cup concentrated beef stock
salt and freshly ground pepper to taste
pinch of sugar

To serve
freshly grated pecorino cheese

Scrape any fat from the back of the tripe and cut it in large strips about 8 cm wide. Place the tripe in a large saucepan with the onions, celery, carrots and salt and fill the pot with water. Bring to the boil, then cover and simmer for 2 hours. Make the sauce while the tripe is cooking.

To make the sauce
In a heavy-based saucepan, sauté the onions in the oil until translucent. Add the remaining ingredients and simmer for at least 1 hour, or until the tomato sauce is thick and red. Taste while cooking to see if more salt, pepper or sugar is needed. Stir frequently to avoid burning.

When the tripe is cooked, remove it from the cooking pot and cut into strips 2 cm x 8 cm. Put the tripe in the saucepan with the tomato sauce and simmer, covered, for 45 to 60 minutes, being careful to stir frequently to avoid burning (add a little water if necessary). Taste again for salt and pepper and remove the sprigs of herbs.

To serve
Serve the tripe lukewarm, as the Italians do, and pass a bowl of grated pecorino cheese to sprinkle on top.

GINGERED BEEF TONGUE
(Serves 8)

3 small corned beef tongues
6 cloves garlic, peeled
8 slices peeled fresh ginger
2 tablespoons brown sugar
2 tablespoons vinegar

To serve
fruit chutney
salad of tomato, cucumber and basil

Wash the tongues well under cold water. Place in a very large boiler with the garlic, ginger, brown sugar and vinegar, and fill the pot with water. Bring to the boil, cover and simmer for 3¹/₂ hours. As the water boils away, add more hot water. Taste the water after 1 hour: if it is very salty, drain off and replace.

When the tongues are cooked, remove from the water, peel off the skin and cut away any coarse meat and small bones. Remove the ginger from the cooking water and cut it into fine slivers.

Arrange the tongues in a bowl or oblong tin, sprinkling in the ginger as you do so. Cover with a board to fit inside the rim of the container and top with heavy weights or cans of food (as if pressing a terrine), or press in a meat press. Cover and refrigerate for 24 hours.

To serve
Unmould the pressed tongue and cut it into fine slices. Serve with a good fruit chutney and a tomato, cucumber and basil salad.

VEAL KIDNEYS WITH MADEIRA
(Serves 2)

1 tablespoon butter
1 small onion, peeled and chopped finely
3 or 4 veal kidneys, depending on size
salt and pepper to taste
2 tablespoons Madeira
1 tablespoon cream

To serve
hot toast

Melt the butter in a frying pan and very gently sauté the onion until soft. While this is cooking, prepare the kidneys. Remove any membranes and fat and cut the kidneys in slices about 5 mm thick, or cut in cubes. Place the kidneys in the frying pan with the onion and butter, add salt and pepper and cook for only 4 to 5 minutes, otherwise the kidneys will toughen. Remove the kidneys from the pan and set aside in a warm place.

Add the Madeira and cream to the pan and, over high heat, reduce the sauce by half. Taste for salt and pepper, and pour sauce over the kidneys.

To serve
Spoon the kidneys and sauce over hot toast and serve at once.

Life at Talbragar had its fair share of dramas. Once I lost the car in the creek. Henry had sent me into town to get some parts on a day when it was pouring with rain. I came to the creek and saw that the water was already very high and swift, so I prudently got out of the car and tore back to the homestead in the pouring rain, drenched. When we got back to rescue the car, it had already disappeared, washed away.

Polo and pony-club picnics were big events in the rural calendar, as were extended family picnics for the district. I seem to remember endless picnics, held for a wide variety of reasons. I was a polo groupie, so polo picnics were very regular in our life. For all these events we took out masses of food. I used to make lemon cheese tarts and apple tarts for every picnic. And we took lots of meringues, lamingtons and other tarts as well, like Neenish Tarts. I was given the recipe for Neenish Tarts by my friend Doctor Bray, who delivered my daughters in the tiny hospital at Cassilis, a small village close to Talbragar. I can always remember Bruce Arnott (the son of Sheila Arnott, my father's cousin) asking what I was bringing to one particular event. 'Neenish Tarts' replied Sheila. Bruce responded, 'Who are the Neenish Tarts, Mum?' Bruce was a handful: once, at a children's party at Tom Baillieu's property, he pushed one of the children's nannies into the pool head-first as she was bouncing one of the children up and down at the side of the pool.

LAMINGTONS

Cake
125 g butter
$^3/_4$ cup castor sugar
2 eggs
pinch of salt
1 teaspoon vanilla extract
1$^1/_2$ cups self-raising flour, sifted
$^1/_4$ cup milk

Chocolate icing
375 g icing sugar mix
$^3/_4$ cup cocoa
3 tablespoons butter
pinch of salt
boiling water

To finish
desiccated coconut

To make the cake
Preheat the oven to 190°C. Beat the butter and castor sugar together with an electric beater and add the eggs, one at a time, beating until the mixture is white and fluffy. Add the salt, vanilla, flour and milk, and beat with a wooden spoon for a few minutes.

Spoon the mixture into a greased and floured baking tin and bake on the centre shelf of the oven for 35 minutes. Turn out onto a cake cooler and allow to cool. Store in an airtight container. (It is easier to make lamingtons if the cake is 24 hours old.)

To make the icing
Mix all the ingredients, except the boiling water, in a bowl. Add enough boiling water to make a very runny icing. Stir until the mixture is smooth.

To finish
Cut the cake into small squares and dip in the warm chocolate icing. Roll each square in a generous amount of coconut and place on a cake cooler to allow the icing to set. Store in an airtight container.

NEENISH TARTS
These are the best Neenish Tarts I have eaten. The bases can be made at least four or five days in advance, and the tarts filled and refrigerated in an airtight container three days ahead.

(Makes 45 tarts)

Tart cases
250 g ground almonds
4 tablespoons icing sugar
7 tablespoons plain flour
pinch of salt
2 eggs, beaten

Filling
300 g unsalted butter
300 g icing sugar
pinch of salt
vanilla extract to taste mixed with 2 tablespoons milk
    (or rum to taste)

Vanilla icing
1 cup icing sugar, sifted
pinch of salt
1 tablespoon unsalted butter
1/4 teaspoon vanilla extract
milk

Chocolate icing
1 cup icing sugar, sifted
pinch of salt
1 tablespoon unsalted butter
1 heaped tablespoon good-quality cocoa
boiling water

To make the tart cases
Preheat the oven to 180°C. Place the almonds, icing sugar, flour and salt in a food processor and process until well mixed. Add the eggs and process until the dough forms a ball. Chill in the refrigerator for 30 minutes. Roll the dough out very thinly on a lightly floured board and cut out rounds with a 7 cm round biscuit cutter and line small tartlet tins. Bake the tarts in the oven for 15 to 20 minutes until crisp and pale biscuit-coloured. Remove the cases from the tin and cool on a cake rack.

To make the filling
Place the butter, icing sugar, salt, vanilla and milk or rum in a bowl and beat together until white and creamy. Fill the pastry cases with the mixture, smoothing the surface with a knife.

To make the vanilla icing
Place the icing sugar in a bowl and add the salt, butter and vanilla. Beat together with sufficient milk to make a spreadable consistency, then with a knife spread the icing over one half of the surface of each tart. Allow it to set before icing with the chocolate icing.

To make the chocolate icing
Place the icing sugar in a bowl and add the salt, butter and cocoa. Mix together with a wooden spoon, adding enough boiling water to make a spreadable consistency.

To finish
Spread the remaining half of each tart with the chocolate icing. Allow the icing to set and store the tarts, preferably in the refrigerator, in an airtight container with greaseproof paper between each layer. Remove from the refrigerator one hour before serving.

LEMON CHEESE TARTS

We also used to fill some of the tart cases with apple.

(Makes 24)

Pastry
1¾ cups self-raising flour
185 g cold butter, cut in cubes
1½ tablespoons icing sugar
1 egg yolk
a little iced water if necessary

Lemon cheese
juice and rind of 3 lemons
6 tablespoons castor sugar
6 egg yolks
100 g butter

Apple filling
4 or 5 Granny Smith apples, peeled, cored and sliced
1 cup sugar
$^{1}/_{2}$ cup water

To serve
thick cream (optional)

To make the pastry cases
Put the flour, butter and icing sugar in a food processor and process until the mixture resembles breadcrumbs. Add the egg yolk and process until the mixture forms a ball: add iced water if necessary. Remove the dough from the processor bowl, wrap in plastic wrap and store in the refrigerator for 1 hour.

   Preheat the oven to 190°C. Lightly butter 24 small tartlet tins. Roll out the pastry very thinly and cut in rounds with a 6 cm biscuit cutter. Line the tins with the pastry rounds, prick the bottom with a fork and cook on the centre shelf of the preheated oven for 12 to 15 minutes or until the pastry is pale golden. Turn out onto a cake rack to cool. The tart cases will keep three or four days in an airtight container.

To make the lemon cheese
Put the lemon juice and rind, sugar and egg yolks in a saucepan and beat together well. Add the butter and cook over low heat, stirring all the time, until the mixture thickens. Pour into a container, allow to cool, cover and store in the refrigerator.

To make the apple filling
Put the apples, sugar and water in a saucepan and simmer until the apples are soft and translucent and the water has evaporated. Remove and allow to cool.

To serve
Just before serving, spoon the lemon cheese or apple fillings into the tart cases and serve with the optional thick cream.

GINGER BISCUITS
125 g butter
$^{1}/_{2}$ cup castor sugar
1 egg
1 cup plain flour
1 teaspoon baking powder
2 teaspoons ground ginger
3 tablespoons finely chopped glacé ginger

Preheat the oven to 180°C. Beat the butter and sugar until white and fluffy. Add the egg and continue to beat until it is well combined. Mix the flour, baking powder and ground ginger together and sift into the butter mixture, beating in with a wooden spoon. Mix in the chopped glacé ginger.

Lightly butter a biscuit tray. Place small teaspoons of the mixture on the tray – not too close together, as they spread while cooking.

Cook on the centre shelf in the oven for 12 to 15 minutes. The biscuits should be golden. Transfer to a cake cooler with a spatula. Allow to cool and store in an airtight container.

PECAN WAFERS
(Makes about 20)

1 cup pecan nuts
3 egg whites
1¹/₃ cups firmly packed brown sugar
1 teaspoon vanilla extract

Preheat the oven to 180°C. Grind the pecan nuts in a food processor until quite fine. Beat the egg whites until they form firm peaks. Gradually add the brown sugar to the egg whites and continue beating until the mixture holds stiff peaks. Fold in the vanilla and ground pecans.

Drop teaspoonfuls of the mixture, well apart, onto a greased and floured baking tray. Bake in the oven for 10 to 15 minutes or until the biscuits are crisp.

Cool on a wire rack and store in an airtight container.

PECAN BISCUITS
(Makes 50)

125 g butter
250 g brown sugar
1 egg
¹/₂ teaspoon vanilla extract
1¹/₄ cups plain flour
pinch of salt
¹/₄ teaspoon baking powder
¹/₂ cup finely chopped pecans

Preheat the oven to 190°C. Beat the butter and brown sugar together until light and creamy. Add the egg and vanilla and beat well. Sift together the flour, salt and baking powder, and beat into the creamed butter mixture. Mix in the pecan nuts.

Place teaspoonfuls of the mixture onto a lightly greased baking sheet and bake in the oven for 15 minutes or until golden. Cool on a wire cake rack and store in an airtight container.

CAROLYN'S NUT WAFER BISCUITS

3 egg whites
$^1/_2$ cup castor sugar
1 cup plain flour, sifted
1 $^1/_4$ cups whole unblanched almonds

Preheat the oven to 180°C. Beat the egg whites until they hold stiff peaks. Gradually beat in the sugar until the mixture is a meringue consistency. Carefully fold in the flour and almonds. Mix lightly.

Place the mixture in a buttered and floured 23 cm loaf tin. Bake on the centre shelf of the preheated oven for 30 to 40 minutes, or until the loaf is firm to the touch. Turn out onto a cake cooler and allow to get quite cold. Wrap in foil and leave for two days.

Preheat the oven to 100°C. Using a very sharp knife, cut the loaf in wafer-thin slices. Place the slices on oven trays and bake in the preheated oven for 45 minutes, or until crisp and lightly coloured. Store in an airtight container.

The family picnic discrimination was huge: you just didn't fraternise with anyone who wasn't a grazier or a descendant of a grazier. These picnics were usually at a spot of great physical beauty in the district, and you never brought just any old thing. The competition among the ladies in food presentation was huge – and unspoken. I remember one picnic when 'Uncle' Chad Martin, Carolyn's godfather, arrived in his bi-plane. He was a much-decorated pilot in the RAAF in World War II.

There were usually about twenty families at any one picnic. We had great food, really – all very country food like roast beef and roast chicken, Aberdeen sausage and potato salad, and – the latest fashion – a tossed green salad. Everyone would take a cake. One of my favourites was a bush cake with whisky icing. I have a wonderful chicken-liver pâté recipe from those days that I still make, which was given to me by Rosemary Thompson.

BUSH CAKE WITH WHISKY ICING

125 g butter
$^3/_4$ cup castor sugar
3 eggs, beaten
1 tablespoon milk
1$^1/_4$ cups self-raising flour
pinch of salt
2 teaspoons vanilla extract

Whisky icing
250 g icing sugar, sifted
pinch of salt
125 g unsalted butter
1 tablespoon whisky
few drops of cochineal colouring
slivered blanched almonds

Preheat the oven to 190°C. Beat the butter and sugar until pale and fluffy. Add the eggs and continue beating until the mixture is thick and creamy. Beat in the milk. Stir in the flour and salt with a wooden spoon and add the vanilla.

Butter and flour a ring cake tin, spoon in the cake mixture and bake on the centre shelf of the oven for 35 to 40 minutes. Turn the cake onto a cake cooler and ice when cold.

To make the icing
Put the icing sugar, salt, butter and whisky into a bowl and beat together well, until the icing is creamy and fluffy. Add enough cochineal to make a very soft pink colour, then ice the cake and sprinkle with slivered almonds.

AUNT ELSIE GRIGOR'S FRANGIPANI CAKE
125 g butter
$1/2$ cup sugar
3 egg yolks
a dash vanilla extract
$1/2$ cup milk
$1^1/4$ cups self-raising flour

Topping
3 egg whites
pinch of salt
$3/4$ cup castor sugar
1 cup desiccated coconut

Beat the butter and sugar to a cream. Add the egg yolks one at a time and beat until the mixture is thick and fluffy. Beat in the vanilla extract. Add the milk and sifted flour alternately, beating with a wooden spoon. Spoon the mixture into a buttered and floured 20 cm square cake tin. (These days this cake would be better baked in a springform tin.)

To make the topping
Preheat the oven to 160°C. Beat the egg whites with the salt until they hold soft peaks. Gradually add the castor sugar and continue beating until the mixture resembles meringue. Carefully fold in the coconut and spoon the mixture on top of the cake batter.

Cook on the centre shelf of the preheated oven for $1^1/4$ hours, or until the cake is cooked. Carefully turn the cake out onto a cooler, then turn it right side up on to another cake cooler and allow it to cool completely.

ROSEMARY THOMPSON'S CHICKEN LIVER PÂTÉ
Make the pâté 24 hours ahead and take out of the refrigerator a little before serving time.

2 small onions, peeled and chopped
2 tablespoons butter
500 g chicken livers, cleaned
$1/4$ teaspoon grated nutmeg
freshly ground pepper to taste
pinch of dried thyme
1 teaspoon chopped fresh marjoram
1 teaspoon salt
1 tablespoon brandy
125 g butter
4 tablespoons cream
melted butter to seal the surface

To serve
toasted bread or French bread
pickled gherkins

Sauté the onions in the butter until soft, then add the chicken livers, spices, herbs and salt and sauté until the livers are lightly cooked but still pink in the centre. Flame with the brandy, add the 125 g butter and the cream, and transfer the mixture to a food processor. Process the mixture until it is smooth, then pour it into a terrine. Seal the surface with melted butter. Allow to cool and store in the refrigerator.

To serve
Serve the pâté as a first course with slices of toast or French bread and gherkins.

ABERDEEN SAUSAGE
This is good served with a potato salad.

500 g minced round or topside steak
250 g rindless bacon, minced
1 onion, peeled and minced
1 cup fresh breadcrumbs
1 tablespoon Worcestershire sauce
1 egg
salt and freshly ground pepper
dry breadcrumbs

Put the minced steak, bacon and onion in a bowl and mix together. Add the breadcrumbs, Worcestershire sauce, egg, salt and pepper and mix until thoroughly combined. Turn the mixture onto a floured board, knead and form into a firm sausage.

Place the sausage on a clean, dry cloth and roll up tightly. Tie each end with kitchen string, making sure the sausage is very tightly encased in the cloth. Seal the edge of the cloth with a poultry pin.

Put the sausage in a large saucepan with plenty of boiling water. Reduce the heat and simmer slowly for 1½ to 2 hours. Remove from the pan and let stand for five minutes in the cloth before unrolling. Remove the cloth carefully. Roll the sausage in dry brown breadcrumbs.

I don't remember wine being the beverage at these early picnics: it was quantities of beer, Pimms Cup for the women, and whisky and gin. I do remember when I first noticed people bringing and drinking wine, because I took a photograph and gave it to my friend, the wine man, Douglas Lamb. It was at the polo at Warwick Farm, and it was a photo of a rubbish bin full of wine flagons. This was when it became smart to drink wine – in the late fifties and early sixties – which also heralded a gradual change in food. We used to drink the most dreadful wine in those days, usually in a flagon, although for dinner parties we would serve good French wine. At that time there were only a few Australian wine connoisseurs – that came later.

Among the local rural community at the time, there was a little sub-group of slightly bohemian people who made my life very interesting. They didn't mix with the traditional or conservative bush society very much. My daughter Sue calls them the 'Bloomsbury Group'. The core of this group included Paul Haefliger, then the art critic for the *Sydney Morning Herald*, and his artist wife, Jean Bellette; Wallace Thornton, the artist, and his partner, Danielle Wunderlich; and Sheila and Matt Carroll, parents of the film producer, Matt Carroll. Sheila changed our steady diet of lettuce and beetroot salads with mayonnaise by teaching me the recipe for a proper vinaigrette dressing. With very few changes I still use the same basic quantities.

SHEILA CARROLL'S VINAIGRETTE

$^1\!/_3$ cup white vinegar
$^1\!/_3$ cup olive oil
$^1\!/_3$ cup peanut oil
good pinch of salt
1 heaped teaspoon Dijon mustard, with or without seeds
freshly ground pepper
2 cloves garlic, skins on, bashed

Place all the ingredients in a screw-top jar and shake well to combine. Store in a cool place and shake well just before serving.

I remember that I met the artist Bill Dobell, who later became Sir William Dobell, with this group. I was in Sydney at the time, and Paul Haefliger was desperate to see Bill's latest work from Bali, which he would not show them. We all went out for a Chinese meal and Wallace asked me to persuade Bill to take us back to his studio around the corner and show us some of his paintings. After a few glasses of wine and a good meal, he did take us to his studio. He had painted all these marvellous things on bits of fibro and the pieces all came together like a Last Supper. I remember beautiful faces and beautiful flowers, even though when it was all repainted eventually it wasn't a great success. Wallace Thornton subsequently painted a portrait of me, and one of Sue as a very small child.

Apart from the picnics, the other stand-out events were the balls, which took place about as frequently. There were Polo Balls (up all night, held after the polo carnivals at places like Maitland or Goulburn where we would stay with friends or in the local pub), Picnic Race Balls, and glamorous, very 'social' Balls in the city held at Show time and in Race Weeks.

In those days, we all had a different gown for each ball and a different outfit for each important day at the races. I have a photo of myself at the showground in a suit by Madame Pellier, a very well-known French seamstress in Sydney at the time, but most of my clothes were from Vera Brand and all my hats from Stella Frankel. I used to come to town to get the gowns fitted for these events. It was all very stylish. Often I would make a special trip to Sydney from Terrigal, on my holiday there in the New Year, and get all my clothes and hats for the following Easter season, the most important social time in Sydney. There was one country lady, Mrs Bolton, who made a beautiful gown for me: the overseer's wife, she was an excellent seamstress. I was 'called in' in that dress at one of the Black and White Balls I attended and it was the dress in which Wallace Thornton painted me.

We stayed at the Hotel Australia during our visits to town. When we came to town, our first stop was a Chinese meal; the kids loved it and I loved it. Chinatown was out of bounds to us in those days, it seemed too scary – little did we know how good it would have been – so we went to a place next door to the Australia, whose name I don't recall. It was magic! We always had Sweet and Sour Pork, Chicken and Almonds and Fried Rice, and we adored it.

CHICKEN AND ALMONDS
(Serves 4)

250 g chicken breast meat, cut in dice
2 tablespoons vegetable oil
salt to taste
3/4 cup chopped bamboo shoots
3/4 chopped Chinese cabbage
8 water chestnuts, sliced
16 button mushrooms, halved
1 1/2 cups hot chicken stock
1 tablespoon soy sauce
2 teaspoons cornflour, mixed with 2 teaspoons water

To serve
toasted blanched almonds
boiled or steamed rice

In a wok, sauté the chicken in the oil with the salt. Add the sliced vegetables, stock and soy sauce. Cover and steam for 2 minutes. Stir in the cornflour and cook briefly until the sauce thickens.

To serve
Sprinkle the chicken and vegetables with toasted almonds and serve with rice.

We had one very exclusive ball in the city called the Country Matrons' Ball, held at Easter. I must have shown some signs of being a caterer and organiser then because I used to organise it every year. Each country matron 'hostess' asked a number of guests to these large and very glamorous dinner dances, held at the end of Show Week so that all the men were available. Each of the twenty or twenty-five hostesses would have a table with their guests at the Ball at Prince's (twice we held them at hotels: the Metropole Hotel and the Hotel Australia, neither of which exist any more). Everyone would be dressed elegantly – women in long ballgowns complete with any diamonds they might have, and men in immaculate tails.

The balls held in the country were slightly less formal, with great big buffets and more of the same sort of food we served at the picnics, only more elaborate. We each contributed and had locals to serve the food and drink. All the tables were dressed with our own local flowers. I remember one of these events occasioning my first cooking disaster. It was the Coolah Matrons' Ball and I made a dubious chicken dish, a fricassée. Not being very experienced I put it in the coolroom and left it to cool down. It had some sort of 'booze' in it (sherry, I think) and canned mushrooms – a fatal combination which produced fermentation. As I went to put it in the fridge before I went to bed, I found it gurgling and bubbling and raised the alarm. Henry and a station-hand went out and killed and plucked turkeys in the middle of the night to replace the ruined chicken. Henry was then woken very early in the morning by the phone ringing, with a message to say that a friend had died suddenly in the middle of the night. So we had a wake instead of a ball, for which I made boiled turkey with celery stuffing, one of the most delicious ways of cooking a turkey.

VICTORIAN BOILED TURKEY

Don't be alarmed if, when you take it from the pot, the turkey looks a mess. Once the sauce goes over the turkey it looks great, and it is a taste sensation – especially for winter dinners.

Stuffing
250 g very finely chopped onion
250 g very finely chopped celery
125 g butter
375 g white breadcrumbs
juice of 1 lemon
grated rind of 2 lemons
4 tablespoons chopped parsley
2 eggs, beaten lightly
salt and freshly ground pepper

Turkey

1 x 5.8 kg turkey
4 carrots, sliced
1 turnip, sliced
1 outside stick of celery
3 onions, peeled and each stuck with 3 cloves
12 black peppercorns
1 heaped tablespoon salt
1 to 2 bay leaves
parsley stalks
water

Celery sauce

1 head of celery
215 g butter
90 g plain flour
600 ml boiling milk
200 ml cream
salt and freshly ground pepper
parsley

To make the stuffing

Cook the chopped onion and celery with the butter over low heat until they are softened but not browned. Remove from the heat and add the remaining ingredients, mixing together well with salt and pepper to taste.

To cook the turkey

Remove the fat from inside the turkey, rinse the turkey with cold water and pat dry with paper towels. Pack some of the stuffing loosely in the neck end, then plug the opening with a crust of white bread and secure with poultry pins. Sew up the opening above the 'parson's nose' with double thread and a darning needle. Pack the remaining stuffing in the tail end of the bird and cover with another crust of bread. Sew up the opening, making sure you sew flesh and skin together. Bend the wings underneath to the back. Tie the 'parson's nose' and legs together with kitchen string, then turn the turkey over and tie the wings together. Tie a piece of string around the wings and over the breast, and another piece around the legs and the back. (The turkey should look like a well-wrapped parcel and should be carefully secured as it is to be well and truly exposed to the elements.)

Put the remaining ingredients in a large boiler. Place the turkey on top, breast side down, and add enough water to cover the turkey. Cover the boiler, bring the water to the boil, reduce the heat and simmer for 2 hours.

To make the sauce and serve

Discard the celery leaves, remove any string from the stalks and break the stalks into rough pieces. Put the celery in a saucepan with 125 g of the butter and cook over low heat until the celery is tender.

In a separate saucepan melt the remaining butter, add the flour and cook, stirring, for a few minutes. Remove from the heat, add the hot milk, whisking constantly, then return to the heat and cook, stirring, until the mixture thickens. Add the celery to the white sauce, then transfer the mixture to a food processor and process until smooth. Add the cream and process again. If the sauce is too stiff, add more cream. Season with salt and pepper, adding extra salt if you want to serve the turkey cold.

To serve

Take the turkey from the pot (you will need rubber gloves for this) and place it, breast side up, on a serving platter. Remove the string and pour over the celery sauce. I improve the look of the turkey by placing bunches of parsley between the legs and the body. Carve and enjoy with boiled baby potatoes. Follow with a good green salad.

I don't remember the famous Romano's or Prince's restaurants very well until after World War II when Henry came home and after Michael, Sue and Carolyn were born. They were the only places we went to – to dine, dance and generally to have great food and a good fun time when we were in the city. At Prince's I remember the food was more inclined to be French-style and by the time we started to go there they had a liquor licence; the bands were wonderful to dance to. Jim Bendroit, who owned Prince's, did a lot of the tableside cooking. The caviar was served with chopped eggs, onions, sour cream and blinis – definitely not done today!

I remember that Frank Packer used to eat huge bowls of prawn cocktail and the favourite dish of the house was a Chicken Kiev so luscious that, when cut open, it exploded in a fountain of melted butter on the plate.

CHICKEN KIEV

Flatten each chicken breast fillet (leave the skin on and the wing bone attached) with the flat side of a meat mallet. Place a finger-sized piece of frozen butter in the centre, roll up the chicken, folding in the ends as you do this, and carefully seal the edges with toothpicks. (The butter must not be able to run out during the cooking.)

Dip the stuffed breasts in flour, then in egg beaten with milk, then in breadcrumbs. Repeat the process, dipping in flour, then the egg mixture and breadcrumbs. Refrigerate the stuffed breasts until ready to cook.

Deep-fry the fillets, a few at a time, in hot vegetable oil for 8 to 10 minutes, until golden-brown. Drain on paper towels, then remove the toothpicks and serve immediately.

PRAWN COCKTAIL
(Serves 6)

300 ml tomato ketchup
250 ml thickened cream
2 teaspoons Worcestershire sauce
juice of $1/2$ lemon
Tabasco sauce
750 g small cooked prawns, shells and digestive tracts
    removed

To serve
small finger sandwiches of brown bread and butter

Mix the ketchup, cream, Worcestershire sauce and lemon juice together and add Tabasco sauce to taste. Add the prawns just before serving.

To serve
Spoon the prawn cocktail into small glass bowls and serve with the brown bread and butter sandwiches.

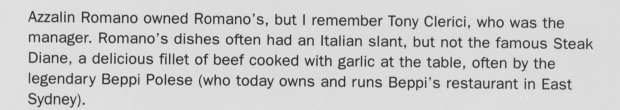

Azzalin Romano owned Romano's, but I remember Tony Clerici, who was the manager. Romano's dishes often had an Italian slant, but not the famous Steak Diane, a delicious fillet of beef cooked with garlic at the table, often by the legendary Beppi Polese (who today owns and runs Beppi's restaurant in East Sydney).

STEAK DIANE
(Serves 1)

1 piece of trimmed fillet steak
2 to 3 tablespoons butter
1 clove garlic, peeled and mashed to a paste
salt and freshly ground pepper
Worcestershire sauce
1 tablespoon finely chopped parsley

With a meat mallet, pound the steak until it is about 3 mm thick. Heat the butter in a heavy-based frying pan. When the butter is sizzling and just starting to change colour, place in the piece of steak. Cook for about 1 minute on one side, then spread on the garlic and sprinkle with salt and pepper. Turn the steak to cook the other side. Immediately sprinkle the Worcestershire sauce on the meat and scatter over the parsley. By this time the steak should be cooked

Place the steak on a warm dinner plate, pour over the contents of the pan and serve at once with sliced boiled baby potatoes and a green salad. Each serving must be eaten immediately while the next one is being cooked.

Another popular venue was the Hotel Australia on Thursday nights, particularly during Show Week or Race Week when we would often gather there for dinner and dancing. Of course, it all went out of fashion eventually and other restaurants, such as Pruniers in Double Bay, became the places to go. Chicken in a Basket became *so* smart! We ate it in a hole-in-the-wall type place in Double Bay: *everybody* went there on Sunday nights for their fried chicken served in a small basket lined with a red checked napkin.

Dinner parties at home usually included roast beef, lamb, or some chicken or duck dish. Fish was impossible to buy anywhere except at the wharves at Pyrmont or outside local pubs. The Sydney Fish Markets at Pyrmont have only been open since the early seventies.

For many years we coasted along in much the same manner, with only the addition of a few Asian restaurants. Then, suddenly, in the mid seventies, nouvelle cuisine came in, as did very French cuisine and our own young chefs' interpretation of that style. At the same time, serious foodies could be seen down in Dixon Street in Chinatown eating real Chinese meals – delicious. We had moved well beyond the sweet-and-sour/chicken-and-almond period.

My children and grandchildren are all good cooks. I think people in the country probably learnt to cook quickly because they had no choice. One had to rely on the garden, the chook yard, meat from the paddock, and when desperate, the local store. Sue has made a very successful career out of her talents and is now Executive Food and Wine Editor of *Vogue Entertaining*. Michael is a legendary camp-oven cook and produces great barbecues, and Carolyn also is very good at everything she decides to cook, especially her marmalade, quite delicious country roasts and great cakes. She tells a funny story about scones and cakes at the local show: there were always events at the show to encourage cooking and the girls would enter cakes and pots of jam. Carolyn, with her daughter, Sarah, recently entered two cakes: a chocolate cake and an orange cake made from recipes that I had passed down to her. Apparently the judges cut into the cakes and said, 'These are obviously packet cakes', and expelled them!

BASIC ORANGE CAKE

In latter years I always baked this cake in a ring tin. It can't sink if there's no middle and it cuts into better slices.

125 g butter
³/₄ cup sugar
3 eggs
1¼ cups self-raising flour
pinch of salt
juice and grated rind of 1 orange

Orange icing
2 cups sifted icing sugar
125 g butter
grated rind of 1 orange
pinch of salt
orange juice

Preheat the oven to 190°C. Beat the butter and sugar until light and fluffy. Beat in the eggs, one at a time, until they are well mixed. With a wooden spoon, beat in the flour, salt, orange juice and rind, alternating the flour with the juice.

Butter a 30 cm x 20 cm cake tin and dust it with flour. Pour in the cake mixture and gently spread it evenly across the tin. Bake on the centre shelf of the preheated oven for 35 to 40 minutes. Turn the cake out onto a rack and leave it to cool. It is better to leave the cake for a few hours before icing.

To ice the cake
Beat the icing sugar, butter, orange rind and salt with enough orange juice to make the icing creamy and fluffy. Spread on the orange cake and let stand for about 1 hour before serving.

WASHINGTON CURRANT POUND CAKE

This recipe was passed to me by Millie Sherman (well-known Sydney cake and chocolate maker) in the eighties. I, in turn, passed it on to my relatives in the country and my grand-daughter Sarah says it's one of the best cakes she has ever made.

500 g plain flour
1½ teaspoons baking powder
1 teaspoon freshly grated nutmeg
½ teaspoon salt
375 g unsalted butter
2³/₄ cups castor sugar
6 eggs
1½ teaspoons vanilla extract
1 cup milk
350 g currants

Preheat the oven to 180°C. Sift the flour with the baking powder, nutmeg and salt. Set aside. Cream the butter and sugar with an electric beater. Add the eggs, one at a time, beating well after each addition. Add the vanilla and continue beating until the mixture is smooth, light and fluffy.

Stir one-third of the flour mixture into the butter and egg mixture with a wooden spoon and add one-third of the milk. Repeat with the remaining flour and milk, mixing only until the ingredients are combined. Stir in the currants. Turn into a greased and floured 25 cm ring tin. (Use a deep tin, such as a bundt tin.)

Bake on the centre shelf of the preheated oven for 1 hour 20 minutes, or until a skewer inserted in the middle of the cake comes out clean. Cool in the tin on a wire rack for 15 minutes before turning the cake out onto the rack. Cool completely.

This cake should be kept in an airtight container for three days before serving. Serve sliced, with a glass of choice, rich malmsey Madeira.

LIGHT FRUIT CAKE
225 g butter
$1^{1}/_{2}$ cups sugar
3 eggs
pinch of salt
$^{1}/_{2}$ cup milk
2 teaspoons vanilla extract
1 cup plain flour
1 cup self-raising flour
125 g sultanas
125 g chopped, mixed candied peel
125 g crystallised cherries, cut in quarters

Preheat the oven to 180°C. Beat the butter and sugar until light and fluffy. Add the eggs one at a time, beating well after each addition, until the mixture is thick and creamy. Add the salt and stir in the milk and vanilla with a wooden spoon. Add a little of the flour to the mixed fruit and mix it in with the tips of your fingers until the fruit is coated. Add the remaining flour to the egg mixture and mix well with a wooden spoon. Add the fruit and stir into the cake mixture.

Butter and flour a large loaf tin and spoon in the cake mixture. Bake on the centre shelf of the preheated oven for $1^{1}/_{2}$ hours or until a skewer inserted in the middle of the cake comes out clean. Turn the cake onto a cake cooler and allow to cool. Store in an airtight container.

Serve with a glass of black sherry or Amontillado or Manzanilla sherry.

COOKING CLASSES

A friend of mine was responsible for starting me in cooking classes. Penny Alexander (now Penny Coombes), then head of the Occupational Therapy Department at Cumberland College of Health Sciences, announced one day that she was bringing six students over to learn the basics of cooking. She wanted these girls to have an occupation. I said I didn't want to give classes, that I didn't know how, and she replied simply that she was bringing them over regardless. It was in the early sixties, I think. Once I started the classes, they never stopped.

My kitchen at the time was the tiniest thing, smaller than it is now. The basic structure of the classes I devised for these girls never changed. Once I got going, I charged sixty dollars for a series of five classes. And everyone got a decent taste of the food, not just a lick off a spoon. I have never used a mirror: I simply tilt the bowl to show what's happening. And I have never given students written sheets of recipes, just a list of the ingredients. I make them write the method down in their own words as I explain it to them. I found this makes them remember and understand more effectively.

I've still got the original pages from those classes with the Cumberland girls and I would still approach teaching the basics in exactly the same way. I divided the classes up into five sections: Commençer (we were so into French – this meant 'starters', of course!), then Vegetables, Beef and Lamb, Chicken and, finally, Dessert. You can't go wrong if you learn from the basics – how to cook a good crêpe, for example. Then one can take a basic crêpe and do something Italian or French or Asian to it. How to cut up chicken. How to cook peas. How to fillet a fish and make gravlax. How to clean octopus. How to cook a fillet of beef. Lots of how-tos. Later, when I was doing special classes like the seafood classes, I always made sure the how-to basics were covered also: how to open oysters and clean scallops; how to cook a crab or a lobster. I found I didn't have to repeat the basic classes all that often, because people started to come who wanted to learn different recipes and themes and ways of doing things. But the basics, to me, are still very important. When Paul Bocuse came out to Australia, I met him and he gave me an invaluable piece of advice: 'If you know how to cook a green bean, you know how to cook anything.' I agree with this principle. Only one person has ever walked out on my classes, and that was a woman who objected to being told how to cook a green bean!

The classes were the most enjoyable thing I did at that time and, I believe, my greatest success. Once I started, the people just kept coming. People who did the basic class would write down their name and suggest other things they wanted to learn more about, and when I had enough people wanting the same thing, I would do a class: seafood, ice-cream, Christmas food, what to serve with drinks, and so on. When I started travelling (and I continued to give classes even when I moved into magazines and newspapers and was able to travel), I would give classes on my return from foreign parts and show some of the wonderful things I had eaten – from Thailand, Italy, France, England, Hong Kong and Singapore. I would either have recipes or reproduce things in my own way.

Even before I started travelling I would use the knowledge I'd picked up from my reading to experiment with flavours, and I used this knowledge for my classes as well. For example, after I had read Waverley Root's *Foods of Italy* I remembered a dish called Sicilian Caponata. I made it up for my class from his description of the dish and taught it in the Vegetable section.

Another great influence was Leo Schofield, then a food columnist and restaurant reviewer for the *Sydney Morning Herald* and a partner in the advertising agency Schofield, Sherbon and Baker. He is now the Director of the Sydney Festival, Chairman of the Sydney Symphony Orchestra, and Artistic Director for the Olympic Arts Festival 2000. On his return from trips overseas, Leo would write columns describing dishes he had tried. I would attempt to make them up from his descriptions. The flavours were quite good, but you should see some of the photographs of them now! I didn't really understand what they should look like.

Later, as my classes grew more popular, my daughter Sue and I would go to the Hunter Valley from time to time, to teach for two days. We were lent a cottage by Peter Meier, who still has a successful restaurant up there in the wine country and who writes for the *Sunday Telegraph*. The wine guys would give us suitable wines to go with the dishes. I also went up to Surfers Paradise several times and taught in private kitchens. But mostly I had my classes at home.

At the classes we could sit twenty to twenty-five students on folding chairs and they were so close to the action they could see, hear and smell everything. It was very domestic. I always felt it was a better way to go than addressing a cast of thousands with a microphone or whatever (although I have done classes like that when invited). I would employ an assistant to finish off, to add ingredients at the correct time, to watch that nothing burnt and, above all, to clean up the mess.

Occasionally, in such a domestic and hands-on setting, we would have a bit of a disaster. One I remember involved using a new tin for a chocolate cake. I made the cake as usual, pulled it from the oven at the end, turned it out with a flourish – and uncooked cake mixture ran all over the front of the bench! The tin was a new variety with a built-in lining, so the cake took longer to cook. Probably my acting ability helped me to ham it up in situations like these!

Following are some favourite recipes I have used in classes over the years, for the original classes I designed for those first six girls and for the specialty classes that followed.

Commençer

BASIC CRÊPE RECIPE
(Makes about 18)

1 cup plain flour
$^1/_2$ teaspoon salt
2 whole eggs
2 egg yolks
$1^1/_4$ cups milk
1 tablespoon melted butter
2 tablespoons brandy
butter for frying the crêpes

Sift the flour and salt into a bowl and make a well in the centre. Add the eggs and egg yolks and gradually whisk in the milk and melted butter until the mixture is smooth and creamy. (Alternatively, place all the ingredients in a food processor and process until smooth.) Let the batter stand for 1 hour. Before cooking the crêpes, add the brandy and, if the mixture is too thick, stir in a little more milk.

Heat a little butter in a crêpe pan of the size required for the recipe and pour off the excess; the butter should only coat the base. Quickly add a small ladleful of the batter, rotating the pan so that the base is completely coated. The crêpe should be very thin. Fry the crêpe over medium-high heat until it is set on top and lightly browned underneath. Loosen the edges of the crêpe with a spatula and quickly turn it. Continue cooking until the crêpe is brown on the other side, then transfer it to a plate.

Repeat with the remaining batter, stacking the crêpes on top of each other with a sheet of greaseproof paper between every second crêpe.

SPINACH FILLING FOR CRÊPES

80 g butter
3 tablespoons plain flour
2 cups boiling milk
salt and pepper
1 kg spinach
$1/2$ teaspoon ground nutmeg

Melt the butter in a saucepan, whisk in the flour and cook for 3 minutes. Add the milk all at once and whisk briskly over heat. Cook, stirring with a wooden spoon, until the mixture comes to the boil and thickens. Simmer for a few minutes and add salt and pepper to taste, then remove from the heat and set aside.

Wash the spinach leaves well and cut out and discard the stalks. Cook the leaves for 10 minutes in salted water. Drain, refresh under cold running water then drain again and squeeze dry. Purée in a food processor with the nutmeg and salt and pepper to taste. Add the puréed spinach to the reserved white sauce and mix until well combined.

Spoon some of the filling onto each crêpe. Roll up and place in an ovenproof dish. Cover the dish with foil and reheat the crêpes in a preheated 150°C oven for about 20 minutes before serving.

FRESH GREEN PEA SOUP

(Serves 6)

1 kg fresh green peas
1 large onion, peeled and chopped
125 g butter
1 medium iceberg lettuce, shredded coarsely
600 ml light chicken stock
salt and pepper
sugar
leaves from 1 sprig of mint
150 ml milk
150 ml cream

Shell the peas and set aside. Cook the onion in butter over low heat until soft and translucent. Add the lettuce and cook just until wilted. Add the peas and stir until well coated with the butter. Add the hot chicken stock with salt, pepper and sugar to taste. Bring to the boil and cook just until the peas are tender.

Process the mixture in a food processor with a little of the fresh mint to taste, until smooth. Return the soup to the saucepan, add the milk and cream, and heat through. (Do not let the mixture boil.) Taste for seasoning and serve hot.

Vegetables

HOW TO COOK GREEN BEANS

Plunge topped and tailed beans into a large pot of boiling water with salt to taste. *Never* put the lid on. Bring quickly back to the boil and cook for 3 to 5 minutes, or until a knife tip can be inserted into the bean. Drain and rinse under cold water to arrest the cooking. Serve the beans at once, or allow to cool if you want to serve them cold.

If you want to cook the beans ahead and reheat, just toss them back into boiling water for 1 minute and drain. (This is very useful when you have a large number of people to cook for.)

BEAN AND MUSHROOM SALAD

(Serves 12)

750 g trimmed and sliced tiny button mushrooms
1.5 kg cooked green beans, topped and tailed
vinaigrette (see recipe on p. 88)
freshly grated nutmeg
salt and pepper

Toss the mushrooms and beans together in vinaigrette. Add plenty of grated nutmeg. Taste for salt and pepper (this salad needs a lot of salt), toss again and serve.

GREEN BEANS WITH CREAM

(Serves 4 to 6)

1½ cups cream
750 g green beans
lemon juice
grated nutmeg
salt and freshly ground pepper

Bring the cream to the boil in a saucepan and cook until reduced by half. Cook the beans in boiling, salted water until just tender. Drain and toss the beans in the hot cream. Season to taste with lemon juice, nutmeg, salt and freshly ground pepper. Serve at once.

SWEET POTATO TIMBALES

(Serves 6)

450 g cooked sweet potato, drained well
40 g unsalted butter
2 large eggs
1 tablespoon brown sugar
$1/2$ cup milk
$1/4$ cup cream
2 teaspoons finely grated orange rind
$1/2$ teaspoon freshly grated nutmeg
pinch of cinnamon
salt to taste

Preheat the oven to 190°C. Mash the sweet potato and beat in the butter and eggs. Add the remaining ingredients and mix together well. Butter six $1/2$-cup soufflé dishes and fill them with the sweet potato mixture. Place the dishes on a baking tray and cook the timbales in the oven until set and golden-brown on top.

RATATOUILLE

This makes a large quantity and the dish can be served hot or cold.

(Serves 12, or makes a very large dish for a buffet table)

$1/2$ cup olive oil
8 medium onions, peeled and cut in quarters
2 large cloves garlic, peeled and mashed with salt using
    the blade of a knife
2 red capsicums, seeds and membranes removed,
    cut in chunks
2 green capsicums, seeds and membranes removed,
    cut in chunks
1.25 kg zucchini, cut in 2 cm chunks
salt and pepper to taste
1.5 kg large red tomatoes, peeled, seeded and cut in
    chunks
sugar

Heat the oil in a large pan, add the onions and garlic, cover and simmer over low heat until the onions are soft. The onions must *not* brown. Add the capsicums and zucchini, and plenty of salt and pepper. Cover and cook until tender: do not overcook.

Just before the mixture has finished cooking, add the tomatoes with a dash of sugar. Turn the heat up to full and taste for salt, adding more if necessary. You should not have too much liquid. Remove from the heat and serve the ratatouille hot or cold.

CARROTS, PARSNIPS AND ONIONS

This is a good dish to serve with lamb.

(Serves 8 to 10)

125 g butter
1 kg even-sized carrots, peeled and cut in 1.5 cm slices
1 kg even-sized parsnips, peeled and cut in 1.5 cm slices
1 kg whole baby onions, peeled and a cross cut in each
 end
2 tablespoons brown sugar
salt and freshly ground pepper to taste
1/2 cup brandy to flame the vegetables

Melt the butter in a large frying pan and add all the vegetables, sugar, salt and pepper. Cover and cook over medium heat for 30 to 40 minutes, adding a dash of water and stirring from time to time as necessary.

Just before serving, place the brandy in a small saucepan and tip over the flame to ignite the brandy, then pour it over the hot vegetables and turn the heat to high for 1 minute. (The dish can be cooked ahead and reheated, but the brandy must be added just before serving.)

OVEN POTATOES

Use pink-skinned potatoes. Peel the potatoes and boil in salted water until cooked. Cut each potato in half and score the whole surface with a fork. Liberally butter a baking dish and put in the potatoes, flat side down. Sprinkle with plenty of salt and freshly ground pepper, and place a nut of butter on top of each half. Cook in a preheated 200°C oven for at least 45 minutes. These are good served with a roast chicken.

BRAISED FENNEL OR LEEKS

Trim off the fennel's hard outside layer and root base. Cut each bulb in quarters, leaving a little of the feathery tops. Heat 125 g butter in a pan, add the fennel quarters and cook, turning frequently, until they brown slightly. Add salt and pepper to taste, and a very little water. Cover and braise the fennel over low heat for 15 to 20 minutes or until soft, turning once.

If you are using leeks, trim off the roots and discard the tough green leaves. Wash the leeks well and cut in halves lengthwise. Cook in the same way as fennel.

STUFFED ARTICHOKES

10 small artichokes
3 cups white breadcrumbs
2 tablespoons chopped parsley
$^3/_4$ cup freshly grated pecorino cheese
2 cloves garlic, peeled and chopped finely
2 eggs, beaten
salt and pepper to taste
$^1/_4$ cup olive oil

Preheat the oven to 185°C. Trim the tops of the artichokes down well and cut off and discard any stalks and coarse leaves. Bash down the tops of the artichokes, spread out the petals and remove any 'chokes'.

Mix together the breadcrumbs, parsley, cheese, garlic, eggs and salt and pepper. Pile the stuffing loosely into the artichokes, then press the outside petals together to firm up the stuffing.

Put the olive oil in a large ovenproof dish, add water to come 1 cm up the sides and heat through. Arrange the artichokes in the dish, side by side and cook in the preheated oven for 1 hour.

PISELLI

(Serves 6)

3 kg fresh peas in the pod
1 medium-sized onion, peeled and sliced thinly
1 large clove garlic, peeled
pinch of salt
pinch of sugar
freshly ground pepper to taste
about $^1/_2$ cup water
$^1/_2$ cup olive oil

Shell the peas and keep a few of the pods. Place the peas and pods in an enamel or stainless steel pot with a lid. Add the remaining ingredients and cook, covered, over very low heat for 2 hours. Inspect from time to time to see if you need to add any more water. Strain, discard the pea pods and garlic, and serve.

SICILIAN CAPONATA
(Serves 8)

1.5 kg eggplants, diced
salt
olive oil
1 bunch celery, leaves and root discarded, sliced
2 red capsicums, seeds and membranes removed,
    cut in 2 cm dice
3 onions, peeled and sliced
3 tablespoons tomato paste
1 tablespoon sugar
1 cup good-quality Italian red wine vinegar
1/2 cup green olives
1 tablespoon capers, or a few more if you like
salt and freshly ground pepper to taste

Place the eggplants in a colander, sprinkling each layer with salt. Set aside over a bowl for at least 1 hour to drain away the bitter juices. Pat dry with paper towels.

Heat a good amount of olive oil in a large frying pan and fry the eggplant cubes until cooked and lightly browned on the outside. Remove with a slotted spoon to a large bowl. If necessary, add more oil to the pan, then quickly fry the celery, sprinkling it with a little salt. The celery should still be crisp. Transfer it with a slotted spoon to the bowl with the eggplant. Fry the capsicum in the same way and transfer to the bowl.

Clean the pan, then add the 1 cup olive oil and fry the onion until it changes colour. Add the tomato paste with a little water and simmer for a few minutes, then add the sugar, vinegar, olives, capers and salt and pepper. Cook just until heated through, then pour over ingredients in the bowl and toss together. Serve at room temperature.

Meats

FILET D'AGNEAU À LA CRÈME DE CIBOULETTE
(Serves 4)

butter
2 boned and trimmed lamb loins

Sauce
60 ml white wine
2 tablespoons chopped spring onions
2 tablespoons chicken stock
$1^1/_2$ cups cream
1 tablespoon purée of watercress
3 tablespoons water
100 g butter
1 tablespoon lemon juice
l tablespoon chopped chives
salt and pepper to taste

Preheat the oven to 220°C. Melt a little butter in a large frying pan and quickly brown the lamb loins on all sides. Transfer the loins to a lightweight oven pan, placing them well apart in the dish. Bake on the top shelf of the preheated oven for 12 minutes. Remove from the oven and set aside to rest in a warm place for 10 minutes.

To make the sauce
Put the white wine and chopped spring onions in a saucepan and cook until reduced to about 1 tablespoon: the mixture should look like marmalade. In a separate saucepan cook the chicken stock and cream until it is reduced by two-thirds.

Beat together the watercress purée, water and butter. Add the cream reduction to the spring onion reduction, then add the watercress mixture, lemon juice, chives and salt and pepper and bring to the boil, stirring until mixed.

Serve the sauce at once with the sliced lamb.

LAMB LOINS WITH GARLIC SAUCE
These days we can get good prepared stocks such as canned Campbell's chicken consommé, which you can use if you want to make this dish in a hurry.

(Serves 4)

1 tablespoon butter
1 tablespoon olive oil
2 lamb loins, boned and trimmed

Sauce

4 large cloves garlic, peeled and sliced finely
100 g unsalted butter
1/2 cup port
1 cup strong lamb stock, or canned chicken stock
salt and pepper to taste

Preheat the oven to 220°C. Heat a little butter in a heavy-based frying pan and quickly sear the lamb loins, turning until browned all over. Transfer the lamb to a baking dish and cook on the top shelf of the oven for 12 minutes. Remove from the baking dish and set aside in a warm place to rest for 10 minutes.

To make the sauce

Cook the garlic very slowly in 40 g of the butter, until soft but not brown. Add the port and stock, bring to the boil and cook until reduced by one-third. Remove any fat from the baking dish, add the sauce and cook over high heat until two-thirds of a cup remains. Whisk in the remaining butter, 1 tablespoon at a time, adding each piece as the previous one is melted. Correct the seasoning and serve at once with the lamb.

TIAN D'AGNEAU NIÇOISE

I ate this dish in Paris, then taught it in a class.

(Serves 4)

1/2 cup olive oil
4 ripe tomatoes, peeled, seeded and chopped
1 onion, peeled and chopped finely
salt and pepper to taste
1 tablespoon chopped basil leaves
200 g tiny button mushrooms, stems trimmed
3 eschalots, peeled and chopped
150 g butter, divided into 4 equal pieces
1 small bunch chives, chopped
500 g spinach
2 lamb loins approximately 250 g each,
    boned and trimmed
1/2 cup white wine
1 tablespoon truffle oil
3 tablespoons water
1 clove garlic, peeled

Heat a little of the olive oil and cook the tomato and chopped onion over low heat until the mixture has reduced. Add the salt, pepper and chopped basil, and set aside.

Heat the remaining olive oil in a pan and cook the mushrooms until they release their liquid. Drain, chop and return them to the pan with one of the chopped eschalots, a piece of the butter, and a tablespoon of chopped chives. Season with salt and pepper and keep warm.

Remove the stems from the spinach leaves, wash the leaves, then blanch in boiling salted water. Drain, squeeze out the excess water and chop the spinach finely. Return to the pan, add another piece of the remaining butter, season with salt and pepper and set aside in a warm place.

Preheat the oven to 200°C. Sprinkle the lamb loins with salt and pepper, spread with a piece of the butter, and cook in the preheated oven for 20 to 25 minutes. Remove and set aside to rest for 10 minutes. Melt the remaining piece of butter in a frying pan and add the two remaining chopped eschalots. Sauté, then add a teaspoon of the tomato mixture, the white wine and truffle oil, and simmer until reduced. Add the water, reduce again, then add the juices from cooking the meat with salt and pepper to taste. You should now have about 150 ml of sauce. Put the sauce through a fine sieve. Set aside and keep warm.

You will need four metal tart rings 12–15 cm in diameter. Rub the tart rings and four heated plates with the garlic clove and place a ring on each plate. Cover the bottom of each ring with a layer of spinach, then add a layer of mushrooms and last, a layer of the tomato. Press down with the back of a spoon. The rings should be three-quarters full with this mixture.

Cut the loins in very thin slices and arrange them inside each ring on top of the tomato layer. Season with salt and pepper.

To serve
Remove the rings and serve the tian surrounded by sauce.

CORNER OF TOPSIDE ROAST
Always choose a good piece of meat complete with its fat (you can cut the fat off before you eat it) if this is not available, buy something else! This roast is very good served cold – at room temperature, not refrigerated.

(Serves 6)

1.75 kg to 2.25 kg corner piece of topside
Dijon mustard
freshly ground pepper
sea salt
vegetable oil
plain flour
1 cup water, or more if necessary
1/2 cup port
1/2 cup cream

Preheat the oven to 190°C. Spread mustard over the top of the meat and sprinkle with freshly ground pepper and sea salt flakes. Pour some oil over the base of a baking dish so that the meat will not stick to the pan and put in the topside fat side up. Place the baking dish on the shelf above the centre and roast the meat in the oven for exactly 1 hour, basting 2 or 3 times.

Remove the roast from the dish and set aside to rest for 15 minutes in a warm place.

Pour off the grease from the baking dish, add a little flour and mix it with the bits on the bottom of the dish. Add the water, port and cream, stir and simmer on top of the stove until the sauce thickens. Taste for salt and pepper and correct seasoning.

Carve the meat very thinly, slicing from the corner. Serve with the sauce and some boiled potatoes.

PAILLARD ALLA MILANESE

Trim the bones, fat and gristle from veal chops, then beat out the meat to about 1 cm thick. Lightly pat on flour with your hands, then shake off the excess flour.

Dip each prepared veal chop into a mixture of egg beaten with 2 tablespoons of water, then dip the meat into a mixture of two parts breadcrumbs to one part freshly grated parmesan cheese and salt and pepper.

Fry the crumbed veal in a mixture of olive oil and butter until golden on the outside and pink (but not raw) in the middle. Do not overcook.

PORK NECK WITH APPLE SAUCE AND POTATOES

The pork neck and apple sauce can be served cold with great success as part of a buffet table. The hot pork neck is a huge favourite when you have friends for dinner.

(Serves 8)

2 pork necks
vegetable oil
cracked pepper
sea salt
good sprinkling of paprika
good sprinkling of caraway seeds

Apple sauce
8 Granny Smith apples, peeled and cored
water
sugar
pinch of salt
125 g butter

Potatoes
2 kg baby potatoes
salt
juice and grated rind of 2 oranges
125 g butter
pepper

Preheat the oven to 190°C. Put the pork necks in a roasting dish and pour over a little oil. Sprinkle with cracked pepper, sea salt, paprika and caraway seeds. Roast, uncovered, on the centre shelf of the preheated oven for 2 hours. Then remove and set aside to rest in a warm place before slicing.

To make the apple sauce
Cut the apples into chunks and place in a saucepan with water about 2 cm deep. Cook until the apples become mushy. Add sugar to taste and a large pinch of salt. Mix in the butter and set aside to cool. Serve at room temperature with the sliced pork.

To cook the potatoes
Boil the potatoes in salted water until tender, then drain, peel and set aside in a warm place. Just before serving, heat together the orange rind and juice with the butter and salt and pepper to taste. Pour over the potatoes.

To serve
Slice the pork neck and pass the apple sauce and potatoes separately.

Poultry

DUCK LIVER TERRINE

Adapted from a recipe by Michel Guérard. This terrine is wonderful served with a chilled Sauternes.

(Serves 6)

full breast from a 1.5 kg duck
1 tablespoon vegetable oil
90 g pork speck, rind removed
325 g duck livers
$1^1/2$ to 2 teaspoons salt
$^1/4$ teaspoon pepper
pinch of quatre épices
250 ml thick cream
4 egg yolks
$1^1/2$ tablespoons Armagnac

To serve
1 tablespoon sugar
1 tablespoon butter
small bunches of sultana grapes (3 to 4 grapes in each)
1 tablespoon Armagnac
hot toast
freshly ground pepper

Preheat the oven to 250°C. Place the duck breast in a baking dish, pour the oil over and cook in the oven for 20 minutes. Allow to cool, remove the skin and dice the breast meat. Roughly chop the speck and put it in a food processor with the duck livers, salt, pepper, quatre épices, cream, egg yolks and Armagnac. Process the mixture until smooth, then pour it into a bowl and add the diced duck breast meat.

Pour the mixture into an earthenware terrine, cover with a double layer of heavy-duty aluminium foil and put the lid on top. Place the terrine in a baking dish, add hot water to come three-quarters up the side of the dish and cook in the oven at 250°C for 30 minutes. Allow the terrine to cool, then refrigerate for 24 hours before serving with a spoon straight from the dish.

To serve
Melt the sugar and butter in a frying pan. Add the grapes and toss quickly for a few seconds. Flame with the Armagnac and serve warm with the terrine, hot toast and pepper.

VOLAILLE AU VINAIGRE
(Serves 6)

12 chicken thighs
180 g butter
$\frac{1}{2}$ cup red wine vinegar
$\frac{1}{2}$ cup white wine
$\frac{1}{2}$ cup chicken stock, or more if needed
1 to 2 tablespoons tomato paste
3 cloves garlic, peeled and chopped finely
salt and pepper to taste

Melt 80 g of the butter in a large heavy-based saucepan, add the chicken thighs, skin side down, and sauté a few at a time until lightly browned. Set aside. Pour off the grease from the pan, then add the vinegar and white wine to deglaze the pan. Add the chicken stock, tomato paste and garlic with salt and pepper to taste.

Return the chicken to the pan and cook, covered, over low heat for 25 to 30 minutes, or until the chicken is cooked, turning the pieces now and then. Remove the chicken to a serving platter and keep warm. Skim the fat from the cooking juices and discard, then strain the juices and return to the pan. Put the pan over low heat and add the remaining butter in small pieces, beating with a whisk. Do not allow the sauce to boil.

Taste for salt and pepper then pour the sauce over the chicken pieces. Serve at once with mashed potatoes and a green vegetable.

SAUTÉED CHICKEN BREASTS WITH A FOIE GRAS SAUCE
(Serves 8)

Sauce
2 cups chicken stock
1 cup port
$^1/_2$ cup cream
1 x 200 g can foie gras
salt and pepper to taste

Chicken
8 chicken breast fillets
plain flour
salt
butter
vegetable oil

To serve
cooked julienne of zucchini, carrots and celery

To make the sauce
Put the chicken stock and port in a saucepan and cook until reduced to $1^1/_2$ cups. Just before serving, beat the cream and foie gras together until smooth and add to the reduction. Cook, stirring, until heated through, but do not allow to boil. Add salt and pepper to taste.

To cook and serve the chicken
Lightly dust the chicken breasts with flour, sprinkle with salt and sauté briefly on both sides in a little butter and oil in a frying pan. Cover the pan and continue cooking over low heat until the breasts are just cooked.

To serve
Serve the chicken breasts with the sauce poured over, and with a cooked julienne of zucchini, carrots and celery.

QUAIL WITH LIME OR LEMON AND GRAPES
(Serves 6)

12 quail
butter
salt and pepper to taste
1 tablespoon brandy
1 cup chicken stock
$1/2$ cup Marsala
a few finely cut lime or lemon slices
1 to 2 teaspoons redcurrant jelly
1 cup seedless green grapes

Cook the quail in a little butter in a large pan until browned, sprinkling with salt and pepper and turning frequently. Flame with brandy, then add the chicken stock, Marsala and lime or lemon slices. Cover and simmer for 10 to 15 minutes, turning frequently, and adding more stock if necessary. Simmer for another 10 minutes or until cooked, then remove the quail to a large platter and keep warm in the oven.

Skim the pan juices to remove any fat. Add the redcurrant jelly and boil quickly. Taste for salt and pepper, then add the grapes and heat through. Pour at once over the quail and serve.

ROLLED TURKEY BREAST
(Serves 4 to 6)

1 boned turkey half-breast
1 clove garlic, peeled and crushed
175 g sliced pancetta
1 tablespoon fresh rosemary leaves
2 to 3 fresh sage leaves
freshly ground pepper
vegetable oil

Sauce
$1/2$ cup cream
1 cup chicken stock
salt and pepper

With a sharp knife, 'butterfly' the turkey meat by slicing it lengthwise through the breast from one side to the other, leaving one side intact so that the breast can be opened out to form one thin slice.

Place the 'butterflied' turkey breast, skin side down, on a board and spread with the crushed garlic, cover with the pancetta, then sprinkle over the rosemary and place on the sage leaves. Sprinkle the breast with freshly ground pepper, then roll it up along the long side like a Swiss roll, so that the skin remains on the outside. Seal the ends with poultry pins and tie up the roll with kitchen string.

Preheat the oven to 200°C. Brush the surface of the roll with vegetable oil and place in a baking dish. Roast in the oven for 45 minutes. Remove the roll from the baking dish and set aside to rest in a warm place.

To make the sauce and serve

Pour off the oil from the dish, add the chicken stock and cream, and boil on top of the stove until the sauce thickens. Season with salt and pepper to taste.

Remove the pins and string from the turkey roll, cut in slices and serve with the sauce.

Seafood

FISH WITH BEURRE BLANC

1 large white fish such as snapper, pearl perch, flathead, or parrotfish, scaled, cleaned and gills removed
salt and freshly ground pepper
white wine

Beurre blanc

8 spring onions, chopped
1 tablespoon very strong fish stock (see recipe on p. 34)
3 tablespoons white wine vinegar
3 tablespoons dry white wine
185 g unsalted butter
salt to taste

Preheat the oven to 230°C. Sprinkle the fish with salt and pepper. Place the fish on a large piece of heavy-duty aluminium foil, pour over a little white wine and wrap the fish tightly, sealing the edges of the foil. Place on a baking tray and cook the fish on the shelf above the centre of the oven for 20 minutes. Do not overcook.

To make the beurre blanc

Put the spring onions, fish stock, vinegar and white wine in a saucepan and cook until reduced to 2 tablespoons. Purée the reduction in a blender or food processor, then return to the saucepan. Cook over low heat, adding the butter a chunk at a time and whisking until the sauce is smooth and creamy. Add salt to taste and serve with the fish.

OYSTERS WITH BEURRE BLANC AND JULIENNE OF MIXED VEGETABLES
(Serves 4)

1 cup mixed julienne of leeks, carrots and celery
butter
24 oysters on the shell

Beurre blanc
strained liquid from the oysters
120 ml white wine
120 ml white wine vinegar
1 small onion, peeled and chopped finely
350 g butter, softened
pepper to taste

Cook the julienne in a little butter in a pan just until it has softened, then set aside. Strain the juice from the oysters and reserve. Dry the shells and put the oysters back in the shells. Place the oysters on a rack that will fit on a baking dish and set aside. (A cake cooler is suitable.)

To make the beurre blanc and serve the oysters
Put the oyster liquid, white wine, vinegar and onion in a saucepan and cook until the liquid is almost evaporated. Remove from the heat and add the pepper. Return the pan to very low heat and gradually whisk in the butter. Stir in the softened julienne and set aside.

Half-fill a baking dish with boiling water and reheat on top of the stove until the water is boiling. Turn off the heat and place the rack of oysters on the baking dish, cover the oysters and baking dish with foil and leave for 60 seconds.

Remove the oysters to warm serving plates, ladle over the sauce and serve at once.

SCALLOPS, PRAWNS AND BUGS WITH VERMOUTH AND PRAWN BUTTER SAUCE
(Serves 10)

1 kg cooked prawns, shelled, cleaned and heads and
    shells reserved
12 cooked Balmain or Moreton Bay bugs, shells, heads
    and digestive tracts removed and discarded and tails
    cut in halves

Prawn butter
125 g butter
reserved prawn heads and shells
1 cup white wine
1 cup dry vermouth

Scallops
1 kg scallops (without roes)
40 g butter
salt and pepper to taste
$^{1}/_{2}$ cup dry vermouth

Sauce
2 cups fish stock (see recipe on p. 34)
$^{1}/_{2}$ cup dry vermouth
1 cup cream, plus a little extra if necessary
reserved prawn butter and stock
salt and pepper

Put the shelled prawns and bugs in a bowl and set aside.

To make the prawn butter
Melt the butter in a saucepan and fry the prawn shells and heads. Add the white wine and vermouth and cook, pressing from time to time with a potato masher, for 15 to 20 minutes. Transfer the mixture to a food processor and process to break up the prawns. Strain the mixture through a fine sieve, pressing well down to extract as much liquid as possible, then discard the solids. Allow to stand until cool, then refrigerate. The prawn butter will come to the top and set on top of the stock.

To cook the scallops and make the sauce
Cook the scallops in a little butter, with salt, pepper and vermouth until just set. Remove the scallops from the pan, mix them in a bowl with the prepared prawns and bugs and set aside.

Add the fish stock, vermouth and cream to the pan and cook until reduced to $1^{1}/_{2}$ cups. Add the reserved prawn butter and prawn stock. Taste for salt and pepper, and add more cream if necessary.

Just before serving, reheat the sauce, add the scallops, prawns and bugs, and quickly heat through. Serve immediately.

Desserts

STRAWBERRY MOUSSE

(Serves 8)

1 cup sugar
$^1/_3$ cup sherry
$^1/_4$ cup rum
4 egg yolks
juice of 1 small lemon
pinch of salt
pinch of nutmeg
1 tablespoon gelatine, dissolved in $^1/_4$ cup sherry
300 ml sour cream
2 punnets strawberries, hulled
4 egg whites

Put the sugar, sherry, rum, egg yolks, lemon juice, salt and nutmeg in a saucepan and cook over low heat, stirring, until the mixture thickens. Remove from the heat and add the dissolved gelatine.

Pour $^1/_4$ cup of this custard into a food processor with the sour cream and strawberries. Process until smooth, then combine with the remaining custard. Transfer to a bowl and chill for 30 minutes.

Beat the egg whites until stiff and fold into the strawberry mixture. Cover and refrigerate overnight.

HOT STRAWBERRY SOUFFLÉS

These soufflés will impress your guests. You can have everything ready and just beat in the egg whites with the sugar at the last minute. By the time you've poured them a delicious glass of suitable dessert wine, the soufflés will be ready to eat.

(Makes 10 x $^3/_4$ cup soufflés)

400 g strawberries, hulled and crushed well
200 g castor sugar
2 tablespoons Fraises des Bois liqueur
12 egg whites
pinch of salt
50 g castor sugar
icing sugar to dust the soufflés

To serve

2 punnets strawberries, hulled and puréed in a food processor with sugar to taste (the sauce should be quite sweet)

whipped thickened cream

Preheat the oven to 200°C. Generously butter ten $^3/_4$ cup soufflé dishes and dust with castor sugar.

Cook the strawberries with the 200 g of castor sugar over medium heat, stirring frequently, until the mixture has the consistency of jam. Stir in the liqueur, transfer the mixture to a bowl and set aside to cool.

Beat the egg whites with salt and the 50 g of castor sugar until the mixture holds stiff peaks. Mix 2 to 3 large spoonfuls of the beaten egg whites into the strawberries to lighten the mixture, then fold in the remaining egg whites.

Spoon the soufflé mixture into the prepared dishes and level each one with a spatula. Place the dishes on a biscuit tray and run the tip of your index finger around the edge of each dish. This will help the soufflés rise evenly.

Cook the soufflés on the centre shelf of the oven for exactly 12 minutes. Remove the soufflés from the oven, immediately dust the tops with icing sugar and serve at once.

To serve

Each person splits open a soufflé at the table, pours in the strawberry sauce and follows with a spoonful of whipped cream. Eat at once and enjoy.

CARAMEL ORANGES

$1^1/_2$ oranges per serving
Grand Marnier or Orange Curaçao
1 cup sugar
water

Peel the oranges, removing all pith and cut in thin slices. Place in a dish and marinate for a few hours liberally sprinkled with either Grand Marnier or Curaçao.

Make a caramel with the sugar and a dash of water and pour over the oranges. Cover and refrigerate for 1 to 2 hours before serving.

You can serve the oranges just as they are, or with ice-cream or cream.

My brother, Ian Harcourt Perry, my mother and me. We were all too fat! My mother made us eat *everything* on our plates!

Above: My mother, aged about 19 or 20, at a picnic in Sydney, probably Kirribilli. She is the one without a hat, in the front row – her hat seems to be on the man next to her.

Far left (top): My mother, Beatrice Austin Greigor before she was married to my father.

Far left (bottom): My father, Arthur Harcourt Perry.

Left: My Great–grandmother Perry holding me, with my father, Arthur Perry, behind the chair and my grandfather, Herbert Perry, with the large moustache.

Opposite: Me, probably aged 2+.

Me, taken just before I went to my 'coming out' ball. Kindly note the hair-set!

Above: Me, playing the lead in *The Prince Who Was a Piper*, during my last year at school at Glennie.

Below: My wedding to Henry White in the tropical Brisbane garden of my great–uncle, George Perry. The wedding party (left to right): Keith Wilson, Marga Harrold, Henry White, me, Chad Martin, Sheila Arnott, Ron Smith, Marjorie Lightbody.

Top left: My son, Michael Charles Hunter White.

Top right: My eldest daugheter, Susan Gai White – now Sue Fairlie-Cuninghame, Executive Editor, Food and Wine, *Vogue Entertaining*.

Bottom left: My youngest daughter, Carolyn Anne White – now Carolyn McKittrick.

Opposite: Me, at the Royal Easter Show in Sydney – my hat from Stella Frankel and my suit from Madam Pellier!

Me, painted by Wallace Thornton in the early 1950s. I am wearing the gown in which I was called in at the Black and White Ball.

CRÈME CARAMEL
(Serves 4 to 6)

Caramel
$^3/_4$ cup sugar
1 tablespoon water

Custard
600 ml milk
150 ml cream
6 eggs
3 heaped tablespoons sugar
1 teaspoon vanilla extract

To make the caramel
Melt the sugar and water in a heavy-based saucepan and cook until the syrup forms a caramel. Pour the caramel into an oven-proof mould and keep turning the mould until the inside is coated. Set aside to cool.

To make the custard
Heat the milk and cream until warm. Beat the eggs with the sugar and vanilla extract, then pour in the warm milk mixture. Strain the custard into the caramel-lined mould. Cover well with a double layer of heavy-duty foil and with a lid if available.

Place the mould in a large saucepan with hot water coming almost to the top of the mould. Cook in just simmering water for 45 minutes. Take out the custard and check that it is cooked: be careful not to overcook or the custard will be watery. Allow to cool, and refrigerate overnight. When ready to serve, turn the crème caramel out onto a serving dish.

CRÈME RENVERSÉE WITH CUMQUATS
Make a custard as for Crème Caramel above. Instead of lining the bowl with caramel, grease it with butter and cook the custard in the same way.

Refrigerate the custard overnight and after turning it out pour over $^1/_2$ cup Grand Marnier and sprinkle with $^1/_2$ cup chopped preserved cumquats.

PETER MEIER'S FLAMBÉED FRUITS

These were always served by Peter at Len Evans' famous wine auctions at Rothbury vineyards in the Hunter Valley.

(Serves 12)

250 g unsalted butter
60 g sugar
3 punnets strawberries, hulled
8 Chinese gooseberries (kiwifruit), peeled and sliced
4 mangoes or peaches, peeled and sliced
200 g fresh lychees, peeled
flesh and juice from 4 passionfruit
juice of 4 oranges
finely shredded zest of 2 oranges
50 ml brandy
50 ml Cointreau

Melt the butter and sugar in a large frying pan. Add the fruits, fruit juices and zest and cook over high heat for a few minutes, until the juices bubble. Pour in the brandy and Cointreau, and tip the pan over the flame. Hopefully it will ignite the alcohol! If you are cooking on an electric stove you will need a box of matches. Serve the fruits as soon as they have flamed.

DAMIEN PIGNOLET'S BUTTERY SHORTCRUST

The best variation on a shortcrust pastry I have discovered.

180 g unsalted butter
240 g plain flour
pinch of salt
60 ml water or mineral water

Remove the butter from the refrigerator 30 minutes before making the pastry.

Sieve the flour and salt onto a marble pastry slab or work bench. Chop the butter into smallish pieces and toss lightly in the flour. Make a well in the centre and pour in the cold water.

Using a pastry scraper, work the paste to a very rough heap of buttery lumps of dough.

Using the heel of your hand, quickly smear the pastry away from you across the board. It will lightly combine. Gather the dough together, press quickly into a flat cake, dust with a little flour, wrap in plastic film and refrigerate for 20 minutes.

Roll out, dusting with flour as necessary. Drape the pastry over the rolling pin and roll over a flan tin.

Prick the bottom with a fork and place the shell in the freezer or refrigerator for at least 20 minutes before baking. Line with a double thickness of foil, pressed well into the corners. Cook for 10 minutes at 200°C, then remove the foil and lower the temperature to 180°C. Cook for a further 10 minutes until quite dry, golden and crisp.

If the pastry is to be filled with a liquid, have the filling hot and pour straight into the tart while the crust is still hot. In this way you will have no seepage of liquid into the base.

Do not fill the tart with beans or rice. Pricking the base will prevent undue rising, and will permit a little bubbling of the surface, which adds to the flaky quality.

Completed shells can be stored in the freezer for days until needed. Do not defrost them. They go straight from the freezer to the oven at 200°C.

Always roll the pastry out after it has been rested for a short time only. It should never be hard. Let it warm up to room temperature if it has been in the refrigerator overnight.

Chill the pastry in the freezer for 20 minutes before baking.

Recipe from Stephanie's Feasts and Stories, *Stephanie Alexander (Allen & Unwin)*

CATERING DAYS

I haven't got the slightest idea how I learnt to cook for large numbers of people. Like everything else, I just did it. When I left the country and came down to Sydney, my life became very different. The most obvious thing was that I now had to earn a living, but from what? I thought about what I could do, and I thought, 'Well, I can cook'. So that's really the beginning of my career in food.

I drove around in a series of mad cars that my children and grandchildren remember with amusement. There was a multi-coloured one – green, pink and brown – with roof racks. And then there was the yellow Datsun station-wagon. The honour of sitting in the back seat caused fights among the kids because there was a gaping hole in the floor through which the road could be seen whizzing by. As a caterer, I never had anything as glamorous as a van with my name on it to go to the glamorous events or homes we catered for.

I married again, Lindsay Campbell, a journalist I met in Sydney. Lindsay had one arm, the other having been torn off in a car accident. I worked with Lindsay throughout our life together. At one stage, he had a small magazine for the country called *Agroscene* to which I contributed recipes, until one night there was a terrible tragedy and the place where the magazine was printed burnt down. Of course, nothing was insured, so the magazine folded. It was through Lindsay that I re-established contact with an old friend, Consuelo Guinness – Perry, her husband, used to drive Lindsay home occasionally from the local pub – and Consuelo and I started catering together.

Consuelo's father was Carlos Zalapa and he was really a good cook. He was Mexican, and had fled the Revolution in 1919. He ran one of Sydney's first ethnic restaurants, La Bodega, a Spanish restaurant in Paddington. So Consuelo grew up surrounded by good food and even ran the restaurant for a while. Carlos was involved in writing one the most influential books of the time, *Oh, For a French Wife!* with Ted Moloney and other members of the Society of Gourmets. They also wrote two other very good books called *Oh For a Man Who Cooks* and *Cooking for Bachelors* – all well illustrated with some very racy graphics. We used many recipes from these books as a basis for our dishes, and they were all consistently successful: fillet of beef with béarnaise sauce, beef stroganoff, bortsch and French onion soup.

FILLET OF BEEF WITH BÉARNAISE SAUCE
(Serves 6 to 8)

Beef
1 fillet of beef, trimmed of all fat and membrane,
 and tied with string to form a roll
125 g butter, melted
sea salt flakes
freshly ground pepper
1 tablespoon boiling water

Béarnaise sauce
³/₄ cup white wine
¹/₃ cup white vinegar
1 tablespoon dried French tarragon
1 small onion, peeled and chopped finely
handful of parsley stalks
small knob of butter
freshly ground pepper to taste
6 egg yolks, beaten
250 g butter, at room temperature

To cook the beef
Preheat the oven to 220°C. Place the beef in a baking tin. Pour over the melted butter and sprinkle with salt and pepper. Cook on the centre shelf of the oven for 5 minutes. Remove the tin from the oven, and pour the boiling water around the meat. Baste the meat well and turn the oven heat down to 180°C. Continue to cook the meat for a further 30 minutes, basting once or twice. Remove the meat from the tin and allow to rest for 15 minutes before serving. The fillet can also be served cold, but is best eaten the day it is cooked.

To make the béarnaise sauce

Place the wine, vinegar, tarragon, onion, parsley stalks, teaspoon of butter and the pepper in a stainless-steel saucepan. Simmer very slowly until the liquid is reduced to about 3 tablespoons. Strain and put in the top of a double boiler with the beaten eggs. Cook over simmering water, stirring with a wooden spoon until the mixture has thickened like custard. (Take care that the top section of the double boiler does not touch the simmering water, or the mixture will curdle.)

Gradually whisk in the butter, in small pieces, until the sauce has thickened. (You can do this with a small hand-held electric beater.) Pour into a container and set aside to cool. (Do not refrigerate.)

Slice the beef and serve with the béarnaise sauce and a simple green salad or vegetable.

BEEF STROGANOFF

Adapted from Ted Moloney's recipe in Oh, for a French Wife!.

(Serves 4)

1 kg trimmed fillet of beef, cut in slices
125 g butter
1 tablespoon chopped onion
salt and pepper to taste
250 g button mushrooms, stalks removed, sliced
300 ml sour cream

To serve
boiled rice or baby new potatoes
green salad

Pound each piece of fillet with a wooden mallet until it is flattened to 5 mm thick, then cut into fingers. Melt the butter in a frying pan with a lid. Add the onion and cook, stirring, over low heat until the onion is soft and yellow. Add the beef, increase the heat and cook quickly for 2 minutes on each side, keeping the pieces on the move. Season with salt and pepper.

Remove the steak with a slotted spoon to a warm casserole and set aside. Add the mushrooms to the butter remaining in the pan. Sauté with the lid on the pan, adding a little more salt and pepper. Return the beef to the pan and immediately everything is completely hot again, stir in the sour cream.

To serve
Beef Stroganoff used to be served with boiled rice, but you can also serve it with baby new potatoes and follow it with a green salad.

FRENCH ONION SOUP
Adapted from Ted Moloney's recipe in 'Oh, For a French Wife!.

Stock
1 boiling fowl or 2 kg gravy beef
1 small bunch of celery, any wilted leaves cut off
1 carrot
2 onions, cut in halves
3.75 litres water
salt and pepper to taste

Soup
750 g peeled and sliced onions
125 g butter
salt and pepper to taste
thin slices of golden toast
grated cheese

To make the stock
Place the chicken or beef in a large pot with the celery, carrot and onions. Don't chop the vegetables into little pieces: the stock will simmer very slowly, so there will be plenty of time for all the flavour of the vegetables to be extracted. (Keeping the vegetables in large pieces will prevent them from getting mushy and they won't 'cloud' the stock.) Add the water, salt and pepper, and bring to the boil, then turn the heat very low and simmer slowly for 4 hours.

Strain the stock into a bowl, discard the vegetables and, if you have used a boiling fowl, put it aside for some other use. (My dog, Chandon, would love it!) Refrigerate the stock overnight to set the fat, and remove it before making the soup.

To make the soup
Very gently fry the onions in the butter. Remove any piece of onion that shows signs of burning. The golden colour of the soup must be preserved: this is a very definite indication of its flavour.

Transfer the stock to a clean pot and, when the onions are soft and golden, drop them into the stock. Taste for salt and pepper, and simmer, covered, for 1 hour.

Preheat the oven to 180°C. Line the bottom of a baking dish with the toast (it must be free of burns) and cover it with a good layer of grated cheese (approximately 5 mm thick). Pour the soup gently into the baking dish so that the cheese-loaded toast floats to the surface with as little disturbance as possible. Add another good, heavy layer of grated cheese to the now-floating toast and put it in the preheated oven for 10 minutes, or until the cheese and toast merge into a light and creamy crust. Take the baking dish straight to the table and serve.

Other stalwart books we relied on were Elizabeth David and Robert Carrier. Cold soups became very fashionable at one stage, and we often relied on Carrier's fresh tomato soup with cream, diced ham and cucumber.

SUMMER TOMATO SOUP, ADAPTED FROM ROBERT CARRIER
(Serves 4)

1 kg ripe tomatoes, washed
1 tablespoon sugar
2 teaspoons salt
1 teaspoon onion juice
grated rind and juice of $\frac{1}{2}$ lemon, or more to taste
150 ml cream, chilled
4 thin slices cooked leg ham, diced
$\frac{1}{4}$ cucumber or 1 Lebanese cucumber, peeled and diced

Purée the tomatoes in a blender or food processor and pass through a sieve. (There should be a little over 600 ml of purée.) Chill thoroughly in the refrigerator.

Just before serving, add the sugar, salt, onion juice and grated rind and juice of the lemon. Stir thoroughly until smooth, then stir in the cream. Add the diced ham and cucumber and serve at once.

In the first days of the catering business, we just ran around delivering home-made pâtés and quiches to private clients. The very first thing I did was a dish of braised pigeon for a private dinner. There was no competition, the market was wide open. No one else was doing simply prepared, gourmet foods in the eastern suburbs. Consuelo and I made quiches with every flavour – so new! so fashionable – served as a first course or with a green salad for bridge lunches.

QUICHE LORRAINE

Pastry
$1\frac{1}{4}$ cups plain flour
pinch of salt
120 g butter
2 to 3 tablespoons iced water

Filling

125 g bacon rashers, rinds removed
3 eggs
300 ml cream
salt, pepper and nutmeg to taste
90 g Swiss cheese, grated

To make the pastry

Place the flour, salt and butter in a food processor and process with an on–off action until the mixture is like fine breadcrumbs. Add the iced water and when the mixture forms a ball remove it from the bowl and wrap in plastic film. Refrigerate for at least an hour.

Place a 23 cm quiche ring on a buttered baking tray. Roll out the pastry on a floured board and line the quiche ring. Refrigerate for at least 2 hours.

To make the filling

Preheat the oven to 190°C. Grill the bacon rashers until crisp, then chop and set aside to cool. Beat the eggs together with the cream, salt, pepper and nutmeg. Scatter the bacon over the base of the tart shell, add the cheese, then pour in the egg mixture. Bake the quiche in the oven, on the shelf above the centre, for 45 minutes.

At that time, chicken was regarded as *the* party dish. At any functions, chicken it was, and often very badly prepared. It was the days of what we called Chicken Sick – a sobriquet coined by the clever advertising man, David Wynne, for the plates of pale, washed-out chicken liberally covered in a dubious white sauce with bits of herb in it. This dish was the universal function dish and regarded as very delicious, which it wasn't.

We did Pink Chicken and a Chicken Salad that were extremely successful. The Chicken Salad developed into one of my most useful dishes.

PINK CHICKEN
(Serves 4)

5 chicken drumsticks and 5 thighs, still on the bone
butter
2 tablespoons finely chopped onion
1 cup white wine
1/2 teaspoon dried thyme
1 tablespoon paprika
salt and pepper to taste
1 cup cream
1 tablespoon plain flour, dissolved in a little milk
finely chopped parsley

Sauté the chicken pieces in a pan in a little butter and, when the pieces are lightly coloured, add the onion and cook for 3 to 4 minutes over low heat. Add the wine, thyme, paprika, salt and pepper. Cover and cook slowly until the chicken is tender.

Remove the chicken pieces to a serving dish and keep warm. Carefully spoon off the fat from the pan juices. Stir in the cream and heat through, then pour in the flour and milk mixture. Bring the mixture to the boil and simmer until the sauce thickens.

Return the chicken pieces to the pan and cook them in the sauce over low heat for 4 to 5 minutes. Sprinkle with a little extra paprika and finely chopped parsley and serve at once with a green salad.

CHICKEN SALAD

I always use S&W mayonnaise in this recipe as home-made mayonnaise can separate when the salad is stored in the refrigerator.

(Serves 10)

Chicken
2 x No. 16 chickens
2 carrots, peeled and chopped
2 onions, peeled and chopped
2 sticks of celery, broken in pieces
salt and pepper

Dressing
2$^1/_2$ cups mayonnaise, more if necessary
1 cup thickened cream
1 to 2 tablespoons soy sauce
curry powder to taste
salt and freshly ground pepper to taste

Salad
freshly cooked chicken meat, chopped
2 x 300 g cans water chestnuts, drained and sliced finely
12 spring onions, sliced finely
2 cups finely chopped celery
$^1/_2$ cup good mango chutney
Italian parsley leaves

To cook the chickens
Place the chickens, breast up, in a large boiler. Scatter in the vegetables, add plenty of salt and pepper and pour in water to come about halfway up the chickens. Bring to the boil, cover and simmer for 1 hour 10 minutes. Test the chickens at the thigh joint to see if they are cooked.

Remove the lid and leave the birds in the pot until they are cool enough to handle. (I used to wear rubber gloves.) Remove the meat and skin and cut in pieces. Place in a bowl, cover and refrigerate.

To make the dressing
Mix all the ingredients together.

To assemble and serve the salad
Mix the chopped chicken with the water chestnuts, spring onions, celery, chutney, parsley leaves and the dressing. Taste for salt and pepper. Cover and refrigerate until serving time.

Eventually our catering got out of hand and each of us decided to go our own way. Consuelo is now Food Editor of *Belle* and also still hard at it catering. She is one of my best friends.

We did well because we served good food – things like fabulous sandwiches, based on the method my mother taught me. She said, and quite rightly, that if people were drinking there should be sandwiches. People don't seem to have them as often now and I think it's because they can't be bothered making them – good sandwiches are time-consuming. Our favourites were chicken, mayonnaise and celery (made with S&W mayonnaise rather than a home-made one, because the texture is better for sandwiches), fresh ham and mustard, beef and béarnaise, beef and chutney, pâté, and egg and chopped stuffed olives. I discovered a marvellous way of preparing the chicken for a chicken sandwich. I separate the meat from the bones of a cooked chicken while it is still hot, wearing rubber gloves. Include all the skin because it keeps the flesh moist (chop the skin separately and then mix it in). Pack all the meat and skin bits tightly into a rectangular plastic container and put it in the fridge until it is quite cold. It will then be a firm mass that can be cut into slices, broken up, chopped, and mixed with whatever you fancy. I noted at a recent function that Belinda Franks had added toasted pine nuts and raisins to the chicken sandwiches and left out the celery. Quite delicious!

I prepared many things for the Art Gallery of New South Wales, including an opening for the British Exhibition of 1977. I remember it was a cocktail buffet where we served big platters of sandwiches. Sue, my daughter, and I had to crawl along underneath the tables to get to the baskets to replenish them, it was so crowded. Other openings we did there were the Chinese Exhibition with 1000 guests, where I catered with the usual food and we had Chinese cooks to do the Chinese-style food.

Another dish we used frequently – and these are limited only by one's imagination and taste – were baby tarts. We started serving them in the days when the vol-au-vent reigned supreme. We made the tart cases ourselves then; now, good ones can be bought and filled. They were my suggestion for the recent opening of *Vogue Korea*, because they are easy, sophisticated and very Australian. Our business manager carried up a few thousand of them by hand on the plane and the caterers filled them according to my suggestions. They were a great success: she said they 'inhaled them'. Baby tarts are great containers for any little thing, and they go straight into the mouth in one pop. We often used egg and bacon, tomato, and mixed mushroom fillings.

TINY TARTS
(Makes 30 cases)

Tart cases
1^1/$_4$ cups plain flour
salt
125 g butter
2 tablespoons iced water

Fillings
Neil Perry's caviar tarts (recipe follows)
seared scallops on creamy cabbage (recipe follows)

To make the tart cases
Place the flour, salt and butter in a food processor and process with an on–off action until the mixture is like fine breadcrumbs. Add the iced water all at once and, when the mixture forms a ball, remove from the bowl and wrap in plastic film. Refrigerate for at least an hour.

Preheat the oven to 190°C. Roll out the dough until thin and cut into rounds with a small biscuit cutter. Line small patty tins with the pastry rounds. Cook in the oven for 12 minutes. Store the tart cases in an airtight container until ready to fill.

NEIL PERRY'S CAVIAR TARTS
Neil said this recipe was never to be given away and I never did until I noted he had published it in his book! Here is the original recipe he gave me when Vogue *had a 'fashion' party at the Prime Minister's residence at Kirribilli on Sydney Harbour when the Keatings were in residence.*

Filling
florets from 1 medium cauliflower
^{1}/$_4$ to ^{1}/$_2$ cup olive oil
1 large onion, peeled and diced
2 large cloves garlic, peeled and chopped
juice of 1 lemon
a little chicken stock
salt and pepper to taste

To serve
tiny tart cases
Osietra caviar

To make the filling
Put all the ingredients for the filling in a heavy-based saucepan and cook, covered, over low heat, stirring occasionally until the cauliflower is tender. Transfer the mixture to a food processor and purée until smooth. Set aside in a bowl to cool.

To serve
Put a spoonful of the cold cauliflower cream in each tart case, top with a little Osietra caviar and serve at once.

SEARED SCALLOPS ON CREAMY CABBAGE
30 scallops without roes
1 tablespoon olive oil
2 tablespoons butter
heart of 1 small Savoy cabbage
2 tablespoons lemon juice
salt and freshly ground pepper
200 ml cream

To serve
tiny tart cases

Dry the scallops with paper towels and toss in olive oil. Set aside.

Melt the butter in a large frying pan and cook the cabbage over very low heat with the lemon juice, salt and pepper until just barely cooked: about 8 minutes. Add the cream and bring to the boil and cook over high heat for 2 to 3 minutes. Taste for salt, pepper and lemon juice.

Salt and pepper the scallops and sear them briefly on each side over high heat on a Le Creuset grill or in a non-stick frying pan.

To serve
Spoon a small pile of cabbage into each tart case, place a scallop on top and serve at once.

I developed a solid private clientele, cooking regularly for many well-known clients, and I regularly donated my services, with Sue's help, in preparing the Melbourne Cup lunch for the Peter Pan Committee. I remember that at all events my tortes, cakes and ice-creams were consumed with gusto. This proved to be something of a strain at one opera dinner held at Lady Mary Fairfax's residence, Fairwater, in Sydney when I was responsible for the desserts and sixty extra guests turned up before the end of dinner!

APRICOT ALMOND TORTE

These tortes were the best catering standby and people always came back for more. Twelve of each of the tortes were made for the Fairwater event.

(Makes 16 slices)

350 g castor sugar
2 teaspoons baking powder
10 Sao biscuits, rolled into large crumbs
   with a rolling pin
250 g almonds with the skins on, chopped finely
250 g dried apricots, chopped finely
8 egg whites

To serve
600 ml thickened cream
vanilla extract to taste
glacé apricots, sliced
angelica, cut in small strips

Preheat the oven to 180°C. Butter a 28 cm springform tin. Line the base with greaseproof paper and butter again.

Mix all the dry ingredients together in a bowl. With your fingertips, break up the chopped apricots so they are evenly distributed throughout the mixture.

Whip the egg whites until they hold stiff peaks and fold carefully into the dry mixture. Pour the mixture into the prepared tin and bake on the centre shelf of the preheated oven for 45 minutes.

When the torte is cooked, loosen the springform and turn the torte onto a wire rack. Remove the paper. If the torte does not seem to be cooked, do not worry: sometimes it appears to be a little sticky. When the torte is cold, slide it onto a serving platter and cover tightly with foil. (The torte can be made two days in advance, or can be frozen successfully for a week.)

To serve
Finish the torte at least two hours before serving. It is easier to serve if you cut it before decorating. With a sharp knife, cut the torte in quarters and cut each quarter into four slices. Whip the cream and flavour it with the vanilla extract. Spread the cream over the torte and decorate with glacé apricots and angelica. If the weather is hot, refrigerate the torte, but it is good served at room temperature.

DATE TORTE

Make this in exactly the same way as the Apricot Almond Torte, substituting walnuts and stoned dates for the almonds and dried apricots. Decorate the cream with finely sliced dates.

CHOCOLATE TORTE

(Makes 16 slices)

350 g castor sugar
2 teaspoons baking powder
pinch of salt
4 tablespoons cocoa
2 cups coarsely shredded coconut
2 cups cornflakes, crushed a little with a rolling pin
250 g walnuts, chopped finely
8 egg whites

To serve
600 ml thickened cream
vanilla extract to taste
coarsely grated dark chocolate

Preheat the oven to 190°C. Butter a 28 cm springform tin. Line the base with greaseproof paper and butter again.

Mix all the dry ingredients together in a bowl. Whip the egg whites until they hold stiff peaks and fold carefully into the dry mixture. Pour the mixture into the prepared tin and bake on the centre shelf of the preheated oven for 45 minutes.

When the torte is cooked, loosen the springform and turn the torte onto a wire rack. Remove the paper. When the torte is cold, slide it onto a serving platter and cover tightly with foil. (The torte can be made two days in advance, or can be frozen successfully for a week.)

To serve
Finish the torte at least two hours before serving. It is easier to serve if you cut it before decorating. With a sharp knife, cut the torte in quarters and cut each quarter into four slices. Whip the cream and flavour it with the vanilla extract. Spread the cream over the torte and sprinkle with the coarsely grated chocolate. If the weather is hot, refrigerate the torte, but it is good served at room temperature.

FERNAND POINT'S PAVÉ AU CHOCOLAT

This was the cake made for my first Vogue lunch.

(Makes 8 to 10 slices)

Sponge cake
4 eggs
3/4 cup castor sugar
2/3 cup plain flour
1/3 cup cornflour
pinch of salt
1 teaspoon baking powder

Chocolate layer
250 g good-quality dark chocolate
1 tablespoon water
6 egg yolks, beaten
250 g very soft butter
6 egg whites, beaten stiffly

To serve
300 ml cream, whipped

To make the cake
Preheat the oven to 190°C. Butter and flour a 28 cm springform tin.

Beat the eggs with an electric beater until thick and fluffy. Gradually add the castor sugar and continue beating until the mixture is thick and white.

Mix together all the dry ingredients and sift over the beaten eggs. Carefully fold together and pour into the springform tin. Bake on one shelf above the centre of the oven for 20 to 25 minutes, or until the cake is cooked. Remove the springform and turn the cake out onto a rack to cool for a few hours.

Transfer the cake to a serving platter and fix folded pieces of strong aluminium foil around the cake with a paper clip, to form a collar. Make sure that the foil is tight, as it will have to contain the chocolate mixture.

To make the chocolate layer
Melt the chocolate with the water in a basin over hot water. Remove from the heat. Beat the egg yolks and blend with the chocolate, beating thoroughly to mix well. Beat in the softened butter. Fold in the stiffly beaten egg whites and immediately pour the chocolate mixture over the cake. Cover and refrigerate overnight.

To serve
Remove the foil collar, spread over the whipped cream and serve cut in slices.

SMALL MERINGUES WITH LEMON BUTTER
Ten quantities of meringues and eight of lemon butter were made for the Fairwater event.

(Makes 80 small meringues or
40 medium-sized meringues)

Meringues
5 egg whites
pinch of salt
375 g castor sugar

Lemon butter
6 egg yolks
100 g sugar or to taste
juice and finely grated rind of 3 lemons
150 g butter

To serve
500 ml thickened cream, whipped until it holds stiff peaks

To make the meringues
Preheat the oven to 100°C. Beat the egg whites with the salt until they hold soft peaks. Continue beating and add half the sugar, 1 tablespoon at a time, until the mixture holds stiff peaks. Add the remaining sugar all at once and beat for a few minutes only.

Butter biscuit trays. Cover with greaseproof paper and butter again. Place meringues on the trays with a spoon (the size depends on how you wish to serve them) and bake on the lower shelves of the oven for 2 to 2½ hours. Cool and store in an airtight container. The meringues can be made at least four or five days before serving.

To make the lemon butter
Beat the egg yolks with sugar until pale and thick. Place in a saucepan with the lemon juice and rind and cook over low heat, stirring constantly with a wooden spoon, until the mixture thickens. Remove from the stove and beat in the butter. Pour into a large, clean screw-top jar and allow to cool. This will keep for at least one week, covered, in the refrigerator.

To serve the meringues
Place the meringues on a large platter with a bowl of lemon butter and a bowl of the whipped cream for guests to help themselves.

POACHED PEACHES
(Serves 6)

3 cups water
3 cups sugar
6 peaches

Put the water and sugar in a large saucepan and bring to the boil, stirring until the sugar has dissolved. Add the unpeeled peaches and return the syrup to the boil. Lower the heat and poach the peaches gently for about 20 minutes, carefully turning them a few times to ensure they cook evenly. Remove the saucepan from the heat and carefully transfer the peaches to a large bowl. Pour in the syrup and set aside to cool, then cover and refrigerate.

To serve, remove the skins from the poached peaches and serve each peach on a plate with a little of the poaching syrup.

I love making ice-cream and I've experimented with a wide range of flavours over the years.

Never whip the cream before making ice-cream in a machine, as the churning can turn the mixture to butter! I had this experience myself once when I was churning the ice-cream as the guests were eating their dinner.

PEACH ICE-CREAM

(Serves 8 to 10)

5 egg yolks
$3/4$ cup sugar
300 ml milk
dash of vanilla extract
550 g fresh yellow peach flesh
300 g poached peach flesh (see recipe on p. 136)
1 cup castor sugar
$1/3$ cup peach liqueur
$1/2$ cup syrup from the poached peaches
300 ml thick cream

Beat the egg yolks and sugar together. Heat the milk, pour a little of the hot milk onto the beaten eggs and mix together. Pour the egg mixture back into the saucepan and cook over low heat, stirring constantly, until the mixture thickens and coats the back of a spoon. Remove from the heat, pour into a bowl, add the vanilla extract and set aside to cool.

Put the fresh peach flesh, poached peach flesh, castor sugar, peach liqueur and poached peach syrup in a food processor and purée until smooth. Mix with the cold custard, add the cream and refrigerate until well chilled. Freeze the peach mixture in an ice-cream maker as instructed by the manufacturer and store, covered, in the freezer until ready to use.

HONEY ICE-CREAM

(Serves 6)

8 eggs
1 cup honey
4 cups cream

Beat the eggs until thick and creamy. Bring the honey to the boil, then pour the hot honey onto the beaten eggs and whisk until mixed. Pour the mixture back into the saucepan and cook over low heat, stirring constantly until the mixture thickens a little. Do not let the mixture boil.

Pour into a bowl and set aside to cool thoroughly. When cold, add the cream and chill in the refrigerator. Freeze in an ice-cream machine as instructed by the manufacturer and store, covered, in the freezer until ready to use.

ORANGE ICE-CREAM
(Serves 20)

12 medium-sized navel oranges
12 egg yolks
2 cups sugar
1.2 litres cream

To serve
thin slices of peeled oranges, quarters of fresh figs or poached fruit

Chop 4 of the oranges roughly and purée in a food processor. (Purée well, as some of the zest should go into the ice-cream.) Extract the juice from the remaining oranges. Mix the juice with the orange purée and push through a sieve. Only a little of the pulp will go through and it is mainly the essence of the zest that is needed.

Beat the egg yolks with the sugar until well mixed. Add the sieved orange juice and cook over medium heat, stirring with a wooden spoon, until the mixture starts to thicken. Pour into a bowl and allow to cool. Cover and refrigerate until very cold.

Add the cream to the orange custard and freeze the mixture in an ice-cream maker as instructed by the manufacturer. Store, covered, in the freezer until ready to use.

An ice-cream machine produces the best ice-cream, but if you do not have one, whip the cream and mix in the orange custard. Pour the mixture into a large cake tin, cover with aluminium foil and put in the freezing compartment of your refrigerator. When the mixture is partly set, take it out and mix around a few times, then return to the freezer.

To serve
Spoon the ice-cream onto individual plates and serve with thin slices of peeled oranges, quarters of fresh figs or poached fruit of your choice.

COFFEE AND PECAN NUT ICE-CREAM
(Serves 4 to 6)

4 egg yolks
3/4 cup well-packed, soft brown sugar
1 cup milk
450 ml cream
2 tablespoons coffee essence
3/4 cup chopped pecan nuts

Beat the egg yolks and brown sugar together. Heat the milk and pour it onto the egg mixture. Return the mixture to the saucepan and cook gently over low heat, stirring until the mixture thickens and coats the back of a spoon. Pour into a bowl and set aside to cool.

When cold, add the cream, coffee essence and chopped pecan nuts. Cover and chill in the refrigerator. Freeze the mixture in an ice-cream maker as instructed by the manufacturer and store, covered, in the freezer until ready to use.

STRAWBERRY ICE-CREAM
(Serves 10)

2 punnets strawberries
6 egg yolks
1 cup sugar, or a little more if the strawberries
    are not fully ripe
900 ml cream
1 tablespoon lemon juice

Hull 1¾ punnets of the strawberries and keep the remainder for serving. Purée the hulled strawberries and set aside in a bowl.

Beat the egg yolks with the sugar. Bring the cream to the boil, pour a little onto the egg mixture and whisk together. Return the mixture to the hot cream in the saucepan and cook, stirring constantly, until the mixture coats the back of a spoon. Strain the custard onto the puréed strawberries, add the lemon juice and taste for sugar. The mixture should be very sweet as the frozen ice-cream loses sweetness and flavour. Chill the mixture in the refrigerator then freeze in an ice-cream maker as instructed by the manufacturer and store, covered, in the freezer.

CARAMEL ICE-CREAM
(Serves 8)

¾ cup sugar
1 teaspoon water
400 ml milk
500 ml cream
5 egg yolks
vanilla extract

Place the sugar and water in a saucepan and cook slowly to a dark caramel. It is from this caramel that you will get the flavour and colour. Be careful not to burn the sugar. Plunge the bottom of the saucepan into cold water to arrest the cooking.

Boil the milk and cream in a separate saucepan and, off the heat and preferably over the sink, pour the hot mixture onto the caramel. Put the saucepan with the caramel mixture back on the stove over low heat and cook until the caramel dissolves.

Beat the egg yolks with a little vanilla, then pour in a little of the hot caramel mixture and stir together. Pour the mixture back into the saucepan and cook over low heat, stirring, until the mixture coats the back of a spoon. Allow the custard to cool, then pour it into a bowl, cover and chill well. Freeze the custard in an ice-cream maker as instructed by the manufacturer and store, covered, in the freezer until ready to use.

CRÈME GLACÉE À LA SARRASINE
(Serves 8 to 10)

12 egg yolks
$1^1/_4$ cups sugar
pinch of salt
1 litre cream
$^1/_3$ cup Armagnac
$1^1/_2$ tablespoons ground cardamom
1 tablespoon vanilla extract

To serve
$^1/_3$ cup sugar
$^1/_2$ cup lightly toasted slivered almonds
$^1/_2$ cup cream
2 tablespoons Armagnac

In a bowl, beat the egg yolks, sugar and salt together. Bring the cream to the boil in a saucepan, then pour a little hot cream onto the yolk mixture and whisk together. Return the yolk mixture to the pan and cook over low heat, stirring constantly, until the mixture coats the back of a spoon. Pour the custard into a bowl and, stirring now and again, allow to cool. Cover and refrigerate for 1 hour.

Add the Armagnac, cardamom and vanilla and whisk until mixed. Cover and refrigerate for at least 2 hours. Freeze in an ice-cream maker as instructed by the manufacturer. Transfer to a covered container and store in the freezer until ready to serve. (This ice-cream will not harden, but will always remain pleasantly soft.)

To serve
Heat the sugar in a frying pan over low heat until it begins to caramelise. Add the almonds and toss. Pour the caramel and almonds onto a tray and leave to cool. When the caramel is cool, break it up into small pieces and store in an airtight jar until ready to use. Lightly whip the cream and Armagnac together.

Spoon the ice-cream into chilled glasses. Pour over a small amount of the Armagnac cream and sprinkle with a few caramel almonds.

BUTTER PECAN ICE-CREAM

(Serves 6)

1 cup brown sugar
$^{1}/_{2}$ cup water
pinch of salt
2 eggs
2 tablespoons butter
1 cup milk
1 teaspoon vanilla extract
1 tablespoon sherry
300 ml thickened cream
$^{1}/_{2}$ cup broken pecan pieces

Place the brown sugar, water and salt in a saucepan, bring to the boil and simmer for 2 minutes. Remove from the heat and add the eggs, beating until the mixture has thickened slightly. Beat in the butter and set the mixture aside to cool. When it is cold, add the milk, vanilla, sherry and, lastly, fold in the cream.

Chill the mixture and then freeze it in an ice-cream maker, adding the nuts when the ice-cream starts to set.

Serve with pecan biscuits (see recipe on p. 83)

We never served food that made anyone sick. We never skimped on ingredients, or on the oil or butter, and everything was always fresh. There was never a question of buying things like seafood the day before the party. However, sometimes one can't control everything. In the early days, it was essential to take everything one could possibly need to the job in question, even washing-up gloves and detergent. So to cater for the opening of Harry Seidler's new building in North Sydney, Consuelo Guinness was sent along complete, as usual, with jars of vinaigrette, mayonnaise, béarnaise and also yellow detergent. Somehow the vinaigrette and the detergent got muddled and the salad was tossed with the latter. People ate a bit of it, but luckily it was whipped off the table and the salad remade with the correct dressing before anyone was severely compromised. We used pink detergent after that.

There were many high-profile events that followed. Marjorie Pagan hosted a dinner for King Hussein of Jordan. Naturally there was fierce security; the place was swarming with troops of armed, uniformed guards patrolling the grounds, and they even had an official taster. We were in the garden in the big double garage preparing for dinner. At this time of my life, I used to get terrible, terrible nerves before big events like these and my stomach would blow up. This time it blew up so much I felt breathless. The waiters had just taken in plates to serve, and I let off explosively, an absolute banger, like a gun shot. Sue, my daughter, who was assisting me, said 'Mum!' in a shocked voice, but I must say I felt much better. However, what I hadn't reckoned on was the security scare that the noise caused. All the guards came running, machine guns at the ready. We pretended nothing had happened as they searched the shed. It really was quite frightening, but very funny at the same time.

I prepared lunches and dinners for many other political figures, which went off without such drama. They included the United States Ambassador and the United States and British Consuls-General, Princess Ira von Fürstenburg, Earl Mountbatten, Sir Michael Redgrave, Glenda Jackson and the Royal Shakespeare Company.

Another VIP dinner at which I catered was a marvellous party held for Dame Joan Sutherland and Luciano Pavarotti, two legends who were singing together in Sydney. It was hosted by Di Heath at Mrs John Lewis' house on the harbour. I made stuffed peaches – *pesche ripieni* – from a recipe by Giuliano Bugialli, and there were two magnificent cakes, one for each guest of honour, prepared by two talented cooks, Dany Chouet (she made a luscious chocolate cake for Pavarotti) and Millie Sherman (a two-tiered cake with butterflies and flowers, Dame Joan's favourite themes at the time). Dame Joan didn't show up, which was in the end a great relief to all of us because her cake collapsed! It was a hot night, really hot, the worst I think we had had in years, and we had fans playing on the cakes to keep them cool. Dame Joan's cake wilted nevertheless – the butterflies took off with the fan and the flowers just fell off. I am very proud to report that the stuffed peaches looked good and tasted delicious. Pavarotti said he had not had peaches like that since his mother made them for him as a child. Photos of Pavarotti eating are rare, and I never got one of him with my peaches, although I later managed to take one of him eating quail at a party in Melbourne for *Vogue*.

GIULIANO BUGIALLI'S STUFFED PEACHES
The peaches are baked just enough so they don't lose their fresh taste. The natural flavour is also enhanced by the stuffing, which has an apricot flavour, complementing the peach taste without covering it.

(Serves 6)

6 large freestone peaches, ripe but not overripe
90 g amaretti biscuits
6 pats butter
1/4 cup sugar
1/4 cup brandy

Preheat the oven to 190°C. Divide the peaches in half and remove the stones. (To halve a peach and remove the stone without breaking the peach, find the line that girdles the peach and follow it in, cutting through with a knife. Place each hand firmly on each of the peach halves. To loosen both halves from the stone, gently turn the two halves in opposite directions until they are free of the stone.) With a teaspoon, enlarge the holes left by the stone a little.

Butter a rectangular Pyrex baking dish (32 cm x 22 cm) and place all 12 peach halves in it. Crush the amaretti into crumbs with a mortar and pestle or blender, then fill the peach holes with the amaretti crumbs. Put half a pat of butter, then a teaspoon of sugar, over each peach half.

Place the baking dish in the preheated oven for 20 minutes, then remove the dish from the oven, add 1 teaspoon of brandy to each peach half, and bake for 15 to 20 minutes more.

Remove the dish and transfer the peaches to a serving dish. Let stand until completely cold; do not refrigerate.

Giuliano Bugialli, The Fine Art of Italian Cooking *(Times Books)*

CHOCOLATE AND RASPBERRY CAKE

Made by Dany Chouet of Cleopatra Restaurant at Blackheath in the Blue Mountains of New South Wales to honour the great tenor, Pavarotti.

5 eggs
125 g castor sugar
100 g powdered almonds
60 g cocoa (Drostes if possible)
50 g plain flour
50 g unsalted butter, melted and cooled
3 tablespoons sugar

Chocolate cream
350 ml cream
450 g dark chocolate

Raspberry syrup
200 ml water
3 tablespoons sugar
3 tablespoons raspberry liqueur (Framboise)
8 teaspoons seedless raspberry jam

Preheat the oven to 200°C and butter a 24 cm round springform tin. Line the bottom with greaseproof paper and butter again.

Beat 3 egg yolks with 1 whole egg and the castor sugar until the mixture is light and white. Sift together the powdered almonds, cocoa and flour, and mix well by hand. Alternately fold the flour mixture and the melted butter into the egg mixture using a large metal spoon.

Beat 4 egg whites until stiff with the 3 tablespoons of sugar until the mixture forms a meringue. Mix 2 or 3 tablespoons of this mixture with the chocolate mixture, then fold in the remaining meringue.

Carefully spoon the cake mixture into the tin. Cook on the centre shelf of the preheated oven for 25 to 30 minutes, until the cake is cooked. Turn the cake onto a cake cooler and leave until thoroughly cold.

To make the chocolate cream

Melt the chocolate with the cream. Allow to cool completely and chill until the mixture is cold and looks like thick cream.

To make the syrup and assemble the cake

Cook the water and sugar together for a few minutes. Allow to cool and add the raspberry liqueur.

Slice the cake horizontally into three layers (a sharp ham knife is best). Place the bottom layer on a serving dish, brush with the syrup, spread with half the raspberry jam, then spread over a quarter of the chocolate cream. Place on a second layer of cake and repeat. Place the last layer on top, paint with a little syrup and spread the remaining chocolate cream over the top and sides of the cake.

Chill, covered, in the refrigerator and remove 1 hour before serving.

I produced a lunch for the Russian ballerina Plisetskaya at the Australia Council. She was in Australia dancing *Carmen* with the Bolshoi Ballet. I concocted a special cake and put it on one of my favourite platters. It was presented in front of her at the appropriate moment and she, not speaking or understanding a word of English, said something in Russian and promptly departed, taking the cake and platter and leaving the lunch! No one got any pudding and I never saw my platter again.

Another interesting lunch presented me with a different sort of culinary challenge: sixty members of the Shanghai Philharmonic Orchestra were to have lunch on a boat in Sydney Harbour. They were the first Chinese musicians to visit Australia officially after the signing of the cultural trade agreement following Whitlam's trip to China in 1974. I devised lunchboxes, all made up with little sausages, hard-boiled egg, other assorted delicacies, and a spice cake. It was a huge job, but I had been told by Pat Yeomans, a friend who knew about such things, that this would be the method of eating the Chinese players would prefer. They ate it all, sang a song, and presented me with a Mao badge.

Another memorable luncheon on the Harbour was for Michel Laclotte, Director of the Louvre, who was entertained by the Australia Council. The lunch was a great success, so much so that my silverware was over-enthusiastically and accidentally thrown over the side of the boat!

I prepared a polo lunch in honour of His Royal Highness, Prince Charles. I did my baked ham, as well as a fillet of beef with chutney and mustard, chicken breasts with lemon mayonnaise, and three salads. Afterwards, we served big baskets of fresh fruits and local cheeses. For afternoon tea I served chocolate and orange cake. Security was tight, if not comic – German Shepherds sniffed the flower arrangements as we delivered them to the royal tent. When I returned to the car I realised I'd forgotten to leave my ham knife. My friend Perry Guinness headed for the royal tent brandishing the 45 cm blade and was pounced on by police guards, hands on holsters. The imperturbable Perry surrendered the 'offensive weapon' with a polite request that it be delivered to Jim Taylor in the royal tent to enable him to carve the Prince's ham.

COLD LEMON CHICKEN BREASTS
(Serves 8)

8 chicken breast fillets
a little plain flour
2 tablespoons butter
1 tablespoon vegetable oil
salt and pepper to taste

To serve
lemon mayonnaise (recipe follows)
fine strips of lemon zest, peeled seedless grapes,
    or finely sliced capsicum
cold green beans or asparagus dressed with vinaigrette

Lightly dust the chicken breasts with a little flour. In a large frying pan with a lid, melt the butter and oil together over low heat. (The chicken fillets must be cooked very slowly to keep them moist and white.) Place the fillets in the pan in one layer, sprinkle with salt and pepper and immediately put on the lid. The chicken should actually poach in the melted oil and butter.

After 5 to 7 minutes, lift the lid. The breasts are ready to turn when they are white around the edges. Turn the fillets over and replace the lid immediately. They will cook very quickly on the second side. To test, lift the division of the breast with a fork. When the meat is all white, it will be cooked. Remove to a large platter to cool.

To serve
Arrange the chicken breasts on a platter and spoon over the lemon mayonnaise and decorate with lemon zest, peeled grapes or sliced capsicum. Serve with cooked, cold green beans or asparagus, dressed with a vinaigrette.

LEMON MAYONNAISE

3 egg yolks
$^1/_4$ teaspoon dry mustard
salt and pepper to taste
1 teaspoon finely grated lemon rind
2 tablespoons lemon juice, or more if necessary
$^1/_4$ cup peanut oil
1 cup olive oil
1 tablespoon boiling water

Beat the egg yolks, mustard, salt and pepper together. Add the lemon rind and juice. Gradually pour in the oils, in a thin stream, beating all the time until the mayonnaise thickens. Add the boiling water. Taste for salt and pepper and lemon juice. The mayonnaise should have a good lemon flavour.

I suppose it is a double-edged honour, but I cooked the last dinner for Malcolm and Tamie Fraser before he was voted out of office as Prime Minister. Emma Woodward Fisher, from England, was my assistant. We were making the dessert, a Chocolate Marquise with Coffee Bean Sauce; she lifted the whizzing beater out of the mixture and there was a chocolate pattern from floor to ceiling! Emma was one of a series of well-bred English assistants that I employed, whom we used to call 'Joan's Sloanes'. They were very nice girls who came out to Australia for some work experience.

CHOCOLATE MARQUISE

Michel Guérard came to Sydney in the late sixties with Paul Bocuse and I learned to make this dessert.

(Serves 6)

150 g plain good-quality dark chocolate
7 egg yolks
250 g castor sugar
300 g softened unsalted butter
160 g unsweetened cocoa powder
500 ml thickened cream
50 g icing sugar
14 to 16 sponge fingers (available in packets)
1 cup of cold, strong, black unsweetened coffee

To serve
coffee bean sauce (recipe follows)

Melt the chocolate in a bowl over hot water. Beat the egg yolks and castor sugar together until light and fluffy. Add the chocolate and gently fold in with a wooden spatula. In another bowl, beat the softened butter until smooth, then gradually beat in the cocoa to make a cream. Add the egg mixture to the butter mixture and carefully whisk together until combined. Beat the cream with the icing sugar until thick, then add it to the chocolate mixture and whisk with a balloon whisk to obtain a perfect mixture.

Brush the sponge fingers with the cold coffee. Butter a charlotte mould or a deep cake tin 20 cm in diameter, and line the bottom with greaseproof paper. Line the bottom and sides of the mould with the moistened sponge fingers. Pour in the chocolate mixture. Cover and refrigerate overnight before serving. When ready to serve unmould the marquise onto a serving plate. Cut it into slices and serve with the coffee bean sauce poured around.

COFFEE BEAN SAUCE
500 ml milk
150 g castor sugar
2 teaspoons medium-fine, freshly ground coffee
6 egg yolks

Put the milk and half the castor sugar in a saucepan and bring to the boil. Remove from the heat, add the ground coffee and leave to infuse for 15 minutes.

Beat the egg yolks with the remaining sugar until light, then pour in the infused milk and whisk together until combined. Return the mixture to the saucepan and cook over low heat, stirring constantly until the sauce thickens and coats the back of a spoon. Pour into a bowl and allow to cool, stirring from time to time.

I prepared a dinner for Yves St Laurent at the Sydney Town Hall, one dish being a Michel Guérard recipe for smoked fish and lentils. I remember some people at one table grumbling and saying, 'Oh, my God, dried beans!' The Town Hall was a great monolith of a place which used to have no facilities to speak of and we struggled for years through various events. I remember one newspaper report of 'Joan Campbell struggling gamely' with the limitations of the kitchen. This report related to the Guy Laroche/Friends of Odyssey dinner, the menu of which, by the way, I still found necessary to write entirely in French.

SMOKED FISH WITH MICHEL GUÉRARD'S LENTIL SALAD
(Serves 4)

Lentil salad
200 g green lentils
1 litre water
1 1/2 teaspoons coarse salt
1 small bouquet garni
pepper to taste
60 g onions, peeled and diced
60 g carrots, peeled and diced
1/2 clove garlic, peeled and chopped

Dressing
4 tablespoons peanut oil
4 tablespoons wine vinegar
1 tablespoon finely chopped eschalot
salt and pepper to taste

To serve
1 tablespoon chopped capers
sliced smoked Tasmanian Atlantic salmon

To cook the lentils
Wash the lentils and drain well, then place in a non-corrodible saucepan with a lid. Cover with cold water, bring to the boil and remove any scum if necessary.

Add the salt, bouquet garni, pepper, onions, carrots and garlic. Cook gently, covered, for about 35 minutes. Drain in a colander, remove the bouquet and set aside to cool.

To make the dressing
Put all the dressing ingredients in a screw-top jar and shake well to amalgamate.

To serve
Add the capers to the cooled lentils, toss with the dressing and spoon the lentil salad onto individual plates. Arrange slices of the smoked salmon on top.

We discovered, as we arrived to prepare the YSL dinner, once again in the notorious Town Hall, that a new kitchen had been installed, unheralded. It hadn't yet been used. I remember there were huge machines we had never seen before, until Margaret Alcock, one of my assistants that night, worked them out: they were giant steamer boxes, the size of a refrigerator. We prepared the new potatoes in these, then we had to find some way to cook chicken breasts. Once again, Margaret found a method. She lifted the stainless-steel trays from the army of new trolleys, arranged the chicken breasts on top of the trays, and slid them into the giant new ovens.

The Town Hall was also the venue for two celebrated events, the Cause Balls of 1978 and 1980. Leo Schofield was instrumental in organising these events: they were run by the advertising community of Sydney, who chose a 'cause' to which they would give the money they raised. Seven hundred people paid $50 a head. The second ball was nearly a disaster, foodwise. Not only were we still struggling with ancient and ill-equipped kitchens (I have a photo of two of my assistants crouching over a gas burner on the loading dock to check if the beans were sufficiently cooked), but the inexperienced hired help nearly ruined the smoked fish. Leo Schofield rang me during the afternoon at home and alerted me by saying, 'I think you'd better get in there, the smoked salmon is being massacred'. I tore in to find that they had decided, mystifyingly, to cut the salmon at this early stage and, more alarmingly, to hack it apart in quite the wrong way. The salmon had been flown in from Tasmania and was the first push of the marvellous range of produce we were to see from that state. I saved enough of it, just in time. The next course, Squab with Honey Raisin Stuffing, was untouched, but they had also started to hack up the dessert of three fruits: orange, strawberry and kiwi fruit, to be served with Margaret Alcock's petit fours. They had cut the fruit so badly I had to go off and buy fresh supplies for Leo's table and the press!

The hired help for this party were strangers with whom I was required to work for this particular job. Usually I was lucky enough to have access to the very professional services of a team of extremely efficient women we nicknamed 'the White Ladies' because they all wore starched, white uniforms and originally came from the same agency. I used them again and again: their names were Mona Priestley, Molly Wagstaff and her niece Val Ender, Peggy Bull, Sally O'Brien and Pat Martin. I don't know what I would have done without them; there was no one else as good as they were.

Other instrumental assistants during my catering days were people like Margaret Alcock, whom I met through attending her Indian Cooking classes. She had lived in India in her twenties and really knew how to make a curry. Margaret later became my assistant and recipe writer at *Vogue Entertaining Guide* for some time. All these women were marvellous under even the most stringent of conditions. Jim Taylor, our head waiter, was also a tower of strength. He would organise the troops, knew how to lay a table and pour a drink, was immaculately dressed and always called me 'Madame'!

Leo Schofield was a huge influence on me – as he has been, I think, on the development of Australian cuisine. His newspaper columns about his travels and the food he ate always fascinated me and well before I met him I would read them avidly and try to reproduce the dishes he wrote about. I first met him just before doing a catering job at the Bonython Gallery for the opening of an exhibition. It was at a planning meeting beforehand; he was sitting at the front and I was sitting at the back. I'd never seen him before. Someone said I was doing the catering and he said innocently, 'Who's Joan Campbell?' I replied from the back stalls, in my best haughty voice, 'I am Joan Campbell'. Incidentally, it was during that job that I lost a front tooth from a jacket crown. I was walking around with a trolley replete with gorgeous gorgonzola and other cheeses when someone asked me a question about it. As I tried to reply, I blew a tooth out!

I did much work for Leo at his advertising agency. In fact, it was at one of these lunches that there was one of the few near-disasters and one of the Worst Moments of my catering career. We had ordered some beef fillet from a very good butcher that I always used and we cooked it in the usual way. Leo cut into it at the boardroom lunch, and sliced straight into a few maggots – the meat was blown. The butcher, when told, was very embarrassed. It was a once-in-a-lifetime thing and the only slip-up I've ever had. Leo quite calmly cut out the maggoty piece, carved up the rest of the good meat, and went on with the lunch with great aplomb; nobody knew anything about it.

LEO SCHOFIELD'S TOMATO SALAD
With a little help from Elizabeth David!

(Serves 6)

6 large, firm, ripe tomatoes
grated rind of 1 large lemon, or to taste
1 tablespoon finely chopped basil
freshly ground pepper
salt to taste
lemon juice
first-press olive oil

Cut the tomatoes in slices about 1 cm thick and spread on a large platter. Scatter over the lemon rind and basil, and grind over some pepper. Cover with plastic wrap and refrigerate for 1 to 2 hours.

Just before serving, sprinkle with salt, squeeze over a little lemon juice and be generous with the olive oil. Serve as a first course with brown bread and butter.

Unfortunately, one of the legacies of my catering days is a chronically bad back. As I drove around madly, carried heavy boxes of food to and fro, and worked, bent over, for hours on end, my back got steadily worse. Two falls didn't help – one while sitting on a high stool at the Bay Tree kitchen shop in Sydney and another while taking a delivery of two huge frozen turkeys at Oscars Restaurant in Surfers Paradise, where I was to give a demonstration. I kept on holding the turkeys as I crashed to the ground with a noise like thunder. The event that finished it off was a charity ball for Holly Kerr in aid of the Children's Hospital Foundation, which I was doing with Anders Ousbäck. It was the leaning over that night that finished me: my right leg gave way the next day and it was all I could do to get to my bed. I couldn't walk properly for the next five or six weeks.

After catering all day, often the last thing I felt like doing was cooking. Lindsay and I would usually grab a bottle and go off to one of our favourite little haunts in East Sydney, Darlinghurst or Kings Cross. Garibaldis in East Sydney was great: we'd have pasta, veal or liver at big, plain, shared tables. The Vietnam War definitely affected eating in the Cross; it was huge for the food industry at the time.

Once again in my life, Americans had an interesting influence on me. I was on a committee that organised the billeting of American soldiers while they were on leave in Sydney. Sometimes I would invite them to our home for a meal; I used to do this once a week in the late sixties and early seventies, and the American Government later sent me a plaque to say thank you. Through the Americans I was meeting, I became aware of the Australian American Association cookbooks and I often made the Fabulous Cheese Casserole and Lasagne Imbottite from one of them. Of course, it became necessary also to comprehend and cook the quintessential hamburger!

FABULOUS CHEESE CASSEROLE
(Serves 4 to 6)

9 slices of bread
salt and pepper to taste
1$\frac{1}{2}$ tablespoons dried minced onion
1$\frac{1}{2}$ tablespoons dried green onion, or eschalots
500 g cheddar cheese
4 eggs
3 cups milk
1 teaspoon Worcestershire sauce
1 teaspoon dry mustard

Cut three slices of bread in three strips each and fit tightly in the bottom of a lightly greased casserole. Sprinkle with salt and pepper, and a third of the white and green onion. Grate a third of the cheese over this, even it out and press down. Make two more layers the same way.

Beat the eggs lightly and add the milk, Worcestershire sauce and dry mustard. Pour over the bread and let sit for at least eight hours, preferably overnight, in the refrigerator.

Remove from the refrigerator two hours ahead of serving time to allow the mixture to come to room temperature. Bake, uncovered, at 170°C for 50 minutes.

The dry ingredients can be prepared two days ahead, and the liquid added the day before serving. This casserole is absolutely foolproof. It puffs like a soufflé, but can be held, reheated or otherwise mistreated. To double the recipe, double all ingredients, but use only five cups of milk.

Recipe by Carole Gygax

LASAGNE IMBOTTITE
(Serves 6)

First you make this good meat sauce:
1 tablespoon olive or vegetable oil
1 medium onion, peeled and chopped
1 clove garlic, peeled and minced
500 g ground (minced) beef
3½ cups canned tomatoes
1 x 140 g can tomato paste
½ teaspoon dried basil
¼ cup water
¼ cup chopped celery
2 tablespoons chopped parsley
2 teaspoons salt
1 teaspoon sugar
few grains of pepper
1 bay leaf
½ teaspoon dried oregano

Heat the oil in a flame-proof casserole, add the onions and garlic and sauté for 5 minutes. Add the ground beef and sauté until brown, breaking the meat up with a fork as it cooks. Stir in the remaining ingredients. Bring the sauce to a boil, reduce the heat and simmer about an hour, or until thick. This freezes beautifully and is a wonderful spaghetti sauce.

Then you cook the noodles:

500 g lasagne noodles, or other very broad
 (4cm wide) pasta
3 tablespoons salt
1 tablespoon vegetable oil

Bring the water to the boil in a large pot. Add the salt and oil and when the water boils rapidly, add the noodles slowly so the boiling doesn't stop. Cook until tender – about 25 minutes. Drain well, quickly turn onto a platter and separate with a fork.

Finally you assemble the dish:

2 cups ricotta or cream-style cottage cheese (about 500 g)
500 g mozzarella or Muenster cheese, sliced
1 cup grated parmesan cheese

(I buy both mozzarella and parmesan in bulk and slice and grate them myself – much better.)

Preheat the oven to 180°C. Butter a 32 cm x 22 cm x 5 cm baking dish. Cover the bottom of the dish with the sauce. Add a single layer of the drained noodles. Mix the ricotta or cottage cheese with about $1/2$ cup of the sauce. Spoon about a quarter of this over the noodles. Top with a quarter of the mozzarella and a quarter of the parmesan. Repeat to make three or four layers ending with the parmesan cheese topping. Bake for 30 minutes or until hot. This is equally delicious if put together ahead of time and merely heated in the oven at the last minute.

Recipe by Grace M. Sieg

Aside from my childhood neighbour, Mrs Dobell, there had been another American influence early in my life. This was a couple called Peggy and Tillman Durdin. I first met Peggy during World War II when I was living at the family beach house at Surfers Paradise and she was in charge of a house of young US airmen who were resting after flying in the South West Pacific. I did not meet Tillman during that time, as he was a war correspondent for the *New York Times*. The second meeting was when Tillman was stringer for the *New York Times* in Australia. Peggy had been born in China with missionary parents and Tillman was always a little vague about his arrival by boat in China.

It was Peggy Durdin who first taught me the strange tastes of Asia and how they could be used in domestic cooking. She used to make the most delicious slow-cooked pork, and gave me the recipe. Other things she cooked were slightly American Chinese, like a bean-shoot, avocado and olive salad, very useful to me for my catering. I lost the Durdins twice. The first time I refound them was when their name was mentioned by a mutual friend at a party in Sydney. I looked them up at once and we all became firm friends during this time. Peggy had some absolutely irreplaceable and uninsurable antique jewellery from China that she used to leave in my cellar whenever they went away. Then Tillman was suddenly called to China on the 'Ping-pong' situation because he knew Chou En Lai and Mao Tse Tung well. We corresponded for a while, but I lost them again. The second time I refound them was by coincidence in Bangkok. I was there for *Vogue* photographing a house that had a very impressive visitors' book. Among the signatures of people such as Jacqueline Kennedy, Jane Russell, Jim Thompson and Sir William McMahon, there was Tillman Durdin's name and address. I wrote them a letter as soon as I got back to the hotel.

PEGGY DURDIN'S CHINESE-STYLE THRICE-COOKED PORK
(Serves 4 to 6)

1/2 cup red bean curd
3 tablespoons brown sugar
1/2 teaspoon five-spice powder
3 tablespoons light soy sauce
1 tablespoon honey
3 medium potatoes
1 kg belly of pork, cut into strips
1 tablespoon vegetable oil
4 cloves garlic, peeled and chopped finely
1 tablespoon peeled and grated fresh ginger
1/2 teaspoon salt
1 tablespoon sherry

Mix together the bean curd, brown sugar, five-spice powder, soy sauce and honey, and set aside. Peel the potatoes and cut into pieces about 5 mm thick by 4 cm square and set aside. Boil the strips of pork belly for 10 minutes, then drain and slice against the grain into pieces about 5 mm thick.

Place a wok or large frying pan over high heat and add the oil, garlic, ginger and salt. Add the pork and stir-fry for 1 minute, then add the sherry and continue to stir. Add the bean-curd mixture and cook, stirring, until the pork is completely coated, then remove from the heat.

Preheat the oven to 190°C. Arrange the pork mixture and potatoes in alternate layers in an ovenproof dish. Cover and bake for 1 hour.

PEGGY DURDIN'S CHINESE MIXED VEGETABLES

(Serves 2)

1 strand dried bean curd
1 tablespoon dried lily buds
8 dried cloud ears fungi
4 dried Chinese mushrooms
12 fresh snow peas
1 cup bamboo shoots
5 water chestnuts
$1/4$ cup carrots
$1/2$ teaspoon sugar
pepper to taste
2 teaspoons cornflour mixed with 2 tablespoons water
2 tablespoons vegetable oil
1 small piece fresh ginger, peeled and grated
1 teaspoon salt
$1/2$ cup chicken stock
1 cup Chinese cabbage, shredded
1 teaspoon sherry

Break the bean curd into 5 cm lengths and boil in water for 30 minutes (or alternatively, soak overnight until soft, then cut into lengths) and drain. Soak the lily buds, cloud ears and mushrooms in hot water for about 30 minutes. Drain, squeeze out the excess water, trim the lily buds and any tough parts from the cloud ears, discard the mushroom stems, then shred the lily buds, cloud ears and mushroom caps and set aside.

Remove the strings from the snow peas and cut in half diagonally. Shred the bamboo shoots and slice the water chestnuts. Peel the carrots, slice diagonally and boil for 1 minute, then drain. Add the sugar and pepper to the cornflour mixture and set aside.

Heat a wok or large frying pan, pour in the vegetable oil, then add the ginger and salt and stir-fry for a few seconds. Add the prepared bean curd, lily buds, cloud ears and mushrooms and stir-fry for a few minutes. Add the chicken stock, then cover and simmer for about 5 minutes. Add the snow peas, bamboo shoots, water chestnuts, carrots and cabbage, cover and cook for a few more minutes. Stir in the cornflour mixture and when the sauce boils and thickens, add the sherry, toss together and serve at once.

BOEUF BOURGUIGNONNE

Another of Peggy's recipes that was a great favourite at winter boardroom lunches.

(Serves 8)

3 kg chuck steak, in 6-cm x 4-cm cubes
plain flour
sugar
160 g butter
4 tablespoons olive oil
$1/2$ cup warmed brandy
salt and pepper
125 g finely diced speck
$1/2$ cup chopped carrots
2 leeks, washed and sliced finely
3 large onions, peeled and chopped
4 cloves garlic, peeled and crushed
$1/2$ cup chopped parsley
2 bay leaves
2 sprigs fresh thyme, or a good pinch of dried thyme
1 bottle burgundy
a little water or stock
36 small onions, peeled
40 button mushrooms, stems trimmed

Preheat the oven to 150°C. Roll the pieces of beef in flour and a sprinkling of sugar. Melt half the butter with the oil in a heavy frying pan and quickly fry the meat, a few pieces at a time, until brown on all sides. Place in a large heavy casserole. Flame the brandy and pour over the meat. Season well with salt and pepper.

Put the speck in a frying pan and fry until light brown. Add the vegetables, garlic and chopped parsley, and fry until the vegetables have browned. Add this mixture to the meat in the casserole with the bay leaves, thyme, burgundy and enough water or stock to barely cover the meat.

Cover the casserole with foil, then put on the lid. Cook the casserole on the bottom shelf of the preheated oven for $2^1/2$ to 3 hours. Remove from the oven, allow to cool and refrigerate, covered, to set the fat.

To serve

Remove the fat from the top of the casserole and reheat the meat in the oven at 150°C for about 1 hour, or until the meat is thoroughly hot and the sauce is simmering.

While the meat is heating, cook the small onions and button mushrooms. Melt 40 g of the butter in a frying pan and brown the onions well. Add a little water, sprinkle with salt and pepper, cover the pan and cook slowly until the onions are just cooked.

In a separate pan sauté the mushrooms with the remaining butter, and salt and pepper to taste. Just before serving, add the onions and mushrooms to the casserole.

A dinner of great importance, for which I was asked to cater in the late seventies, arose from a request from the Chinese to meet the former Prime Minister Gough Whitlam, a very significant political event. Gough, his wife Margaret and only twenty or so guests were there, with their interpreters, both Chinese and Australian. We knew that Gough had a sweet tooth, and we were only a minute away from Australia Day in January, so we decided to do a selection of puddings including a pavlova and some sort of fruit salad. Gough had a bit of everything and, being very diplomatic, the Chinese followed suit. Wong Latoo, a personal friend of Mao's, who had been with him on the Long March, sat at the table with Gough. The dinner was arranged by Patricia Yeomans and held at Jean Battersby's house. I remember feeling how extraordinary it was watching both men, large in both physical and political stature, sitting there at a card table in suburban Sydney and eating everything we put in front of them!

The first time that my friend Simon Johnson, Purveyor of Quality Foods, flew in fresh truffles from Pebeyres in Cahors, France, in 1993, he gave a dinner party that would be very hard not to remember. He invited a large group of foodies to sample the truffles at his warehouse in Pyrmont, where we were greeted with truffle sandwiches and champagne. The sandwiches are one of Simon's specialities, but this night the chef in charge was Neil Perry (Rockpool, and Wokpool restaurants and MCA catering). This was before Simon had his new kitchen built and Neil cooked the meal under fairly primitive conditions. The whole dinner was delicious – new food to Australian foodies. Before this, unless we went to France or Italy, we ate truffles out of a can.

TRUFFLE SANDWICHES
(Makes 4)

2 slices good-quality sourdough bread (sliced finely – no
    more than 3 mm thick)
good-quality unsalted, cultured butter
20 g fresh truffle, peeled and rubbed with a cut clove
    of garlic and sliced finely with a truffle slicer or
    a sharp knife
fleur de sel

Grill the bread slices on one side only and allow to cool. Lightly butter the untoasted side of each slice. Place one slice of bread, butter side up, on a baking sheet. Put the truffle slices on top and sprinkle with a little *fleur de sel*. Cover with the other slice of bread, butter side down, and put in a preheated 150°C oven for 2 minutes to let the butter melt. Remove from the oven, cut the sandwich in quarters and serve at once as an appetiser.
    Recipe by Simon Johnson

TRUFFLE AND LEEK TARTS
(Serves 4)

1 leek, white part only, washed, trimmed and julienned
1 tablespoon butter
30 ml olive oil
6 thin slices prosciutto, chopped
freshly ground pepper and salt
4 x 5 cm pre-baked pastry cases
30 g fresh truffle, peeled and sliced finely with a truffle
    slicer or a sharp knife

Sauté the leek in the butter and olive oil until soft, then add the prosciutto and sauté a little longer. Season with pepper and set aside in a warm place. Fill the pastry cases with the leek and prosciutto mixture and arrange some sliced truffles on top. Sprinkle over a little of the leek cooking liquid and serve at once.
    Recipe by Neil Perry

Here are some more catering recipes that everyone loved.

PRAWNS WITH MUSTARD
(Serves 6)

36 medium king prawns
1 teaspoon bicarbonate of soda
4 tablespoons vegetable oil
salt and freshly ground pepper
6 to 8 spring onions, chopped
$\frac{1}{2}$ teaspoon dried tarragon
$\frac{1}{2}$ cup dry sherry
$\frac{1}{2}$ cup cream
250 g unsalted butter, cut in small pieces
2 tablespoons Dijon mustard
1 tablespoon chopped chives

Shell the prawns, remove their digestive tracts and soak the prawns in water with the bicarbonate of soda for 30 minutes.
    Heat the vegetable oil in a large frying pan and sauté the prawns until opaque, then remove them from the pan with a slotted spoon, sprinkle with salt and pepper, set aside and keep warm.

Add the spring onions to the pan and fry for a few seconds, then add the tarragon, sherry and cream, and simmer over low heat. Beat in the butter and mustard with a whisk, taste for salt, add the chives, then add the prawns, heat through and serve at once.

TRUFFLE AND POTATO SALAD
We used to use canned truffles. Of course, fresh truffles would make a much better dish.

(Serves 10 to 12 as part of a buffet table)

3.5 kg baby new potatoes

Truffle mayonnaise
4 egg yolks
1 teaspoon Dijon mustard
salt and pepper
2 tablespoons truffle oil
1½ cups peanut oil
1 tablespoon boiling water

To serve
2 truffles, peeled and rubbed with a clove of garlic
    (reserve the peel to flavour rice for a risotto)

Cook the baby potatoes in boiling, salted water until tender. Drain, allow to cool and peel.

To make the mayonnaise
Put the egg yolks, mustard, salt and pepper in a food processor. Process until well mixed. Mix the truffle oil with the peanut oil. With the motor running, pour in the oil in a slow steady stream until you have a thick mayonnaise. Add the boiling water all at once.

To make the salad and serve
Cut the truffles into fine julienne. Mix the mayonnaise with the potatoes and half the truffles, and taste for salt and pepper. Serve on a large platter, sprinkled with the remaining truffles.

STUFFED LOIN OF PORK WITH APRICOTS AND PRUNES

This is a very good dish, either hot for a dinner party or sliced cold and plattered for a buffet table.

(Serves 8)

3.5 kg loin of pork, rind removed, boned and rolled

Stuffing
250 g dried apricots
250 g prunes
1 large onion, peeled and chopped finely
150 g butter
2 cups fine white breadcrumbs
130 g pine nuts
salt and pepper to taste

To cook the meat
$^1/_2$ cup orange juice
$^1/_4$ cup lemon juice
grated rind of 1 orange
1 cup port
$^1/_2$ cup sugar

Ask your butcher to bone, skin and roll the loin of pork. Cut the strings and spread out the meat on a large board.

To stuff the pork
Cut a quarter of the dried apricots and a quarter of the prunes into slivers and reserve. Put the remaining apricots in a bowl with a little water and set aside. Place the chopped onion in a frying pan with the butter and cook until the onion is soft but not coloured. Add the breadcrumbs, reserved slivered apricots and prunes, pine nuts and salt and pepper. Spread the stuffing evenly over the meat and tie it into a neat roll again. You can do this easily by following the marks left by the butcher's string.

To cook the meat
Preheat the oven to 180°C. Place the roast on a rack inside a baking dish and pour the orange and lemon juices and grated orange rind into the dish. Sprinkle the meat well with salt and pepper, and place the baking dish on the centre shelf of the oven. Cook for 30 minutes then, basting every 15 minutes, cook for a further $1^1/_2$ hours. If you think the orange juice is evaporating, add some more; bottled juice will do. If the top of the meat looks too brown, cover with aluminium foil.

Towards the end of cooking time, prepare the remaining dried apricots and prunes. Drain the apricots that have been soaking in water. Add half the port and half the sugar, and simmer gently until they are soft but not mushy. Place the prunes in another pan with the remaining port and sugar. Simmer until they, too, are soft but not mushy.

Cool the fruit and drain, reserving the juices. When the meat is cooked, remove it to a large platter and keep warm in the turned-off oven. Skim all the fat from the pan juices. Add the prune and apricot juices, and deglaze the pan. Serve this sauce and the fruit with the roast.

PASSIONFRUIT SNOW EGGS
(Serves 6)

2 cups milk
6 egg yolks
$1/2$ cup sugar
1 teaspoon vanilla extract
6 passionfruit
6 egg whites
pinch of salt
$2/3$ cup sugar

Caramel
1 cup sugar
1 teaspoon water

Boil the milk in a thick-bottomed saucepan. Beat the egg yolks with the $1/2$ cup sugar. Pour a little boiling milk into the egg and sugar mixture. Mix well and return to the milk in the saucepan. Cook over low heat, stirring, until the mixture coats the back of a spoon. Strain into a bowl and allow to cool. Add the vanilla and either the pulp and seeds of the passionfruit, or the strained juice. Cover and chill.

About two hours before serving, make the poached meringues. Beat the egg whites and salt until they hold stiff peaks. Gradually add the sugar and beat until the mixture is like a meringue. Three-quarters fill a wide, deep frying pan with water and bring to the boil. Turn the heat down until the water is only just simmering. With two tablespoons, form blobs of meringue and drop carefully onto the simmering water. (The water should only just move as you cook the meringues.) Cook two or three at a time – too many in the pan will make them run into each other, as they puff a little. Cook for 3 minutes on each side. Remove with an egg slice and drain on paper towels. When all the meringues are cooked, float the snow eggs on the custard.

To make the caramel
Cook the sugar and water until it is caramel coloured and pour over the snow eggs. Cover the bowl with plastic wrap and refrigerate until ready to serve.

OEUFS À LA CHATELAINE
(Serves 6)

9 hard-boiled eggs
2 teaspoons gelatine
1 x 160 g can beef consommé
1 teaspoon Madeira
1 teaspoon brandy
$^1/_2$ cup sour cream
$^1/_2$ cup mayonnaise
salt and pepper to taste

To serve
250 g cooked prawns, shelled and digestive
   tracts removed
150 g salmon eggs
1 small bunch chives, chopped very finely

Remove the shells from the eggs and cut in half lengthwise. Arrange, cut side down, in a shallow dish. Heat $^1/_2$ cup of the consommé and dissolve 1 teaspoon of the gelatine in it. Beat together the sour cream, mayonnaise, the $^1/_2$ cup of consommé with gelatine, the Madeira and brandy. Taste for salt and pepper, and pour over the eggs. Cover and refrigerate for 6 to 8 hours.

Dissolve the other teaspoon of gelatine in the remaining consommé and, when the liquid starts to thicken, carefully spoon it over the egg mixture. Cover and refrigerate for at least 8 hours, until the gelatine has set firmly.

To serve
Place a large spoonful of the egg mixture on each serving plate and top with the prawns, salmon eggs and chopped chives.

MAGAZINES

As well as catering, I wrote a page for the *Sunday Telegraph* and a column for the *Daily Telegraph* on Wednesdays. I was one of the first people in Australia to write restaurant reviews consistently. I have heard that people are a bit scared of me because I am known as being outspoken, but my policy on restaurant reviews was then as it is now: I never try to destroy a restaurant. If I don't like it, I just walk away and refuse to deal with the place. As for chefs, I have never had the least interest in how they run their business. All I am interested in is the food on the plate. That's what I was there to do: as a critic, assess the food in front of me, plus the service and the look of the restaurant, bistro or café.

I called the Wednesday page, which was in the women's section, 'Campbell's Kitchen'. Looking back at these columns, I must say I'm impressed. I had forgotten how much work and thought went into them, and I can't believe how good all the recipes were! How did I do it all? I don't know!

Here is a selection of the best recipes from those columns.

CARAMEL PEARS

(Serves 6)

6 pears
1 cup sugar
$\frac{1}{2}$ cup rum
1 tablespoon butter
175 ml cream

Preheat the oven to 220°C. Peel the pears, cut in quarters and remove the seeds. Simmer gently in water for 5 minutes and drain.

Place the pear quarters close together in an ovenproof dish, sprinkle over the sugar, then the rum. Cook on the centre shelf of the oven until the sugar is a dark golden-brown. Baste once or twice while the pears are cooking.

When the sugar has caramelised, pour in the cream, stand for 10 to 15 minutes and serve warm.

SPICED CHICKEN LEGS

12 chicken legs
1 tablespoon peanut oil
1 clove garlic, peeled and crushed
1 tablespoon honey
1 tablespoon soy sauce
2 teaspoons grated ginger
2 teaspoons hoi sin sauce
2 tablespoons sherry
good grinding of black pepper
good pinch of salt

Place the chicken legs in one layer in an ovenproof dish. Mix all the remaining ingredients together and pour over the chicken. Cover the dish and marinate the chicken in the refrigerator overnight.

The next day, turn the chicken legs around in the marinade, allow to come to room temperature and cook in a preheated 180°C oven for 45 minutes.

PINEAPPLE RICE PUDDING

(Serves 6 to 8)

flesh of 1 pineapple, cut in small dice
sugar
3 cups cooked rice
$^3/_4$ cup walnut pieces
500 ml thickened cream, whipped
$^1/_2$ cup icing sugar
1 teaspoon vanilla extract

Mix the pineapple with sugar to taste and chill in the refrigerator for a few hours.

Put the rice and walnuts in a large bowl. Add the pineapple and toss the mixture gently. Fold in the whipped cream, with the icing sugar and vanilla extract.

Cover the pudding and chill for two to three hours before serving.

BRAISED BEEF WITH ANCHOVIES

(Serves 4)

6 anchovy fillets
30 g butter
750 g topside beef
2 onions, peeled and chopped roughly
1 leek, washed and sliced
3 sticks of celery, sliced
6 peppercorns
2 bay leaves
3 sprigs mixed fresh herbs, chopped, or $^1/_2$ teaspoon
   dried mixed herbs
$1^3/_4$ cups beef stock (or use 1 can of beef consommé)
pepper and salt to taste

Preheat the oven to 175°C. Mash half the anchovies with half of the butter, then melt the anchovy butter in a frying pan and brown the meat on all sides. Remove the meat and set aside. Melt the rest of the butter in the pan. Add the vegetables and sauté for 5 to 8 minutes, then add the remaining anchovies, the peppercorns, bay leaves, herbs and stock, and bring to the boil. Transfer the stock and vegetable mixture to a casserole and place the meat on top.

Cover the casserole with a lid and braise the meat on the centre shelf of the oven for 2 to $2^1/_2$ hours or until the meat is cooked. Season to taste with pepper. Be careful with the salt as the anchovies may be sufficient.

How did I get into magazines? I just slithered into them. It was actually via Ita Buttrose. Ita's father, Charles, was a friend of Lindsay Campbell's and I went to Ita's wedding. She vanished for a few years to live in London and have two children. Then Frank Packer asked her back to Australia to start *Cleo* magazine.

I catered for Ita's dinner parties, really as a friend, when she was too busy to do them herself. One night I was reading the food section in *Cleo* while I was waiting to plate up the food. I thought to myself, 'I could do that', so I spoke to Ita and she told me the job was up for grabs. But she didn't automatically give it to me: I applied for the job in the usual way, and then got it.

My first page was about lamb. I overwrote it, and was mortified to find it cut drastically when published. Lindsay used to quote Churchill's aphorism to me; 'Had I had more time I would have written you a shorter letter'. But I soon learnt the style. Incidentally, many people thought that Lindsay wrote my pieces for me. He didn't. Sometimes, though, if I was desperate I would ask him to help me find a lead.

WARM SALAD OF SMALL GREENS AND DUCK LIVER
(Serves 4)

Sauce
yolks of 2 hard-boiled eggs
1 teaspoon Dijon mustard
salt and freshly ground pepper to taste
1 tablespoon lemon juice
4 tablespoons olive oil

Salad
cos lettuce
mignonette lettuce
a handful of very small green beans
2 small spring onions
100 g button mushrooms, trimmed and sliced finely
1 tablespoon lemon juice
6 fresh duck livers
1 tablespoon butter or goose fat (available in cans at
   specialty delicatessens)
salt and freshly ground pepper to taste
1 tablespoon red wine vinegar

To make the sauce
Crumble the egg yolks in a bowl and mix with the mustard, salt, pepper and lemon juice. Gradually beat the oil into the mixture, as you would to make a mayonnaise, and set aside.

To make the salad
Wash and drain the lettuces and refrigerate to crisp the leaves. Top and tail the beans and cook in boiling salted water until just tender. Rinse under cold water to retain the bright green colour. Slice the baby onions into fine rings. Sprinkle the sliced mushrooms with lemon juice. Arrange all the salad greens and vegetables on four serving plates.

Cut the duck livers into slices about 5 mm thick. Heat the butter or goose fat in a frying pan and cook the slices of duck liver very quickly – only 1 minute on each side. Add salt and pepper. Arrange the slices of liver on the salad plates (three or four slices are enough).

Pour off the fat from the frying pan and deglaze the pan with the vinegar. Pour the pan juices over the salads. Spoon a little of the reserved sauce over the greens and serve at once.

PRAWN AND BEAN SPROUT SALAD
(Serves 6)

1 kg cooked prawns
500 g fresh bean sprouts
4 spring onions, finely sliced, including some
    of the green tops

Dressing
3/4 cup mayonnaise
1 teaspoon curry powder
a little crushed garlic
1 tablespoon lemon juice
2 tablespoons soy sauce
2 tablespoons sour cream

To serve
Lebanese cucumbers, sliced
vinaigrette
salt and pepper to taste

Peel and clean the prawns and if they are too large, cut in pieces. Mix the bean sprouts, spring onions and prawns together.

To make the dressing
Mix the mayonnaise, curry powder, crushed garlic, lemon juice, soy sauce and sour cream together.

To serve
Pour the dressing into the prawn mixture and toss. Serve with sliced cucumbers dressed with a little vinaigrette, salt and pepper.

My entry into *Vogue* (then Bernard Leser Publications Pty Ltd) was via catering. I was asked by Mary Ellen Ayrton, who was doing the public relations for *Vogue* at the time, to cater for a *Vogue Entertaining Guide* lunch at Gordon Barton's boardroom in the city. Gordon Barton was the founder of IPEC, and *Vogue Entertaining Guide* had just started. The menu I gave them was a Lobster Loaf, Chicken Breasts with Lemon Butter Sauce, baskets of cheese, and a Chocolate Mousse Cake like Fernand Point's pavé au chocolat.

My daughter, Sue, came with me into a kitchen the size of a large cupboard. The table was set by Carolyn Lockhart (not yet Editor of *Vogue Entertaining Guide* and known as Charlie), and I had never seen anything more stylish. It was my first sighting of things *Vogue*. At this stage no one at *Vogue* had ever heard of me – I'd just done catering, the *Telegraph* columns and a bit of magazine work in *Cleo*, although *Vogue* had also featured some of my handiwork in the form of decorative flower trees, which were used in a fashion shoot in 1968.

In spite of curdling the sauce and frantically beating it back from scrambled eggs to a creamy texture, we got the lunch out. Afterwards June McCallum, then Editor-in-Chief of the *Vogue* stable, asked me to join the team. I was very unsure of myself and it took me three more months to ring her and say, 'Do you still want me?' Which she did. So I went to Ita, who generously told me that was where I should be and let me go with her blessing. She wrote me a letter which I have long treasured.

TERRINE OF LITTLE VEGETABLES WITH LOBSTER
(Serves 8)

1 small bunch English spinach
225 g very small beans, topped and tailed
2 medium carrots, peeled and cut in julienne
1 cup celery, cut in julienne
1 cooked lobster
2½ cups strong, strained chicken stock or consommé,
   free of all fat
2½ tablespoons gelatine
salt and pepper

Tomato sauce
1 onion, peeled and chopped finely
3 tablespoons peanut oil
1 kg tomatoes, peeled, seeded and chopped
1 tablespoon finely chopped basil
salt and pepper to taste

Remove the spinach leaves from their stems and cook the leaves in boiling salted water for a few minutes until wilted and slightly soft. Drain in a colander, rinse under cold water, drain again and chop coarsely.

Cook the beans in boiling salted water until tender. Drain and rinse under cold water. Dry on paper towels. Cook and prepare the julienne of carrots and celery in the same way.

Remove the lobster meat from the shell and rinse the head end in cold, salted water. Dry thoroughly and cut in slices. Heat the chicken stock and dissolve the gelatine in it. Allow it to cool completely.

Lightly oil a 1-litre non-stick terrine or loaf tin. Mix the vegetables together with a fork, being careful not to break them. Put a third of the vegetables on the base of the can, add salt and pepper, and pour in a little of the stock and gelatine mixture. Put a row of lobster pieces down the centre and add another layer of vegetables with more salt and pepper and more stock. Add the remainder of the lobster and cover with the rest of the vegetables and some salt and pepper. Fill the tin with the remaining stock. Cover with a layer of plastic wrap, then with aluminium foil and refrigerate overnight.

To make the tomato sauce and serve
Cook the onion in the oil until soft. Add the tomatoes, basil and salt and pepper. Cook over high heat for 10 minutes, then transfer the mixture to a blender and blend until smooth. Remove and allow to cool, then refrigerate until ready to serve.

To serve, pour a small amount of the tomato sauce on each plate and place a slice of the terrine in the centre.

I was Food Editor of *Vogue Entertaining* and *Vogue Australia*. In the beginning I worked from home, but they started renovating a house next door so I moved into the visitors' office on the *Vogue* premises and there I stayed. Since Lindsay died in 1983, I really have been at *Vogue* full-time.

Entertaining guests and VIPs has always been very much part of the *Vogue* culture. From the very first lunch, I used to do the food or was responsible for planning it with an outside caterer. We always produced delicious meals for the Melbourne Cup lunches. Nowadays they run the Cup later in the afternoon so we have afternoon teas instead. We prepared many dishes, but the most famous recipes from these lunches are two chicken salads. First was my chicken salad from catering days, and when we got sick of that Belinda Franks, our *Vogue* caterer, came up with the Vogue Boardroom Chicken Salad.

VOGUE BOARDROOM CHICKEN SALAD
(Serves 6)

6 medium chicken breast fillets
vegetable oil
60 g finely sliced prosciutto, cut in strips
¼ cup pine nuts, roasted in the oven
¼ cup sliced sun-dried tomatoes
2 tablespoons finely shredded fresh basil leaves
salt and freshly ground pepper

Dressing
1 tablespoon balsamic vinegar
4 tablespoons oil from the tomatoes
½ teaspoon Dijon mustard
salt and freshly ground pepper to taste

Preheat the oven to 200°C. Brush the chicken fillets lightly with vegetable oil and place on a baking tray. Bake in the oven for about 12 minutes, or until just cooked. Remove the chicken from the tray, transfer to a plate and allow to cool to room temperature. (Do not refrigerate.)

Slice each chicken breast into diagonal slices and arrange in a large, shallow serving dish. Cover the chicken with a layer of prosciutto strips, then add the roasted pine nuts, dried tomatoes, basil and salt and pepper to taste.

To make the dressing and serve
Place all the ingredients in a jar and shake thoroughly to amalgamate. Drizzle the dressing over the salad and serve at once.

Sometimes we would entertain visiting chefs at home. I once made a lunch for Jeremiah Tower at my house: the menu featured Prawns with Mango and we made Bellinis in the back garden with a kitchen whizz. I remember him being very impressed with Australian cheeses, rating them much more highly than American ones.

Another dinner was held at the home of Carolyn Lockhart for Marcella and Victor Hazan's visit. We had designed a very Australian menu, with Lamb in a Salt Crust as the main dish. I didn't know it at the time, but we nearly had a disaster: Charlie's stove wouldn't work. They rushed the lamb down the road to a friend's place and pretended nothing had happened. The next day Charlie, found that the element in her stove was just a bit loose and the stove henceforth worked perfectly.

LEG OF LAMB IN A SALT CRUST WITH LAMB ESSENCE SAUCE

(Serves 4 to 6)

Sauce:

1.5 kg lamb shoulder or lean trimmed breast, cut in very
    small pieces
olive oil
2 onions, peeled and sliced
1 carrot, chopped finely
1 stick of celery, chopped finely
250 ml dry white wine
water, or light veal stock
bouquet of thyme, rosemary, bay leaf and lemon peel
4 cloves garlic, smashed
Madeira
cider vinegar
freshly ground pepper

Lamb

1 leg of lamb
freshly ground black pepper
700 ml cold water
1 kg plain flour
1 kg coarse salt (available from the butcher)
2 cloves garlic, peeled and sliced
4 good sprigs rosemary
4 good sprigs thyme
finely peeled zest of 1 lemon

To make the sauce

Make the sauce one day ahead. Fry the lamb pieces in a wide, deep pan over high heat with as little olive oil as possible, until very brown and caramelised. Do not overload the pan and remove the meat as it is done, reserving it in a bowl. Add the vegetables to the pan and cook until well browned, being careful not to burn the onions. Return the meat to the pan with the onions, increase the heat and add the wine to deglaze the pan.

Add water or stock to cover and the bouquet of herbs and garlic cloves. Bring to the boil and cook briskly for 3 hours. Keep the sauce well skimmed and replace the evaporated liquid with more stock or water as necessary. Strain, discarding the solids, return the sauce to a clean pan and reduce until rich and syrupy. Allow to cool and store in the refrigerator.

When ready to serve, reheat the sauce, taste and add a little Madeira, a few drops of cider vinegar and pepper to taste. (No salt should be necessary.)

To cook the lamb

Preheat the oven to 220°C. Trim the leg of all fat and skin and season liberally with freshly ground black pepper.

Mix the water with the flour and salt, and knead well to make a smooth dough. Roll out the dough to about twice the surface area of the lamb. Scatter the garlic, rosemary, thyme and lemon zest over both sides of the leg and place it on the dough. Fold the dough over to encase the lamb, making sure the pastry edges are well sealed. Transfer the leg at once to a baking dish and cook in the oven for 1 hour. When cooked, remove from the oven and allow to rest for 30 minutes before serving, cutting open 4 cm from the bottom of the crust to retain the juices in the meat.

Recipe by Belinda Franks

Vogue has never had a test kitchen, so my most of my cooking and photography has been done at my house. My first shoot for *Vogue* was a fish, in photographer Patrick Russell's studio. I remember that June McCallum was there. After that, I did my first big shoot for *Vogue Entertaining Guide* with the same photographer. This time it was a Christmas turkey and Charlie brought me large quantities of silver, pink and blue Christmas balls, silver tinsel, and fancy plates. I still think back on that turkey platter and cringe: it took me just that one photo session to learn that one doesn't precook meat and expect it to look succulent and warm.

I had done a bit of photography before with Howard Jones for *Cleo* magazine, and with Tony Schmaeling for a series of books he produced on the cuisines of the world. Incidentally, Tony Schmaeling – an architect by trade and a very good cook by passion – was responsible for me being the first woman ever invited to attend and comment upon the monthly dinner of the all-male Escoffier Society.

I wasn't particularly worried about learning to put food in front of a camera – you've either got it or you haven't. It's not so different from other photography: you look through the hole and see what's happening and then you get the picture. I was lucky, though, because I worked with the most marvellous photographers at *Vogue*: Patrick Russell, Michael Cook, Rodney Weidland, George Seper, Geoffrey Lung, Quentin Bacon and, more recently, Petrina Tinslay. They made it very easy for me.

I remember one of the first big feature pieces I did in 1980 for *Vogue* magazine. It was called 'Traditional Australian Cooking'. Apparently this was the epitome of what June McCallum thought the magazine should be about. Working for someone like June, who had such vision, was a dream ride. In all the time I worked for her, we never had a disagreement. She is still one of my closest friends and one of the most stylish women I have ever encountered.

I worked closely with photographer Michael Cook for a long time. I remember producing a photo in my bathroom for one of the *Vogue* cook books. Michael was lying on the floor in the sitting-room meditating, sort of out of this world, while I was fiddling around. I called out 'Michael', thinking this would wake him up: he came through and nearly had hysterics at the sight of me balanced in a most uncomfortable position in the shower alcove holding a white orchid over a plate with a background of white tiles. Of course, the picture looked great.

Another photograph we took, which became a cover of an annual *Vogue* cook book, featured an urn with Michael's grandfather's ashes in it. One photo caused us to be sued. We photographed a vanilla bavarois in front of a painting of a view of a harbour and ships in Wales done by Lindsay's ex-wife, who sued us for breach of copyright. The damages were not considerable.

VANILLA BAVAROIS

(Serves 8)

300 ml cream
3 cups milk
3 vanilla beans, split lengthwise
$1^1/_2$ cups sugar
12 egg yolks
$1^3/_4$ tablespoons gelatine, dissolved in $1/_4$ cup water
900 ml thickened cream, whipped

To serve
fresh raspberry, strawberry or passionfruit purée

Place the cream, milk and vanilla beans in a saucepan and bring to the boil. Turn off the heat and allow the mixture to stand for 1 hour.

Remove the split beans to a plate and scrape all the seeds and flesh from the beans. Return the seeds and flesh to the milk mixture and discard the pods. Beat the sugar and egg yolks until they are well amalgamated. Bring the vanilla milk to the boil, pour a little into the egg mixture and whip with an egg whisk. Pour the egg mixture back into the saucepan and cook over low heat, stirring constantly, until the mixture coats the back of a spoon. Stir in the dissolved gelatine, then pour the mixture into a bowl and allow to cool.

Transfer the mixture to a blender and blend until all the vanilla flesh is amalgamated with the custard. Return the mixture to the bowl and, when it is completely cold and just starting to thicken, fold in the whipped cream. Pour the mixture into an oiled mould, cover and refrigerate overnight.

To serve
Unmould the bavarois and serve with a fresh raspberry, strawberry or passionfruit purée.

Another time we had spread props all over the floor of Michael's house and found they were infested with paper lice that swarmed out of a stuffed bird. We both became very ill and our bodies were alive with the creatures. Itch, itch, itch. I don't know why I think it funny now, because it was very uncomfortable and quite serious.

Michael and I had years of good stories together. Once we had to go to northern Queensland and photograph a lot of bulls. I was at home with the bulls and the meat, but Michael was a vegetarian at that time. In getting there I was convinced we were lost and kept saying, 'For God's sake, Michael, this is not the way, turn back, we'll run out of petrol, it's not the way, turn back'. We pulled up at a river where there was a sign saying, 'STAY IN THE CAR, CROCODILE-INFESTED RIVER', or something. 'This is your last stop,' Michael said to me, 'Joan Campbell last seen here!' Michael got into trouble on that trip because he accidentally chained the hired car to a post in a garage in Rockhampton and drove off without knowing, leaving the bumper bar behind.

Michael was responsible for one particularly memorable meal. We were photographing John and Caroline Laws' home in Cloud Valley. They had made some fresh pasta and Michael, who had lived for six years in Italy, made a delicious sauce from a few bits in the fridge: garlic and a few sprigs of broccoli. He asked for some olive oil (this was in the days when we all still cooked in butter) and John said he had a can somewhere that someone had sent him from Italy. We opened it and I had never seen such oil – it was beautiful, dark green with bits floating in it. We'd only seen bottles of stuff that looked and tasted like castor oil. So, with those simple things, Michael concocted a most amazing meal.

Another photographer I worked with extensively was Rodney Weidland. He helped me with a big job, a series of meat promotions which generated lots of interest and were very challenging to prepare. We didn't use a stylist and we photographed a lot of my own things. One of the photos was supposed to be of a picnic, but on the day it was pouring with rain. Rodney went out, collected plants, turned on his bright lights and set up a beautiful garden in the sitting-room. Sometimes photos aren't quite as they seem!

VITELLO TONNATO

This recipe was given to me by Adrienne Lusso who now lives in Italy.

(Serves 8)

1 x 45 g can anchovy fillets
1 shoulder veal, boned, rolled and tied by your butcher
1 x 185 g can Sirena tuna in oil
2 carrots, peeled and sliced
1 onion, peeled and chopped
2 sticks of celery, sliced, and a handful of celery leaves
2 cloves garlic, peeled and crushed
6 cloves
2 litres chicken stock
$^1/_2$ bottle white wine
pepper and a little salt

Mayonnaise
6 egg yolks
juice of $^1/_2$ lemon
1 teaspoon Dijon mustard
salt and freshly ground pepper to taste
300 ml peanut oil
450 ml olive oil

Marinade
1 x 185 g can Sirena tuna in oil
2 tablespoons baby capers packed in salt, washed in
    several changes of water and drained
reserved oil from the anchovies
2 tablespoons olive oil
ground pepper
1 cup of the mayonnaise

To serve
remaining mayonnaise
stock
1 x 95 g can Sirena tuna in oil (optional)
freshly ground pepper
lemon juice
1 tablespoon baby capers packed in salt, washed in
    several changes of water and drained

Drain the anchovy fillets and reserve the oil. Tie the fillets on the meat with fine kitchen twine. Put the tuna, vegetables, garlic and cloves in a large, heavy-bottomed, non-corrodible pot and place the veal on top. Pour in the stock and white wine, and season with pepper and a small pinch of salt. Bring the liquid to the boil, cover the pot, turn down the heat and simmer the veal gently for $1^3/4$ hours. Turn off the heat, remove the lid and set aside the meat and stock in a cool place overnight. The next day, remove the veal from the stock and place it in a deep dish, reserving the stock.

To make the mayonnaise

Place the egg yolks, lemon juice, mustard, salt and pepper in a food processor and blend well. With the machine running, gradually add the oils until the mixture is emulsified.

To marinate the veal

Place the tuna with its oil, the capers, reserved oil from the anchovies, olive oil and pepper in a food processor and blend to a purée. Mix the purée with 1 cup of the mayonnaise and pour it over the veal. Cover the veal and refrigerate for 24 hours. Strain the reserved stock into a clean saucepan and cook until a quarter of the stock remains. Transfer the reduced stock to a bowl, cover and refrigerate.

To serve

Remove the veal from the sauce and scrape all the sauce from the meat back into the dish. Rinse the meat with the stock over the dish of sauce, then pat the meat dry with paper towels and set aside. Reserve the sauce and stock.

Place the remainder of the mayonnaise in a food processor, add the reserved sauce and stock, and blend until smooth. If the sauce is too thin, add a small can of drained tuna and blend again. The sauce should be the same thickness as mayonnaise. Add pepper and lemon juice to taste.

Cut the veal in thin slices and arrange on a platter. Pour over the sauce and serve sprinkled with capers.

ARMENIAN LAMB
(Serves 8)

1 tablespoon oil
2 tablespoons butter
1.5 kg trimmed lamb leg steaks, cut in 5-cm cubes
3 onions, peeled and sliced
2 cloves garlic, peeled and crushed
1 to 2 tablespoons plain flour
$1^1/2$ tablespoons ground cumin
3 teaspoons ground allspice
2 tablespoons tomato paste
1 x 420 ml can beef consommé mixed with 200 ml water
salt and pepper

To serve
rice pilaf (recipe follows)

Preheat the oven to 190°C. Heat the oil and butter in a frying pan and brown the meat a few pieces at a time. Remove the meat to a casserole and set aside. Add the onions and garlic to the pan and cook for 5 minutes. Sprinkle in the flour and spices, stir in the tomato paste, beef consommé and water.

Add the sauce to the meat, taste for salt and pepper, then cover and cook in the oven for 1 to 1½ hours. Check from time to time and add more water if necessary, stirring once or twice during the cooking. Serve the lamb with the Rice Pilaf.

RICE PILAF
90 g butter
2 small onions, peeled and chopped finely
400 g long-grain rice
900 ml chicken stock (this can be 2 cans Campbell's
    chicken consommé or 1 can plus 1 can of water)
salt and freshly ground pepper to taste
175 g fresh dates, stoned and cut in slivers
175 g pistachio nuts, shelled and halved
chopped coriander leaves
finely shredded zest of 2 large limes

Melt the butter in a large, heavy saucepan, add the onion and sauté until soft, but not brown. Add the rice and cook until translucent. Pour on the hot stock, season and, stirring all the time, bring to the boil. Cover the saucepan and cook the rice over low heat for 30 minutes, or until cooked. When testing the rice, stir it with a fork to avoid breaking up the grains. Add extra butter or stock if necessary.

When the rice is cooked, mix in the dates, pistachio nuts, coriander and lime rind. Serve around the Armenian Lamb.

NOISETTES OF LAMB SERVED ON ONION SOUBISE WITH MELTING MINT BUTTER
(Serves 6)

Mint butter
250 g butter, softened
3 tablespoons finely chopped fresh mint
juice of ½ lemon
pepper

Onion soubise
3 large onions, peeled
1 tablespoon butter
1 tablespoon plain flour
¾ cup milk
pinch of grated nutmeg
salt and pepper to taste

Noisettes
6 lamb noisettes
1 tablespoon butter
1 tablespoon oil

To make the mint butter
Place all the ingredients in a food processor and blend for a few minutes. Form the butter into a roll, wrap in plastic film and store in the refrigerator until firm.

To make the onion soubise
Cook the whole onions in salted water until soft. Drain and set aside. Melt the butter in a small saucepan, add the flour and cook for 1 minute. Pour on the hot milk and whisk over heat until the sauce is thick and free from lumps. Season with nutmeg, salt and pepper. Place the onions and sauce in a food processor and blend until the sauce is smooth. Return the soubise to the pan and keep warm.

To cook and serve the noisettes
Melt the butter and oil in a frying pan until very hot. Add the noisettes and cook for approximately 8 minutes on each side, turning frequently.

To serve, spoon the hot onion soubise onto heated plates, place a noisette on the soubise and top each noisette with a slice of the mint butter. Serve at once with crisp green vegetables of your choice.

Sharyn Storrier Lyneham is my current editor at *Vogue Entertaining* and also a director of Condé Nast Australia and we have worked together since I joined *Vogue*. She was then Art Director of *Vogue Living* and of *Vogue Entertaining Guide* (as *Vogue Entertaining* was called in those days). We've been through some funny times and some sad times, and though they say you can't work as closely as we have without some conflict we have agreed about most things, and always the important ones. I've enjoyed working with Sharyn. I think the worst thing we've done together was to put the wrong bottle of wine on the cover of a cook book; *not* the advertiser's bottle! I understand it cost a lot to remedy the situation and our editor at the time was *not* amused!

Everything that is put into the magazine with my name attached is photographed at some stage and therefore everything is tested by me in the kitchen. Then I write the recipes. I don't know how I learnt to write recipes; I just had a brain that picked it up, I just sat down and wrote them. I was already writing recipes for my classes and I had to make them very clear, so it wasn't difficult. Recipes should be short, succinct and to the point. People don't want to cook recipes if they look long and difficult, even though they are, in fact, technical.

I use many recipes from many sources. If I adapt a recipe, I make sure I mark it 'adapted from', and if I copy a recipe I make sure I get permission to print it and acknowledge the name and source. You've only got to change one or two things in a recipe to make it your own, theoretically, if you are foul enough, but that's not my style.

We're always saying that eating habits have changed dramatically. *Vogue* featured a risotto in a 1984 cook book; it was terribly modern then. About the same time we were saying 'how modern' about my mushroom tartlet with a mixture of dried wood-ear mushrooms (soaked in water to soften) and common little mushrooms. But I remember books that I was looking at before I even started at *Vogue*: Ted Moloney's *Good Living Cook Book* and *The Garrulous Gourmet* by William Wallace Irwin. The former was a great influence in the early seventies, and is an absolute classic. Really, it's about what we're all aiming for: creating gourmet foods with a minimum of fuss. The second of these books was even earlier and was still rather French in its approach, but it didn't just copy the French culture – it was for Australians, and focused on produce we had here at the time. Both of them were very modern and eclectic for their time, in terms both of ingredients and of approach. Most importantly, none of the food was contrived or silly or arranged.

TARTLETS WITH MUSHROOM RAGOUT

Today fresh Asian mushrooms are available and these have been substituted for the dried and canned ones I used to use. This tart was on the cover of the first Vogue Wine and Food Cookbook *in 1983.*

(Serves 8)

Tartlets
2½ cups plain flour
pinch of salt
250 g butter
3 tablespoons iced water

Mushroom ragout
400 g tiny button mushrooms
175 g butter
3 cups fresh black fungi, trimmed and cut in
   bite-sized pieces
freshly ground pepper
1 cup red wine, or more if necessary
1 cup strong chicken stock, or more if necessary
200 g fresh enoki mushrooms, trimmed
a little salt

To make the tartlets

Place the flour, salt and butter in a food processor and process with an on-off action until the mixture is like fine breadcrumbs. Add the iced water all at once and, when the mixture forms a ball, remove from the bowl and wrap in plastic wrap. Refrigerate for at least an hour.

Roll the pastry out on a floured board (it should be quite thin) and line eight tartlet cans, each 8 cm in diameter, bringing the pastry well up the sides as you will get some shrinkage during cooking. Re-roll the remaining pastry and make a few extra tartlet shells in case of accidents. Place the tartlets in the refrigerator to firm for 30 minutes before cooking.

Preheat the oven to 190°C. Prick the tartlets well to stop them rising in the middle. Bake on the centre shelf of the oven for 12 to 15 minutes. Carefully turn out on to a cake rack and allow to cool. Store in an airtight container until ready to use.

To make the ragout

While preparing the ragout, place the tartlets in a 150°C oven until heated through. Trim the stalks off the button mushrooms, brush off any dirt and, if you think they are too large, cut them in half.

Melt the butter in a large frying pan and sauté the button mushrooms for 3 or 4 minutes. Add the black fungi and sauté for a further 1 or 2 minutes, then sprinkle with pepper. Pour in the red wine and stock, and simmer for a few minutes. Remove the mushrooms and fungi with a slotted spoon and keep warm.

If you think it necessary, add some more red wine and stock to the pan. Reduce the sauce to about 1¼ cups. Return the cooked mushrooms and fungi to the pan with the enoki mushrooms and simmer for 5 minutes to combine all flavours. Taste for salt and add a small lump of butter to make the sauce shiny.

To serve

Place a tartlet case on each plate, spoon in the mushroom mixture and serve at once.

TONNO CON SALSA DI POMODORO

750 g fresh tuna
salt to taste
plain flour
¼ cup olive oil
1 onion, peeled and sliced
1 clove garlic, peeled and crushed
3 canned anchovy fillets, chopped
1 tablespoon finely chopped parsley
150 ml dry white wine
1 x 450 g can tomatoes, drained and puréed
250 ml water
1 bay leaf
1 teaspoon chopped fresh basil
1 teaspoon chopped fresh oregano

Cut the tuna into 2.5 cm slices. Sprinkle with salt, roll in flour and fry in 2 tablespoons of the oil until lightly browned. Remove from the pan, add the rest of the oil to the pan and brown the onion. Add the crushed garlic, anchovies and parsley and cook just a little. Add the wine and cook until it evaporates.

Add the tomato purée, water, bay leaf, basil and oregano and cook for 15 minutes. Return the browned fish to the pan and simmer for 10 minutes.

FENNEL SOUP
(Serves 6 to 8)

3 bulbs fennel
40 g butter
1 onion, peeled and chopped
1.5 litres chicken stock
150 ml cream, or more if you wish
1 tablespoon Pernod
salt and pepper

Wash and trim the fennel, and chop coarsely. Melt the butter in a large saucepan and sauté the fennel and onion until the fennel is slightly browned. Pour in the chicken stock and cook until the fennel is soft. Purée the mixture in a food processor or blender.

Pour the soup back into the pot and add the cream and Pernod. Bring to the boil, add salt and pepper to taste, and serve.

DUCK WITH ORANGES
This was a great favourite of mine when I had dinner guests.

(Serves 8)

2 ducks, each weighing 1.5 kg
salt and pepper to taste
crushed garlic to taste
250 g butter, melted
3/4 cup honey
2 oranges, sliced
juice of 1 orange
1 cup brandy

Clean the ducks thoroughly, removing the neck bone, any feathers and the fat from the interior. Dry thoroughly with paper towels. Rub the ducks with salt, pepper and crushed garlic and let stand for 1 hour.

Preheat the oven to 190°C. Place the ducks in a large baking tin and pour over the melted butter. Cook in the preheated oven for 1 hour, basting occasionally. While the ducks are cooking, put the honey, sliced oranges, orange juice and half of the brandy in a saucepan and simmer gently until the liquid has reduced and the oranges are cooked a little. They should be like orange conserve.

When the ducks are cooked, pour off all the fat from the baking tin and flame them with the remaining brandy. Pour over the orange–honey mixture and return to the oven to cook for a further 15 minutes, or more if necessary. The ducks must be basted frequently.

Remove the birds from the tin and cut in four with a pair of kitchen scissors, not forgetting to remove the bone that runs from the neck end to the 'parson's nose'. Return the duck pieces to the baking tin, baste well with the orange sauce and reheat for 10 minutes before serving.

PRAWN RISOTTO

(Serves 6)

600 g peeled, small green prawns, digestive
   tracts removed
1 teaspoon bicarbonate of soda
1 onion, peeled and chopped
2 cloves garlic, peeled and chopped
4 tablespoons olive oil
salt and pepper to taste
$1\frac{1}{2}$ cups white wine
$\frac{1}{2}$ cup brandy
60 g butter
500 g Arborio rice
1 litre hot fish stock (see recipe on p. 34)
a little extra olive oil

Wash and soak the prawns in water with the bicarbonate of soda for 30 minutes. Drain and pat dry with paper towels. Fry the onion and garlic in oil until they are light brown. Add the prawns and fry gently. Add salt and pepper, then pour in the wine and brandy. Cook the sauce slowly for about 10 minutes. Strain the sauce, reserve the prawns, onion and garlic in a warm place and reheat the sauce to boiling point.

Melt the butter in a large, heavy saucepan. Add the rice and cook over low heat, stirring constantly, until the rice absorbs the butter and dries out a little. The grains should be evenly coloured.

Gradually add the hot fish stock and the prawn sauce to the rice, a little at a time, until the rice is cooked. When the rice is cooked, stir in the reserved prawns, onion and garlic and add a little olive oil. The risotto should be creamy and the rice firm to the bite but not chalky. Serve at once.

QUEEN VICTORIA'S FAVOURITE RICE PUDDING
(Serves 4)

1 cup brown rice
salt
250 g preserved figs, chopped
1 cup thick cream
¼ cup honey

Cook the rice in boiling salted water for about 20 minutes, or until tender. Drain well and allow to cool, then place it in a bowl with the chopped figs. Whip the cream with the honey and mix through the rice. Chill in the refrigerator until ready to serve.

I find that things change but they don't change much at all. Good food is always good food. Sometimes I have done some dishes that have been very *chichi*, and I still can do that. But I always very quickly end up back at simplicity.

When I look back on my time at *Vogue*, I think the biggest change has been in terms of flavours. First of all it was French food – the old-fashioned dishes. Then there was *nouvelle cuisine*. Then we discovered Asian tastes. And, of course, we experimented with Italian, Moroccan and Greek. We don't do much traditional French food any more apart from bistro and brasserie-style dishes; people are not interested in taking that much time. Wok cooking and pasta have been revolutionary. People don't have time to learn rigorous new methods. They are interested in a 'taste of'. So there are ingredients that can be thrown in to give the requisite 'taste'. I must say I've enjoyed these changes. I've found all the new influences very, very interesting. I've never been to Morocco, for example, but I love the flavours I taste from there.

It's important to remember that we, at the magazines, do not lead the restaurants or the chefs. We pick up our ideas from them: we pick up on the barometer, the bigger picture, and make it into recipes that domestic cooks can manage and enjoy. I remember, for example, finding out about Mark Armstrong and Greg Doyle. When I did the first story on Mark in *Vogue Entertaining* in 1981 – he was a fresh little dewdrop then – I had no influence on his cooking at all, but he had an influence on mine. He was without doubt cooking the best food in Sydney at the time and he taught me a lot, which I tried to pass on to readers in the recipes we published and in my classes.

MARK ARMSTRONG'S CRAB SALAD WITH TRUFFLE MAYONNAISE
(Serves 8)

Mayonnaise
4 egg yolks
salt and pepper to taste
liquid from 1 x 50 g can of truffles, reserve the truffles
   for the salad (you can now buy fresh truffles and
   truffle oil)
1³⁄₄ cups peanut oil, or 1¹⁄₂ cups peanut oil and
   2 tablespoons truffle oil
lemon juice

Salad
curly endive
4 large blue swimmer crabs, cooked (alternatively,
   today you can buy freshly cooked crab meat packed
   in cryovac from your fishmonger)
2 tablespoons dried Japanese hijiki seaweed, soaked in
   water
1 tablespoon soy sauce
4 carrots, cut in fine julienne
1 punnet mustard cress
1 to 2 tablespoons Japanese rice wine
salt and freshly ground pepper to taste
8 x 50 g eggs

To serve
chopped truffle
mustard cress

To make the mayonnaise
Place the egg yolks in a food processor, add salt and pepper and the truffle liquid and process together. With the motor still running, gradually pour in the oil until the mayonnaise is thick. Add lemon juice to taste and set aside.

To make the salad
Wash the curly endive and refrigerate in a plastic bag.

Remove the crab meat from the crab and place in a bowl. Drain the soaked seaweed and toss with the soy sauce over high heat in a non-stick frying pan. Allow to cool. Toss together the crab, carrot julienne and clipped cress with a dash of rice wine and salt and pepper. Poach the eggs in salted water until set, but with the yolk still runny in the centre. Drain the eggs and trim to make an even, round shape.

To serve

Arrange the curly endive on eight individual plates. Place the crab mixture in the centre with a poached egg on top. Spoon the truffle mayonnaise over the egg, sprinkle mustard cress around the edges of the salad and scatter over the chopped truffles.

Greg Doyle gave me my first real taste of *nouvelle cuisine* at the Balmain Bakery, where he started in 1977. I was most impressed, and I would like to say that Greg still cooks the best duck I have ever eaten. At *Vogue*, we tried to distil the essence of *nouvelle*, which was its exciting, open-minded approach, and present it to readers in a way they could readily interpret.

GREG DOYLE'S CREAM OF SCALLOP SOUP WITH SPRING VEGETABLES
(Serves about 12)

Scallop stock
2 carrots, chopped
½ bunch spring onions, chopped
24 green peppercorns
4 basil leaves
4 sorrel leaves
4 sprigs lemon thyme
4 sprigs marjoram
12 sprigs parsley
butter
1 kg scallops
500 ml white wine
1.5 litres fish stock

To finish and serve
butter
2 carrots, peeled and diced
6 eschalots, peeled and diced
300 g oyster mushrooms, diced
2 leeks (white parts only), washed and diced
1 bunch chives, chopped finely
1 cup fresh green peas, blanched
600 ml cream
6 scallops without roes per serving
chopped chervil

To make the scallop stock
Cook the vegetables and herbs in a saucepan with a little butter over very low heat until they are softened but not browned. Add the scallops and sweat until they are overcooked. Add the wine and fish stock. Bring the mixture to the boil and simmer for 15 minutes. Strain, reserving the stock and discard the solids, including the scallops.

To finish and serve the soup

Melt a little butter in a saucepan, add all the vegetables except the peas and cook gently over very low heat until tender. Add the scallop stock and peas, and simmer. In a separate saucepan, bring the cream to the boil and simmer gently until it is reduced by half.

Add the cream to the stock and bring the soup to near boiling point. Place 6 raw scallops in each soup bowl and pour over the hot stock. Serve at once sprinkled with chopped chervil.

There are many people who make claim to it, but I'm afraid I was, with Greg Doyle, the instigator of the Sticky Toffee Pudding. That first recipe was from the Lygon Arms, outside London. They sent me the recipe, typed up on a piece of Lygon Arms notepaper, and I took it to Greg and asked him to prepare it for a feature on hot puddings for *Vogue Entertaining*. He did so and he put it on his menu, where it remained for some time. I have seen this recipe metamorphose into Sticky Date Pudding.

LYGON ARMS STICKY TOFFEE PUDDING
(Serves 6)

Pudding
375 g chopped dates
250 ml boiling water
1 teaspoon bicarbonate of soda
60 g butter
175 g sugar
2 eggs
250 g self-raising flour

Sauce
1 litre thick cream
60 g butter
125 g dark-brown sugar

To serve
cream

To make the pudding

Add the dates to the boiling water and when the water returns to the boil, cook the dates for 4 minutes. Add the bicarbonate of soda, remove from heat and allow to cool.

Preheat the oven to 200°C. Cream the butter and sugar together and add the eggs, one at a time, beating until smooth. Pour the date mixture into the egg mixture, add the flour and beat well. Pour the mixture into a greased baking dish and cook in the preheated oven for approximately 25 minutes or until the pudding is firm.

To make the sauce
Bring all the ingredients to the boil, stirring until the sugar is dissolved. Pour the sauce over the hot pudding, reserving some of the sauce to serve separately.

To serve
Slice the pudding into squares and serve on individual plates with the remaining sauce and cream.

Another chef (or, should I say, ex-chef, as he is now a restaurant consultant and a potter of some renown) I particularly admire is Anders Ousbäck. His food is so simple, but elegant as well as tasty. His famous roast chook and bread sauce was one of the first meals he cooked for me in his own home, and it was perfection. At another meal at his home we had roasted garlic and feta cheese, with toasted brioche, as a first course. It was so good. Then we had a small piece of fish. The last course was the most elegant of all: polished purple figs in an exquisite, grape-coloured, oddly shaped glass platter. Other times I've dined with him in the kitchen and he will cook something like grilled peppers with olive oil, serving them as a starter with a bit of fabulous bread. Some people have no idea how to serve elegant food. They think they need to dress it up. What Anders achieves is simplicity.

ANDERS OUSBÄCK'S ROASTED GARLIC WITH GOAT'S MILK FETA
fresh garlic bulbs, cut in halves horizontally
olive oil
goat's milk feta
freshly ground pepper
loaf of good Italian bread
bowl of rocket leaves
a cruet with virgin olive oil and balsamic vinegar

Preheat the oven to 190°C. Have ready a small square of aluminium foil for each garlic half. Spoon a little olive oil on each piece of foil and lay the garlic on top, cut side down. Twist the foil to seal and place the foil packages on a baking sheet.

Roast the garlic packages in the oven for 30 minutes or until the garlic flesh is soft and the cut surface is a light golden colour. Remove from the oven and set aside for at least 30 minutes before serving.

Remove the garlic halves from the foil and place them on a serving dish, cut-side up. Cut the goat's milk feta in slices and arrange on the dish. Grind over some pepper and serve with slices of Italian bread. Make a salad of rocket leaves and toss with the olive oil and balsamic vinegar to serve with the dish.

Simplicity really can be the key to everything in a meal. Nothing could be simpler than a jar of salmon eggs, for example. Whenever I get hold of one, I eat it in spoonfuls piled on top of buttery toast. I remember one memorable occasion, a Boxing Day, with Leo Schofield, June McCallum, Simon Johnson and a can of Osietra caviar. All dressed in our gardening gear, we took the toaster, the breadboard, some French butter and a bottle of Krug champagne, sat around my dining table and spooned the caviar straight from the can onto hot buttered toast.

It seems fitting to conclude here with a selection of recipes that I have particularly enjoyed making and which show the introduction of new flavours over the years.

THAI SEAFOOD SALAD
(Serves 4)

Dressing
$1/2$ cup fresh lime juice
$1/4$ cup fish sauce
$1/4$ cup palm sugar
1 or 2 fresh chillies, seeded and sliced finely
1 clove garlic, peeled and crushed
100 ml coconut cream

Salad
1 cup fresh cooked crab meat
25 cooked medium prawns, peeled, digestive tracts
   removed and prawns cut in half lengthwise
4 red eschalots, peeled and sliced
1 stalk lemon grass, tender centre part only, sliced finely
3 kaffir lime leaves, shredded
150 g fresh black fungi, cut in pieces
150 g fresh shimeji mushrooms, trimmed
leaves from 1 bunch coriander
leaves from 1 bunch mint
a small handful mizuna leaves
8 spring onions, cut in 2 cm lengths

To make the dressing
Put all the ingredients in a screw-top jar and shake well to combine.

To assemble and serve the salad

Prepare the salad ingredients and just before serving place them in a bowl and toss together. Pile onto a large serving plate, pour over the dressing to taste and serve at once.

ASIAN MUSSELS
(Serves 4)

$1/2$ bottle white wine
3 cups fish stock (see recipe on p. 34)
2 stalks lemon grass, tied together
6 kaffir lime leaves
1 bunch coriander, with roots
3 red chillies, seeded and sliced
8 eschalots, peeled and sliced finely
a 5 cm piece ginger, peeled and cut into julienne
fish sauce to taste
48 mussels, scrubbed well and beards removed
$1/2$ cup torn mint leaves

Place the wine and fish stock in a large saucepan with the lemon grass, lime leaves and the roots and stems of the coriander (reserve the leaves). Bring to the boil, reduce the heat and simmer for 10 minutes.

Stir in the chillies, eschalots, ginger and fish sauce. Add the mussels and cook, stirring frequently, until they open, removing them with a slotted spoon to a bowl as they do so. Discard any mussels that do not open.

Remove and discard the lemon grass and the coriander roots and stems. Stir the mint and coriander leaves into the hot broth and taste for fish sauce.

Divide the mussels between four bowls, pour over the hot broth and serve immediately.

OCEAN TROUT WITH MOROCCAN SPICES
(Serves 4)

2 tablespoons finely chopped coriander leaves
1 tablespoon chopped parsley
3 cloves garlic, peeled and crushed
2 level teaspoons salt
$1^{1}/2$ teaspoons ground cumin
2 teaspoons paprika
pinch of cayenne pepper
1 teaspoon powdered saffron
1 teaspoon harissa (a spicy red sauce available
    from delicatessens)
6 tablespoons olive oil
2 tablespoons lemon juice
1 ocean trout, filleted, bones and skin removed and fillets
    cut in halves

Combine all the herbs and spices, harissa, olive oil and lemon juice and rub into the pieces of fish. Place the fish in a non-corrodible dish, cover and set aside for 1 hour.

Preheat the oven to 200°C. Wrap each piece of fish loosely in aluminium foil, place in a baking dish and bake in the oven for about 5 to 7 minutes.

Unwrap the foil, slide a piece of fish, along with some cooking juices, onto each heated serving plate and serve at once.

QUAIL SALAD WITH SOY AND CHILLI MARINATED CUCUMBER
(Serves 4)

16 quail eggs
salt and freshly ground black pepper
4 quail
juice squeezed from garlic cloves
olive oil
4 Lebanese cucumbers
3 tablespoons vegetable oil
1 clove garlic, peeled and crushed
2 tablespoons soy sauce
2 tablespoons white wine vinegar
1 tablespoon palm sugar
pinch of chilli flakes
mixed salad leaves
chervil sprigs

Hard-boil the quail eggs and, when they are cooked, drop them in iced water to make them easier to peel. Slice the peeled eggs in halves lengthwise and set aside.

Preheat the oven to 200°C. Sprinkle salt and pepper over the quail and squeeze over a little garlic juice. Place the quail in a baking dish and pour over some olive oil. Roast in the preheated oven for 25 to 30 minutes or until cooked to your liking. Allow to cool, then cut the quail into quarters.

Wash the cucumbers, leave the skin on and, with a vegetable peeler, slice lengthwise into thin strips. Place in a bowl. Put the vegetable oil, crushed garlic, soy sauce, white wine vinegar, palm sugar and chilli flakes into a screw-top jar and shake together until well amalgamated. Add salt to taste. No more than 10 minutes before serving, pour the dressing over the cucumber slices and leave to marinate.

To assemble the salad, toss the mixed salad leaves and chervil with salt and pepper and a little olive oil. Spoon half the marinated cucumber onto four serving plates and place the tossed salad leaves and chervil in a pile on the cucumber. Arrange the sliced quail eggs and the quail quarters on each salad and add a pile of the remaining cucumber strips on top. Grind over some black pepper and serve at once.

DUCK SALAD
(Serves 6)

1 Chinese barbecued duck, or a home-roasted duck
4 fresh kaffir lime leaves, shredded finely
2 stalks lemon grass tender part only, sliced finely
1/2 cup fried garlic flakes
6 spring onions, cut in 2 cm lengths
1 tablespoon freshly grated ginger

Dressing
juice of 1 or 2 limes
2 teaspoons Thai fish sauce (nam pla)
2 teaspoons palm sugar
2 tablespoons Thai sweet chilli sauce

To serve
flesh from 2 mangoes, sliced lengthwise
leaves from 3 witlof

Remove all the flesh and skin from the duck, slicing it in irregular small pieces, and place in a bowl. Add the kaffir lime leaves, lemon grass, fried garlic, spring onions and grated ginger.

To make the dressing
Mix the lime juice, fish sauce, palm sugar and chilli sauce together in a small bowl.

To finish the salad
Just before serving toss the duck mixture with the dressing. Add the mango slices and witlof leaves and toss gently.

ALGERIAN POTATOES WITH OLIVE OIL
(Serves 6 to 8)

1.5 kg potatoes
150 ml olive oil
5 cloves garlic, peeled and sliced finely
1 tablespoon tomato purée
1 teaspoon harissa
1 tablespoon cardamom seeds
a good pinch of chilli flakes
salt to taste
2 cups hot water

Peel the potatoes and cut in thick slices. Heat the oil in a large frying pan with a lid. Add the potatoes, garlic, tomato purée, harissa, cardamom seeds, chilli flakes and salt and stir well.

Add the water, bring to the boil, cover and simmer for 20 to 30 minutes. The water will be absorbed into the potatoes.

Serve hot as a first course, or with a main course, or cold as a salad.

LAMB TAGINE WITH FRESH DATES
(Serves 6)

3 tablespoons olive oil
2 tablespoons butter
2 large onions, peeled and chopped
2 cloves garlic, peeled and chopped finely
6 lamb shanks, trimmed
plain flour
1 teaspoon ground ginger
1 teaspoon ground cumin
1 cinnamon stick
a pinch of saffron threads
1 x 425 ml can chicken consommé
250 ml water
salt and freshly ground black pepper
2 quarters of preserved lemons, the flesh and pith
    discarded and the rind rinsed
12 fresh dates

To serve
couscous with chickpeas and pine nuts
    (recipe follows)

Preheat the oven to 175°C. Heat the oil and butter in a large frying pan and cook the onions and garlic until golden. Remove with a slotted spoon and transfer to a large casserole. Dust the lamb shanks with plain flour and fry in the same pan, adding a little extra oil if needed. When the shanks have browned, place them in the casserole and add the ginger, cumin, cinnamon stick and saffron threads. Add the chicken consommé, water, salt and pepper to taste, stir to mix then cover the casserole and place in the oven. Cook until the lamb is tender, approximately 1$\frac{1}{2}$ hours.

Remove the fat from the liquid. Cut the preserved lemon rind into small, thin strips and add to the casserole with the dates and reheat. Serve the lamb mounded on the centre of a platter of the couscous with the sauce poured over.

COUSCOUS WITH CHICKPEAS AND PINE NUTS
(Serves 6)

Cook 500 g of instant couscous, following the instructions on the packet and using chicken consommé instead of water.

Drain and rinse 1 x 375 g can of chickpeas, heat through and toss with the cooked couscous. Transfer to a serving platter and sprinkle with $\frac{1}{2}$ cup toasted pine nuts.

MALAYSIAN CHICKEN CURRY
(Serves 6)

4 tablespoons vegetable oil
2 onions, peeled and sliced
2 cloves garlic, peeled and chopped
1 tablespoon chopped fresh ginger
3 stems lemon grass, tender centre parts only, sliced
    (reserve the remaining stems)
3 large red chillies, seeded and sliced
$1^1/_2$ teaspoons ground turmeric
1.5 to 2 kg chicken thighs, trimmed of fat
3 cups coconut milk
1 walnut-sized piece dried tamarind pulp, crumbled
6 curry leaves
6 green cardamom pods, bruised
1 teaspoon palm sugar
salt
2 tablespoons fresh lime juice
chopped coriander leaves

Heat 2 tablespoons of the oil in a large pan and fry the onions until soft and golden.
Add the garlic, ginger, lemon grass, chillies and turmeric and fry until aromatic. Transfer
the mixture to a mortar and pound to a paste, or process in a blender, until the mixture
forms a paste.

   Return the paste to the pan, add the remaining oil and heat over medium heat. Add
the chicken and turn the pieces until coated with the paste. Add the coconut milk,
tamarind, curry leaves, cardamom pods, reserved lemon grass stems, palm sugar and
salt to taste. Cover and simmer for 35 minutes or until cooked, turning the chicken
pieces in the sauce.

   Stir in the lime juice, transfer the curry to a serving dish, sprinkle with coriander
leaves and serve with steamed white rice.

COFFIN BAY SCALLOPS WITH TOMATO SALSA
(Serves 4)

24 Coffin Bay scallops in their shells
2 tablespoons hoi sin sauce
2 tablespoons olive oil
1 clove garlic, peeled and crushed
freshly ground pepper

Tomato salsa

6 tomatoes, peeled, seeds removed and
    flesh chopped coarsely
1 chilli, seeds removed and flesh chopped coarsely
leaves from $^1/_2$ bunch coriander
1 small red onion, peeled and chopped coarsely
salt and freshly ground pepper to taste
1 tablespoon olive oil

Cut the scallops from their shells with a sharp knife so that they remain in their positions on the shells. Place the shells on a flat baking tray. Combine the hoi sin sauce, olive oil and garlic and pour about $^1/_2$ teaspoon of the mixture over each scallop. Grind over some pepper and set aside.

To make the salsa

Purée all the ingredients except the olive oil in a blender. With the motor running, pour in the olive oil and blend the mixture to a smooth sauce.

To cook and serve the scallops

Preheat the oven to 200°C.

Place the scallops on the centre shelf of the oven and cook for no more than 3 minutes. Place 6 scallops on each serving plate and spoon over some salsa. Put the remaining salsa in a bowl and pass it at the table.

FETTUCCINE WITH A SAUCE OF SUN-DRIED TOMATOES, CREAM AND PRAWNS

(Serves 4)

Sauce

3 tablespoons oil from sun-dried tomatoes packed in oil
3 cloves garlic, peeled and crushed
750 g medium sized, green king prawns, shelled and
    digestive tracts removed
$^1/_4$ cup peeled and thinly sliced eschalots
$1^1/_2$ tablespoons chopped fresh basil
$^1/_2$ cup sun-dried tomatoes packed in oil, drained and cut
    in slivers
$^1/_4$ teaspoon freshly ground white pepper
1 cup chicken stock
$^3/_4$ cup dry vermouth
1 cup cream
$^1/_2$ cup freshly grated parmesan cheese

Pasta

320 g fettuccine
salt
3 litres water

To make the sauce

Heat the oil from the sun-dried tomatoes with the garlic in a frying pan. When the oil is hot, add the prawns and cook for a few minutes, stirring frequently, until the prawns are opaque. Remove the prawns from the pan and set aside.

Add the eschalots, basil, sun-dried tomatoes, pepper, stock, vermouth and cream to the pan and cook over high heat until the sauce has reduced to about $1\frac{1}{2}$ cups. Add the cheese and cook for 1 to 2 minutes more. Return the prawns to the sauce and heat through just before serving.

To cook the pasta and serve

Bring the salted water to the boil, drop in the pasta and cook it until just tender. Drain the pasta well, then add it to the sauce in the pan, toss with two forks to blend well and serve at once.

STEWED CALAMARI WITH PEAS

(Serves 6)

100 ml olive oil
2 cloves garlic, peeled and crushed
1 kg calamari, cleaned and cut into strips
1 cup dry white wine
6 canned anchovy fillets, chopped finely
2 x 450 g cans Italian tomatoes, puréed and sieved
300 g shelled peas
salt and freshly ground pepper
2 tablespoons chopped Italian parsley

Heat the oil in a large, heavy-based frying pan and fry the garlic gently until golden. Add the calamari and toss, then pour in the wine and simmer for 5 to 10 minutes.

Add the anchovies and prepared tomatoes and cook for about 20 minutes. Add the peas and continue to cook until the peas are tender and the calamari is cooked.

Season to taste, stir in the parsley and serve at once with a good Italian bread.

POSTCARDS

I was very lucky to be able to travel with the *Vogue* card in my pocket because it certainly opened doors to experiences I would not otherwise have had. I was not so terribly influenced on these trips by particular people as by particular dishes and tastes. I did find it irritating sometimes to meet some chefs who thought (some still do, I suppose) that Australian food is a joke. Little did they know! The trips gave me a chance to sample the real flavours of cultures I had been reading about for years. I collected some marvellous recipes and I was inspired to make my own recipes calling on the vivid memories of the flavours I had come across. This is probably the closest thing to Australian-style food anyway – we have adopted and adapted, picked up as we've gone along, pinched ideas and made them our own.

Here are some of the most memorable places and tastes from my trips.

From Tahiti

When June McCallum sent me with photographer Michael Cook to Tahiti, we stayed on the island of Papeete at the Tahara'a Hotel. I met the chef of the hotel, Thierry Bretherau, who prepared three special desserts for our visit: Pithiviers, a puff-pastry dish filled with almond cream; Tuile Tahara'a, with lemon sorbet and strawberry sauce; and a gateau prepared with crème bavarois and oranges. I met another cook, Evelyn Arbelot, also of French descent, who prepared a traditional Tama'ara'a feast, the preparation of which is similar to a Maori Hangi. We then went across to Bora Bora, which is where I ate my first-ever fresh heart of palm and I visited a vanilla-bean plantation with Michael Cook. There was a little French store there where they made their own French breads and flew in great delicacies such as foie gras, French cheeses and butter. I loved Bora Bora, it was so incredibly beautiful.

Tahara'a Hotel

CLAIRFONTAINE
(Serves 8)

Crème bavarois
250 ml milk
1 vanilla bean
grated rind of 1 orange
100 g sugar
2 egg yolks
1 tablespoon gelatine, dissolved in a little water
20 ml Grand Marnier
300 ml cream, whipped

To line the can
4 oranges, sliced thinly
2 thin circles of plain butter cake or sponge cake,
    made in a 28 cm round tin
Grand Marnier

Chocolate sauce
250 ml water
250 g sugar
50 g cocoa
50 ml cream

To make the bavarois
Bring the milk to the boil with the vanilla bean and orange rind. Beat together the sugar and egg yolks. Pour a little of the hot milk into the egg mixture and whisk. Return the mixture to the saucepan with the milk and cook over low heat, stirring constantly, until the mixture coats the back of a spoon.

Remove the saucepan from the heat, add the gelatine and stir until the gelatine dissolves into the mixture. Pour into a bowl and add the Grand Marnier. Set aside to cool, then remove the vanilla bean and refrigerate the bavarois until it begins to thicken. Fold in the whipped cream.

To line the tin and assemble the dessert
Line an oiled, 28-cm round cake tin with the orange slices. Pour in half the bavarois mixture. Place a circle of cake on top and sprinkle with Grand Marnier. Pour in the remaining bavarois, cover with the second circle of cake and sprinkle with Grand Marnier. Cover and refrigerate for at least 6 hours to set.

To make the chocolate sauce
Mix together all the ingredients in a saucepan and simmer until the mixture thickens slightly. Set aside to cool.

To serve: turn out the dessert onto a serving plate, cut into slices with a sharp knife and serve on the chocolate sauce.
Recipe by Thierry Bretherau

From Thailand

I went several times to Thailand and I loved it. In terms of food, it changed my perspective absolutely: I picked up new tastes and it introduced me to a whole new look. Real Thai food was very different to what was being served in Australia in the early eighties. One of the best things I've ever eaten in my life, unexpectedly, was in Thailand. A group of journalists and foodies and I were taken on a tour of the island (Panuyi) they were supposed to blow up in a James Bond movie. We travelled there on one of the long, skinny, rat-tailed boats. On this trip we visited a temple built over the water, which smelled very strongly and unpleasantly of fish paste. Around this temple was a Moslem village called Samard, where fishermen caught fresh fish and prepared it immediately for eating. The other journalists wouldn't eat the fish because of the strong smell hanging in the air, but Claude Forell (restaurant reviewer for the *Age* in Melbourne) and I sat down to sample it and it was absolutely delicious: steamed fish with fresh shallots and fresh ginger, and some sort of sauce. The variety of the fish was unknown to us, but it was fresh from the sea and that was what made it so special.

One of the other features that fascinated me was the differences within the culture. In some parts of the peninsula, for example, they seemed only to barbecue things very simply, while elsewhere they used quite a lot of spices. I stayed in Phuket at the Yacht Club, which was an interesting experience: very beautiful, but I noticed one night that there were a lot of guards on each floor.

I was vigilant enough to make a note of the telephone number for reception and put it beside my bed. I had been leaving the door open; I locked it that night. Sure enough, in the middle of the night, something disturbed me by jumping on the roof. I dialled reception and in four seconds flat there were three guards in my room. They told me the noise was a monkey, but I think it was someone wandering around.

On that trip I visited the Kata Thani, one of three marvellous resorts owned by the same company on Kata Beach. The owner, Khun Pramook Achariyachai, and his English wife introduced me to the kitchen and to the whole family. They made the most wonderful meal for which I was given the recipes, including Son-in-law Eggs.

Phuket Yacht Club: Quarter Deck, Chart Room

FRIED WHOLE FISH IN CHILLI SAUCE
(Serves 4 as part of a meal)

Sauce
1 clove garlic, peeled
1 tablespoon finely chopped fresh red chilli
2 coriander roots
1 cup sugar
$1/2$ cup fish sauce (nam pla), or to taste
1 teaspoon tamarind concentrate
2 tablespoons vegetable oil
1 cup water, or to taste

Fish
1 x 500 g to 750 g whole fish, such as ocean perch,
    coral trout, bream, snapper or other reef fish,
    scaled and cleaned
cornflour
vegetable oil for deep frying

To make the sauce
Grind the garlic, chilli and coriander root in a blender or food processor, then add the sugar, fish sauce and tamarind concentrate and process until combined. Heat the vegetable oil in a frying pan and add the blended mixture. Fry for a few minutes until the mixture is aromatic, then add the water and cook for a few minutes more until the sauce thickens. Set aside and keep warm while you cook the fish.

To cook and serve the fish

Wash the fish and wipe it dry with paper towels. Cut three diagonal slashes through the skin on either side and coat the fish in cornflour. Heat sufficient oil in a deep fryer to cook the fish. Carefully slide in the fish and fry for about 10 to 12 minutes until golden brown and crisp.

Remove the fish with a wire spatula and drain on paper towels. Place on a serving platter, pour over the hot sauce and serve at once.

Kata Thani, Phuket

SON-IN-LAW EGGS
7 eggs, hard-boiled and peeled
vegetable oil

Sauce
2 cloves garlic, peeled and crushed
a little oil
2 to 3 slices of fresh red chillies or to taste
$\frac{1}{2}$ cup liquid tamarind concentrate mixed
    with 1/2 cup water
$\frac{1}{2}$ cup palm sugar or brown sugar
4 tablespoons fish sauce (nam pla)
2 tablespoons ready-fried red eschalots

Deep-fry the hard-boiled eggs in vegetable oil until golden. Remove, cut in half lengthwise and place on a serving plate.

To make the sauce
Fry the garlic in a little oil, add the chillies, tamarind water, sugar, fish sauce and fried eschalots. Simmer until the sauce thickens. Pour the sauce over the eggs and serve immediately

I went to the world's first Gastronomic Summit held at the Oriental Hotel in Bangkok. There I met Henri Gault, Paul Bocuse and many other famous gastronomes. They talked for three days, with earphones provided for the translation. I found it fascinating because I met so many interesting food people. I discovered on this trip the place in the world where I most love to have breakfast: the Verandah Restaurant at the Oriental Hotel looking out over the Chao Praya, the 'River of Kings' where boats ply back and forth peacefully. It's absolutely magnificent. On another visit I did classes at the famous Oriental Hotel cooking school with Chalie Amatyakul.

Oriental Hotel Cooking School, Bangkok

BALLS OF MINCED PORK IN GOLDEN THREADS

500 g pork, minced finely
1 tablespoon each of chopped coriander root, peeled and
    chopped garlic, salt and pepper, all blended together
1 egg, beaten
1 tablespoon plain flour
1 cup mixed vegetables such as water chestnuts, bamboo
    shoots, mushrooms and onions, all chopped finely
egg noodles
vegetable oil

To serve

spicy cucumber sauce (recipe follows)

In a bowl mix together the pork, blended coriander root mixture, egg, flour and mixed vegetables. Form into small balls.

Cook the noodles in plenty of boiling water until tender, drain, then pour over a spoonful of vegetable oil to make them easy to handle. Wind the noodles around the meatballs until they are well covered.

Deep fry the noodle-covered meatballs in vegetable oil, two or three at a time, until the noodles are crisp and brown and the meat is cooked. Drain on paper towels. Serve with spicy cucumber sauce.

Recipe by Chalie Amatyakul

SPICY CUCUMBER SAUCE

2 Lebanese cucumbers, peeled and sliced finely
1 tablespoon sugar
2 tablespoons Thai fish sauce (nam pla)
$^3/_4$ cup water
1 tablespoon coriander root and leaves, chopped
1 or 2 red chillies, sliced finely

Combine all the ingredients and allow to stand for 30 minutes before serving.

Recipe by Chalie Amatyakul

CHICKEN SATAYS WITH PANAENG SAUCE

30 satay skewers
6 boneless chicken half breasts

Marinade

1 cup coconut milk
1 teaspoon turmeric powder
$^3/_4$ teaspoon curry powder
1 teaspoon salt

Dipping sauce

1 cup thick coconut cream
2 tablespoons panaeng paste (recipe follows)
3 tablespoons ground roasted peanuts, or crunchy
    peanut butter
salt and sugar to taste

To marinate the chicken

Slice the chicken breasts in strips across the grain. Mix all the marinade ingredients together and marinate the chicken for 1 to 2 hours.

To make the dipping sauce

Heat the coconut cream in a frying pan until the oil runs, then fry the panaeng paste. Add the ground peanuts or peanut butter and the salt and sugar. Transfer to a serving bowl and keep warm.

To cook the satays

Thread three strips of chicken breast on each bamboo skewer and grill for a few minutes. Do not overcook, or the chicken will be dry and tough. Serve immediately with the dipping sauce.
    Recipe by Chalie Amatyakul

PANAENG PASTE

10 dried chillies, cut in pieces and soaked in hot water
    until soft
1 stalk lemon grass, sliced finely
1 teaspoon lime rind, chopped
10 coriander roots, chopped
7 cloves garlic, peeled and chopped
1 eschalot, peeled and chopped
10 peppercorns
1 teaspoon shrimp paste

Put all the ingredients in a blender and blend until the mixture is a fine paste. Place in a covered container and store in the refrigerator.
    Recipe by Chalie Amatyakul

PRAWN ROLLS

25 medium-sized, green king prawns

Marinade

2 tablespoons Thai fish sauce (nam pla)
2 teaspoons chopped coriander root
2 teaspoons peeled and chopped garlic
2 teaspoons ground pepper

To cook the prawns
25 wonton skins, soy bean skins, or thin pancakes
1 egg, beaten
vegetable oil

Dipping sauce
sweet chilli sauce

Remove the heads and shells from the prawns, leaving the tails intact. Slit the back of the prawns with a sharp knife and remove the digestive tracts. Wash the prawns well, drain and pat dry with paper towels.

To make the marinade
Place all the ingredients in a blender and blend to form a paste. Spread this paste over the prawns and marinate for 30 minutes.

To cook the prawns
Remove the prawns from the marinade and wrap each one in a wonton skin. Seal with beaten egg. Just before serving, fry the prawns, a few at a time, in hot oil until they are brown and crisp. Drain on paper towels and serve while hot with a sweet chilli sauce.
Recipe by Chalie Amatyakul

From Hong Kong

In 1985 I went to Hong Kong at the invitation of the Mandarin Hotel for their twenty-first birthday. It was a once-in-a-lifetime experience and I was very honoured; I was the only person invited from Australia. There were forty-six of us and I think it was one of the last 'grand' occasions for food people. We were all flown in first class and had suites filled with flowers, fruits, chocolates and champagne; there were hire cars at our disposal, afternoon tea parties and, at night, magnificent banquets. The chefs had been flown in from China and they had brought exotic foods with them. We had many, many courses over three nights of banqueting at tables decorated lavishly with flowers; in the Chinese manner, there were pink tablecloths. Among the most notable guests were Remi Krug, Robert Carrier, Paul Levy, Fay Maschler from London, Fred Ferretti from the USA, Christian Millau of Gault and Millau, the restaurant critics. For someone who was not familiar with the breadth of Chinese cuisine, it was a great experience.

We had some strange food on those three nights. Willie Mark (who was then heavily involved with the Hong Kong Tourist Association) chose the food, which he said was 'historically correct'. There were certainly things I had never heard of people eating: cordyceps, which pop up like mushrooms and turn into a worm in winter; shredded turtle; civet; sea cucumber; bears' paws; ducks' tongues; the linings of the ovaries of snow frogs.

Mondavi wines (from the USA) were served on the first night. On the second night of feasting, Remi Krug chose the wines – what a treat! Six Krug champagnes, Clos de Mesnil, Blanc de Blanc and Rosé. This night, the decor included orchids, water lilies and goldfish with the pink cloths. The big dish was Braised Civet, Imperial Court-style, served with the head on the platter. As I had two dogs and a pussy cat at home, I was not terribly impressed with that dish, needless to say! They told me a civet is like a fox, but looking at that little head...I don't know.

On the third and last night we were provided with Chinese robes. Mine was blue satin and still hangs in a cupboard. This was the night we had the ducks' tongues (a great delicacy), bears' paws (a bit like pigs' trotters) and the lining of the snow frogs' ovaries (served in a light soup and a bit like tapioca to eat). The wines were Chinese. This was a great experience and one of the highlights of my food life.

On another trip to Hong Kong, I visited Pinocchio Restaurant in Macau where I had Curry Crab, Pudim Flan and Back Filled Prawns. The crab was so fresh I felt it had crawled straight out of the Yellow River onto my plate.

Pinocchio Restaurant

PUDIM FLAN
(Serves 8)

Caramel
90 g castor sugar
1 tablespoon water

Custard
6 whole eggs
3 egg yolks
150 g castor sugar
500 ml milk
30 ml cream
30 ml Cointreau

To make the caramel
Put the castor sugar and water in a saucepan and cook, slowly, shaking the pan occasionally, until the mixture forms a good brown caramel. Immediately pour into a 25 cm flan tin and, lifting the tin with a tea-towel so that you do not burn your hands, turn it until the caramel is set on the sides and bottom of the tin.

To make the custard

Preheat the oven to 200°C. Beat the whole eggs and egg yolks with the castor sugar until the eggs are well beaten. Pour in the milk, cream and Cointreau, and beat until the mixture is of a uniform consistency.

Strain the custard into the flan tin, cover well with foil and place in a baking dish. Pour boiling water into the baking dish until it reaches halfway up the flan tin. Bake on the centre shelf of the oven for 30 minutes, or until the flan is just set in the centre. Remove from the baking dish, place on a rack and allow to cool, then cover and refrigerate overnight.

To serve: turn the flan out onto a serving dish and very carefully cut in slices like a cake.

CURRY CRAB FROM MACAU (CARIL DE CARANGUEJOS)

The owner of Pinocchio, who was Portuguese, gave me this recipe. The large full-of-flesh crabs appeared to be the same variety we get in Australia.

(Serves 6)

5 medium-sized mud crabs, cooked

Curry
8 medium brown onions, peeled and chopped coarsely
1 cup olive oil
6 cloves garlic, peeled and chopped finely
4 bay leaves
5 tablespoons Madras curry powder
1 tablespoon ground turmeric
1 teaspoon five-spice powder
salt to taste

Break up the crabs in the usual way. Crack the claws with a mallet and cut the body pieces in half, leaving the legs intact. Wash the body well in salted water. Set aside in a colander to drain thoroughly.

To make the curry
Cook the chopped onions in olive oil in a large pot over a low heat until translucent. Add the garlic and cook for a little longer, being careful that the garlic does not burn. Add the bay leaves, curry powder, turmeric, five-spice powder and salt and continue cooking, tasting frequently to see if more curry powder or salt is needed, until you have a good hot curry sauce.

Add the crab and continue to cook over low heat until the crab is hot and well coated with the sauce. Serve at once.

Recipe from Pinocchio Restaurant, Macau

I was absolutely fascinated by the Hong Kong markets: all the wonderful types of onions, the specialist stalls selling snakes. I will never forget the sight of a fishmonger catching a live fish for a customer, pulling it out of the tank and splitting it in two, in one side the heart still beating.

From Singapore

En route to London on one trip, I visited Singapore and stayed at the Raffles Hotel with photographer Rodney Weidland and Marion von Adlerstein. I remember that Rodney took a durian back to his room, where it stank dreadfully! Highlights of the trip were a visit to the Apollo Banana Leaf Curry House where we ate fish-head curry, and a wonderful breakfast at Smith Street. On my return I was determined to make fish-head curry, and here is the recipe I remembered.

Apollo Banana Leaf Restaurant

FISH-HEAD CURRY

This was served to me on a large piece of banana leaf and the condiments, etc. were passed and spooned around the edge. You could eat it with your left hand or with a spoon and fork. When you finished, you just folded the leaf in half and they took it away!

(Serves 6)

vegetable oil
a piece of ginger, half the size of your thumb,
    peeled and shredded finely
4 cloves garlic, peeled and chopped finely
4 onions, peeled and sliced finely
8 tablespoons curry powder, mixed to a paste
    with 225 ml water
3 cups coconut milk
2 to 3 teaspoons salt
3 to 4 teaspoons sugar
6 tomatoes, cut in quarters
2 tablespoons tamarind paste, mixed with 200 ml water
3 curry leaves (available at Asian food stores)
6 small red chillies, halved and seeds removed
8 small green chillies, halved and seeds removed
500 g okra
2 kg snapper heads, or 2 or 3 whole small snapper

Heat a little oil in a large pot and fry the ginger until light brown. Add the garlic and fry for 30 seconds. Add the sliced onion and fry until soft and translucent. Add the curry paste and half the coconut milk. Cook until the oil comes through from the coconut milk.

Add the salt, sugar, tomatoes, tamarind water, curry leaves, chillies and okra and continue to cook over low heat. Add the remaining coconut milk and simmer for 5 minutes. Add the fish heads or fish, cover the pan and simmer until cooked.

From London

I drove down the A40 to Oxford to visit Le Manoir au Quatre Saisons with Emma Woodward Fisher, one of 'Joan's Sloanes'. The trip reminded me of the road to Bowral in spring. Le Manoir is just like a gracious country home, with a garden full of glorious flowers. The water garden is also quite beautiful and people play croquet on the lawns. I think the food was some of the best I ate at that time. We both had a tiny iced cucumber soup in a cup with a few chives floating, then I had smoked salmon with a little horseradish soufflé served with lemon butter. It sounds very old-fashioned now but, as they say, everything that goes around comes around, and this style of food is rapidly becoming popular again. Emma's courgette (zucchini) with its peas and pea shoots purée was poached and served in a truffle-juice sabayon and looked spectacular. It was served with baby morels and two tiny clumps of chopped, barely cooked mushrooms. My main course was a ginger duck, cooked in a light pastry and served with onion marmalade, the first onion marmalade I had ever tasted. We had dorado, wood-smoked, with a fine tomato coulis scented with anchovy oil, and there was very finely chopped and blanched cucumber in the butter sauce around the fish. We were served delicious ice-creams and little tiny tarts to finish the meal.

The reason for this particular visit to London was a luncheon at the Hyatt Carlton Towers Hotel, in Cadogan Place. Jacques Reymond from Melbourne had won an important competition judged by several of us in the Hyatt Hotels of each capital city in Australia. I went over with him to do a story for *Vogue Entertaining*. Jacques was to cook a luncheon with all the important English food and wine people as guests, using Australian ingredients and served with Australian wines.

Carlton Towers Hotel

FRICASSEE OF SCALLOPS
(Serves 4)

1 large red capsicum, halved and seeded
16 scallops without the roe, cut in half horizontally
185 g butter
1 medium eschalot, peeled and chopped
$^1/_2$ cup Noilly Prat
$^2/_3$ cup cream
salt and freshly ground pepper
1 small cucumber, cut in julienne and blanched
butter
leaves from 2 sprigs coriander

Preheat the oven to 200°C. Place the capsicum, cut side down, on a greased baking tray. Cook in the preheated oven for about 20 minutes, until the skin blisters and the flesh is cooked. Remove from the oven, cover and when cool, remove the skin. Purée the flesh in a blender or food processor and reserve.

Toss the scallops very quickly in a greased non-stick frying pan until just cooked. Remove from the pan and keep warm until required. Add the butter and eschalot and toss for a few minutes. Deglaze the pan with Noilly Prat and reduce a little. Add the cream, season to taste with salt and pepper, and reduce again until the mixture has a sauce-like consistency. Add the reserved capsicum purée and simmer until heated through.

Toss the blanched cucumber julienne quickly in a pan with a little butter. Strain the hot sauce onto warm serving plates. Arrange the scallops in the centre of each plate, place the cucumber julienne on top and scatter over some coriander leaves.

We went that night to Alastair Little's restaurant in Soho and had a delicious dinner, the highlight of which was real French foie gras. It was the first time I have ever eaten Alastair Little's food. It was simple and good, and he still cooks in the same style.

ALASTAIR LITTLE'S BABY BEETS AND SPRING ONIONS STEWED IN CREAM
450 g baby beetroots
1 eschalot
1 spring onion
30 g butter
juice of 1 lemon
about 300 ml double cream
salt and pepper

Utensils
large saucepan
wide, shallow saucepan to hold the beets
    in a single close-packed layer

Put a large pan of lightly salted water on to heat. If necessary, trim the leaves off the beetroots, leaving about 1 cm of the stalks protruding. Cut off the straggly root tip. Chop the eschalot finely and cut the spring onion across into rings.

Cook the beetroots for about 30 minutes in lots of the boiling water until tender (remember even young beetroots can be very woody). Refresh in cold water and peel while still warm.

Melt the butter in the wide shallow saucepan and sweat the eschalot in it until translucent. Add the beetroots, lemon juice and salt and pepper, and turn to mix and coat. Pour round the cream to come half way up the beets and stew, stirring from time to time, until very hot and the cream has turned an entrancing regal colour.

Transfer to a warmed serving dish, scatter with the spring onion rings and bring to the table immediately.

Recipe from Alastair Little – Keep it Simple, *by Alastair Little and Richard Whittington (Conran Octopus)*

The next morning I drove out to Lygrove Estate to see Kirsten McKay, who had worked with Anders Ousbäck in Sydney.

Lygrove Estate

GOAT'S CHEESE MOUSSELINE
(Serves 6)

butter
zucchini flowers
500 g fresh goat's cheese
salt and pepper
2 eggs
200 ml crème fraîche

Dressing
50 ml virgin olive oil
crushed garlic to taste
juice of 1 lemon
a few fresh basil leaves

To serve
rocket or watercress leaves

Lightly butter 6 dariole moulds and line with petals from the zucchini flowers. Place the fresh goat's cheese in a food processor and process for a few seconds until the cheese is a smooth paste, adding salt and pepper to taste. Add the eggs, process for a further few seconds, then slowly incorporate the crème fraîche.

Preheat the oven to 180°C. Transfer the mixture to the dariole moulds, cover with buttered foil and cook in a water bath in the oven for 25 minutes, or until firm to the touch.

To make the dressing

Just before serving, put the olive oil, garlic, lemon juice and basil leaves in a saucepan and warm through slightly.

To serve

Arrange the rocket or watercress leaves on individual serving plates. Unmould the mousselines and gently pour over the dressing.

Recipe by Kirsten McKay

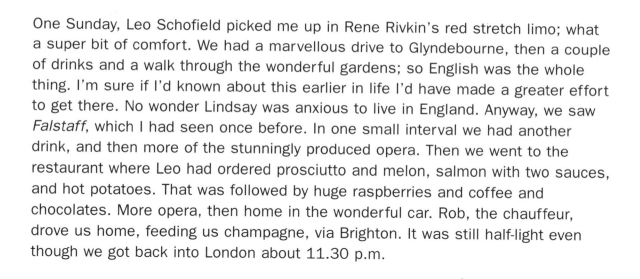

One Sunday, Leo Schofield picked me up in Rene Rivkin's red stretch limo; what a super bit of comfort. We had a marvellous drive to Glyndebourne, then a couple of drinks and a walk through the wonderful gardens; so English was the whole thing. I'm sure if I'd known about this earlier in life I'd have made a greater effort to get there. No wonder Lindsay was anxious to live in England. Anyway, we saw *Falstaff*, which I had seen once before. In one small interval we had another drink, and then more of the stunningly produced opera. Then we went to the restaurant where Leo had ordered prosciutto and melon, salmon with two sauces, and hot potatoes. That was followed by huge raspberries and coffee and chocolates. More opera, then home in the wonderful car. Rob, the chauffeur, drove us home, feeding us champagne, via Brighton. It was still half-light even though we got back into London about 11.30 p.m.

The Savoy Hotel

SUMMER PUDDING

I ate this for dinner when I was staying at the Savoy Hotel in 1988. Of course, we can get such good-quality loose, frozen fruit here in Australia that this is a pudding you can make all year round. For better results, do not let the fruits defrost totally and just drop them into the boiling sugar syrup.

(Serves 4)

6 large slices white bread
100 g sugar
3 cups water
800 g soft summer fruit (raspberries, strawberries,
    red and black currants, loganberries)

Purée of summer fruits
80 g raspberries
80 g black currants
1/2 cup syrup from cooking the fruit
juice of 1/2 lemon

To serve
reserved fresh fruit
20 g icing sugar
1 cup whipped cream

Remove the crusts from the bread and cut the slices into neat finger-sized pieces. Put the sugar and water into a saucepan and heat slowly until the sugar dissolves. Reserve a little of each fruit to serve with the pudding and add the remainder to the sugar syrup. Simmer very gently for approximately 2 to 3 minutes. Remove from the heat.

Line the base and sides of individual one-cup moulds with the bread fingers and spoon in the fruit with a little of the liquid, filling to halfway. Cover with more bread fingers and fill the moulds to the top with the rest of the fruit. Reserve the remaining fruit syrup. Cover the fruit with a small coffee-cup saucer to fit just inside the rim of each mould, and put a weight on top. Refrigerate overnight.

To make the purée
Put the raspberries and black currants in a blender or food processor with 1/2 cup of the reserved fruit syrup and the lemon juice. Process until smooth, then pass through a sieve and discard the seeds. Adjust the taste and thickness of the purée by adding more fruit syrup if necessary.

To serve

Turn the puddings out onto serving plates and pour over the fruit purée. Arrange some of the reserved fresh fruit on top. Dust with icing sugar and serve with whipped cream.
Recipe by Anton Edelmann

Richard Cawley, an English foodie friend of mine who has written several books about food and writes about food in magazines, and who is part of a food programme on the BBC called 'Ready Steady Cook', invited me to a 'welcome' dinner on one of my trips to London. He and his partner, Andrew Whittle, invited twelve people including David Sassoon (Richard's old boss, the Sassoon of the fashion design house, Bellville Sassoon) and Lady Jane Wellesley, a BBC television producer and the Duke of Wellington's daughter. The night was hilarious; the food – as usual with Richard – very special. He printed special folders with the menu: Salmon Three Ways, Chèvres with Cranberry Sauce in Puff Pastry, Quail with Green Ginger and English Strawberries with Fromage Frais.

RICHARD CAWLEY'S QUAIL WITH GREEN GINGER
(Serves 6)

6 medium-sized slices of onion about 1 cm thick
6 quail
90 g butter
salt and freshly ground black pepper
150 ml green ginger wine
150 ml chicken stock
1 × 225 g jar of Chinese stem ginger in sugar syrup

To serve
a selection of steamed fresh vegetables, such as miniature
    sweetcorn, artichokes and cauliflower florets

Preheat the oven to 220°C. Place the onion slices in the bottom of a medium-sized roasting tin and place a quail on each, making sure that the birds are not touching each other. Smear the breast of each bird with 15 g of the butter and season with salt and pepper. Pour the wine and stock around the birds in the pan. The onion slices will keep them above the liquid so that they will brown all over.

Roast for about 30 minutes, basting frequently, or until golden brown and cooked through. Meanwhile slice about six pieces of ginger from the jar and reserve. Remove the cooked quail to a platter and keep warm. Discard the onion. Add 3 tablespoons of the syrup from the ginger jar to the liquid in the roasting tin and reduce by half over high heat. Add the reserved sliced ginger pieces for the last few seconds.

To serve

Place one quail on each of six large heated dinner plates and spoon over some of the reduced sauce with some of the ginger slices. Serve immediately with the steamed vegetables.

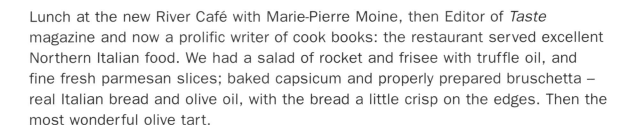

Lunch at the new River Café with Marie-Pierre Moine, then Editor of *Taste* magazine and now a prolific writer of cook books: the restaurant served excellent Northern Italian food. We had a salad of rocket and frisee with truffle oil, and fine fresh parmesan slices; baked capsicum and properly prepared bruschetta – real Italian bread and olive oil, with the bread a little crisp on the edges. Then the most wonderful olive tart.

The River Café

OLIVE, CRÈME FRAÎCHE AND THYME TART
(Serves 6)

Pasta frolla
$2^3/_4$ cups plain flour
1 teaspoon salt
250 g butter, chilled and cut into pieces
2 tablespoons iced water

Filling
1 red Spanish onion, peeled and chopped finely
3 cloves garlic, peeled and crushed
a handful of fresh thyme, including stalks,
    leaves and flowers
20 g butter
750 g silverbeet or spinach, ribs removed, leaves
    washed thoroughly and chopped
2 eggs plus 1 egg yolk, beaten lightly
6 tablespoons crème fraîche
salt and freshly ground black pepper
375 g black Kalamata olives, stones removed

To make the pasta frolla

Place the ingredients in a food processor and process until the mixture forms a ball. Wrap the pastry in plastic wrap and refrigerate for 20 minutes.

   Preheat the oven to 190°C. Roll out the pastry to fit a 30 cm tart tin, press it into the tin and prick the base with the tines of a fork. Bake blind in the preheated oven for 20 minutes or until the pastry is golden. Remove from the oven and allow the pastry to cool in the tin.

To make the filling and cook the tart

Sauté the onion, garlic and most of the thyme in the butter until the onion is translucent, then set aside. Steam the silverbeet until just tender, drain in a colander and allow to cool.

Spread the silverbeet over the pastry base and top with the onion mixture. Combine the eggs with the crème fraîche and salt and pepper to taste, and pour over the onion. Scatter the olives and remaining thyme on top.

Bake the tart in a preheated 190°C oven for 20 minutes, or until it is cooked and the top is puffed and golden.

Recipe by Rose Grey, The River Café

Dinner with Camellia Punjabi and her mother and Paul Levy and his wife at the Bombay Brasserie. Had curries of crab, lobster and mutton. Breads very good. My pudding – the milky thick stuff with pistachios – was delicious.

Bombay Brasserie

MACHI DAHIWALA
(Serves 4)

4 pieces ling, or fillets from any similar thick fish
salt
30 ml vegetable oil
1 bay leaf
2 small green cardamom pods
2 cloves
1 small piece cinnamon stick
1 large onion, peeled and chopped
½ teaspoon ginger paste
½ teaspoon peeled and crushed garlic
⅛ teaspoon ground turmeric powder
1 teaspoon red chilli powder
1 teaspoon peeled and grated fresh ginger
2 fresh green chillies, split lengthwise
250 g plain yoghurt (full-cream), beaten
pinch of sugar (optional)
2 tablespoons chopped fresh coriander leaves

Wash the fish fillets in cold water, sprinkle with salt and allow to stand for 10 minutes. Drain well.

Pour the oil into a shallow, flat pan and heat until it is very close to smoking point. Add the bay leaf, cardamom pods, cloves and cinnamon stick and cook, stirring frequently, until light brown. Add the chopped onion and cook over medium heat, stirring occasionally, until browned. Add the ginger and garlic pastes, turmeric, red chilli powder, grated ginger and green chillies and cook for 1 minute. Add the beaten yoghurt and cook, stirring, until the sauce thickens. (If the yoghurt is very sour, add a pinch of sugar.)

When the sauce is fairly thick, add the fish pieces, cover and simmer for a few minutes until the fish is just cooked. Adjust the salt and serve the fish sprinkled with the chopped fresh coriander leaves.

LEMON RICE
(Serves 4)

$1/4$ cup vegetable oil
$1^1/2$ teaspoons black mustard seeds
1 tablespoon peeled and grated fresh ginger
2 large green chillies, seeds removed, chopped
2 teaspoons urad dal (available from Indian food stores)
12 fresh curry leaves
1 teaspoon ground turmeric
$1^1/4$ cups long-grain rice, cooked, drained and
    allowed to cool
juice of 2 large lemons
cashew nuts

Heat the oil in a pan and add all the ingredients except the rice, lemon juice and cashew nuts, and stir. As soon as the ingredients begin to splutter, remove from the pan and allow to cool. Add the cooked rice and lemon juice, and mix until combined. Transfer to a bowl and serve sprinkled with cashew nuts.

Visited Heidi Lascelles at Books for Cooks. Her bookshop near Portobello Road is marvellous, stacked with works from all over the world. The kitchen at the back is used to create dishes from the books or from customers' ideas or even unusual ingredients picked up while travelling.

ALAPHIA'S CHOCOLATE CAKE

250 g unsalted butter
300 g dark chocolate
5 eggs, separated
25 g castor sugar
25 g plain flour
1 teaspoon baking powder
sifted icing sugar

Preheat the oven to 125°C. Melt the butter and chocolate together and mix until smooth. Allow to cool a little. Add the beaten egg yolks, castor sugar, flour and baking powder, and mix well. Beat the egg whites until they hold stiff peaks and carefully fold the chocolate mixture into the egg whites.

Pour into a well-greased, 23 cm round cake tin and bake in the oven for 45 minutes, or until the cake is firm to the touch. Allow to stand in the cake tin for 5 minutes, then turn out onto a wire rack. Sprinkle with sifted icing sugar just before serving.

Recipe by Alaphia Bidwell, Books for Cooks

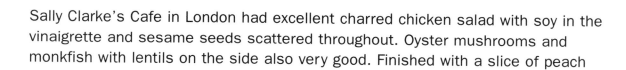

Sally Clarke's Cafe in London had excellent charred chicken salad with soy in the vinaigrette and sesame seeds scattered throughout. Oyster mushrooms and monkfish with lentils on the side also very good. Finished with a slice of peach tart.

I really like the atmosphere at Inn on the Park, where I went for lunch and consumed a delicious piece of turbot. It is a fabulous fish, and was cooked beautifully with a light butter sauce and lots of julienne veg. Later, I went to Beauchamp Place and was very disappointed in the shops except for Ken Lane's jewellery. I had trouble getting a cab home. Apparently they were all taken up with guests being ferried to a garden party at Buckingham Palace!

Very impressed on my first visit to the Hotel Capital in Basil St, Knightsbridge. I stayed there on a later trip to attend *Vogue*'s 30th Birthday celebration, when I helped to supervise the food for the party. The chef at the Capital was Philip Britten, a nice, impatient young man who somehow reminded me of young Australian chefs I had met. He had some strange ideas like no salt and pepper on the tables, that he picked up from Nico Ladenis of Chez Nico with whom he did his apprenticeship.

The Capital Hotel

PHILIP BRITTEN'S LEMON TART
(Serves 6 to 8)

Sweet pastry
125 g plain flour
100 g cold unsalted butter, diced
35 g ground almonds
35 g castor sugar
1 egg yolk
pinch of salt
zest of 1/2 small orange, grated finely
zest of 1/2 small lemon, grated finely
1/2 tablespoon dark rum
1 tablespoon orange juice

Filling
250 ml lemon juice (about 6 lemons)
zest of 4 lemons
200 g castor sugar
250 ml water
40 g cornflour, blended with 2 tablespoons cold water
6 egg yolks
100 g butter, diced and softened

To make the pastry
Preheat the oven to 220°C. Place all the ingredients in a food processor and process until the mixture forms a mass. Remove the mixture from the machine and wrap in plastic wrap. Allow the pastry to rest in the refrigerator for at least 4 hours, then roll it out and line a tart tin 23 cm in diameter. Prick the bottom with a fork and refrigerate for 20 minutes. Bake blind in the oven for 20 to 25 minutes, then set on a rack to cool.

To make the filling
Bring the lemon juice and rind, water and sugar to the boil and leave to infuse for 20 minutes. Stir in the cornflour and bring the mixture slowly back to the boil, stirring until the mixture thickens. Simmer for 1 to 2 minutes, then remove from the heat. Beat in the egg yolks and then the butter.

Strain into a bowl and allow to cool. Pour the cooled mixture into the baked pastry case and serve cold.

Vogue Australia's 30th Birthday was celebrated with an exhibition at the Victoria & Albert Museum. We had a very Australian theme for the food at the event: Tasmanian oysters, mango daiquiris, platters of prawns, lobster sandwiches, mini-hamburgers, curried vegetable tartlets and char-grilled lamb cutlets with chutney. It was an enormous success. Bernard Leser, who was then the Chairman of Condé Nast, and June McCallum, then Editor-in-Chief of the *Vogue* magazines in Australia, hosted the party.

PETER ROWLAND'S VEGETABLE TARTS

Tart cases
2 loaves thinly sliced white sandwich bread
125 g butter, melted
2 cloves garlic, peeled and finely crushed

Filling
1 cup finely julienned celery
1½ cups finely julienned carrot
1 cup finely julienned leek, white part only
1½ cups finely julienned zucchini
40 g butter
2 teaspoons Madras curry powder, or more to taste
¼ teaspoon ground turmeric powder
2 teaspoons peeled and grated ginger
1 tablespoon finely chopped coriander leaves and root
1 cup coconut milk, or more if necessary
salt to taste

To make the tarts
Preheat the oven to 190C. Cut the crusts from the bread with a sharp knife and flatten each slice by rolling with a rolling pin. Mix the butter and garlic. Brush the bread with the garlic butter, then cut each slice with a round cutter to fit small, 5 cm diameter, tart tins. Press well into the tins and bake on the centre shelf of the preheated oven for 15 minutes, until the tartlet cases hold their shape.

Remove the cases from the tins, place on a flat baking sheet and return them to the oven to bake until pale golden and crisp, about another 10 minutes.

To make the filling
Sauté the vegetables in butter for a few minutes. Add the curry and turmeric powders, grated ginger, chopped coriander and coconut milk and cook for a few minutes until the flavours mingle and the liquid is a sauce consistency. Add salt to taste.

Fill the tart cases with the warm vegetable mixture just before serving.

BLAKES BLINIS

One night, Marion von Adlerstein, Director of Travel at Condé Nast in Australia, and I went to Blakes Hotel to taste their famous blinis with caviar.

(Makes 8 blinis)

1 teaspoon sugar
15 g dried yeast
150 ml warm water
140 g buckwheat flour
salt
2 egg yolks
75 g plain flour
150 ml warm cream
2 egg whites
150 ml whipped cream
butter for frying

To serve with each blini
1 thin slice Scottish smoked salmon
1 tablespoon sour cream
10 g Osietra caviar
chives
wedge of lemon

Dissolve the sugar and yeast with warm water. Add the buckwheat flour. Leave in a warm place for 20 minutes. In a separate bowl combine the salt, egg yolks and plain flour with the warm cream, then add to the first mixture. Allow the combined mixture to stand for a further 20 minutes.

Beat the egg whites and add to the mixture. Add the whipped cream and leave the mixture for 10 minutes. Heat a little butter in a frying pan and drop in good-sized tablespoons of the batter (cooking one at a time) and fry the blinis until golden and crisp on the outside and light and fluffy on the inside. Remove the blinis as they cook and set aside to cool to room temperature.

To serve
Lay a slice of smoked salmon on top of each blini. Add a tablespoon of sour cream and spoon the caviar on top. Serve scattered with chopped chives and with a lemon wedge.
Recipe from Blakes Hotel

I visited Gravetye Manor, a magnificent sixteenth-century guest-house in East Sussex. The gardens are glorious. Gravetye was originally built as a wedding present for Katherine Infield in 1598. When I visited it, Leigh Stone-Herbert was working closely with the chef but he is now living back in Sydney, Australia, with his own large catering company.

Gravetye Manor

CHICKEN LIVER PARFAIT WITH GREEN PEPPERCORNS
(Serves 10)

200 g cleaned chicken livers
milk to soak livers
1½ tablespoons Madeira
1½ tablespoons port
4 tablespoons sultanas
200 g clarified butter, melted and slightly warm
12 green peppercorns in brine, drained
salt and freshly ground pepper
500 g pork back fat, sliced thinly
1 sprig fresh thyme

To serve
toasted brioche

Soak the chicken livers in milk, cover and refrigerate overnight. Pour the Madeira and port over the sultanas and leave to soak overnight.

Drain the milk from the chicken livers and place the livers in a food processor. Process to a smooth purée, adding the clarified butter. Stir in the soaked sultanas, green peppercorns and salt and pepper to taste.

Preheat the oven to 150°C. Line a terrine with thin slices of the pork fat. Place a sprig of thyme on the slices of fat, then pour in the liver mixture. Place the terrine in a baking dish of hot water and cook in the preheated oven for 1 hour.

Test by pressing the top: the parfait should be firm. Chill in the refrigerator and serve sliced with warm toasted brioche.

Recipe by Leigh Stone-Herbert

POACHED FILLETS OF WHITING ON NOODLES WITH LOBSTER AND CHIVE BUTTER
(Serves 4)

8 small fillets of whiting
1 cooked lobster, about 750 g in weight

Chive butter sauce
¼ cup white wine vinegar
½ cup white wine
2 eschalots, chopped finely
1 tablespoon cream
150 g butter, cut in small pieces
salt and pepper
chopped chives

Noodles
185 g fresh noodles
60 g julienne of carrot, leek and celery
2 tomatoes, peeled, seeded and centre soft part removed
a little butter
salt and pepper

To cook and serve the fish
a little fish stock
snow peas, trimmed, each cut in four pieces
  and blanched

Skin the fillets with a sharp knife and cut in half. Remove the lobster meat from the tail and cut in medallions. Reserve the best four medallions and chop the remaining lobster meat.

To make the chive butter sauce
Place the vinegar, white wine and eschalots in a stainless-steel saucepan and simmer slowly until about 2 tablespoons of liquid remain. Strain. Return to the pan, add the cream and bring back to the boil. Remove from the heat and with a small wire whisk, beat in the butter, piece by piece. Add salt, pepper and chopped chives to taste. Set aside in a warm place.

To cook the noodles and vegetables
Bring a large saucepan of salted water to the boil and cook the noodles until al dente. Refresh under cold, running water. Blanch the carrot, leek and celery julienne and refresh under cold, running water. Cut the tomatoes into strips, reserving a little tomato for serving.

To cook and serve the fish
Poach the fillets in the fish stock. Put a little butter in a large frying pan and add the noodles, toss well to warm through. Add the carrot, leek and celery, tomato strips and chopped lobster meat. Toss well together and season with salt and pepper. Cut the reserved tomato strips into dice.

Brush the reserved lobster medallions with a little melted butter and put under a hot griller for a few seconds to warm through.

Place the noodle mixture in the centre of four warmed plates. Arrange the fillets of sole on top and place a medallion of lobster in the centre. Spoon over the chive butter sauce and scatter over the snow peas and diced tomato.

Recipe by Leigh Stone-Herbert

From Paris

Enjoyed lunch at La Coupole. I had a wonderful grilled lobster flamed with whisky. The butter sauce, delicately laced with a whisky flavour, was served in a jug and the lobster was covered with a fine julienne of red and green peppers and onion, deep-fried like a frizz. I made this recipe up from what I remembered.

La Coupole

GRILLED LOBSTER HALVES WITH WHISKY BUTTER SAUCE
(Serves 6)

Whisky butter sauce
$1/2$ cup fish stock (see recipe on p. 34)
4 tablespoons whisky
6 eschalots, peeled and chopped finely
250 g unsalted butter, cubed
salt and freshly ground pepper

Vegetables
1 carrot, peeled
1 leek, centre white part only, washed
$1/2$ red capsicum, seeds and membranes removed
$1/2$ green capsicum, seeds and membranes removed
vegetable oil for frying

Lobster
6 small or 3 medium-sized lobsters, cut in half
    and cleaned
salt and pepper
melted butter

To make the sauce
Place the fish stock, whisky and eschalots in a small stainless-steel saucepan and simmer until reduced by half. Strain, discard the solids and return the liquid to the saucepan. Set aside.

To cook the vegetables
Cut the vegetables into fine julienne strips, 6 cm long. Deep-fry in hot oil, a small amount at a time, until they are 'frizzy', and drain on paper towels. Set aside in a warm place.

To cook and serve the lobsters

Cover a griller tray with lightly oiled aluminium foil and place the lobsters on the foil, shell side up. Cook for 4 to 5 minutes, depending on their size. Turn the lobsters over, sprinkle salt and pepper on the flesh and brush with a little melted butter. Cook the flesh for a further 4 to 5 minutes, longer if necessary.

Just before serving, reheat the reserved liquid for the sauce. Lower the heat and whisk the butter into the hot liquid over very low heat until the sauce thickens. Add salt and pepper to taste. Do not allow the sauce to boil or it will separate.

Put the lobster halves on individual plates and place the 'frizzy' vegetables in the head cavity of each half. Place a small pot of the sauce on each plate to pour over the lobster as it is eaten.

Had dinner at Le Télégraphe, where I found it interesting to see what the young, rich Parisian trendies like to think is smart, 'in' stuff. I had quite good asparagus with mousseline sauce. Another good and very trendy bistro I ate at was Le Boeuf sur Le Toit: 'the cow on the roof'!

Visited the de Cossé Brissacs at their marvellous château just near Chartres. Lisa is a Queenslander who completed a Cordon Bleu cooking course, apprenticed herself to a traiteur in Paris, met Emanuel, and is now a countess. She is doing catering and he is farming grain. Lisa made a magnificent lunch, presented on antique Herend china that she had found in a forgotten attic.

LISA DE COSSÉ BRISSAC'S AMARETTO PEACHES
(Serves 8)

Peach mousse
225 ml milk
200 ml cream
3 egg yolks
4 tablespoons castor sugar
4 peaches, blanched, peeled and stoned
1 tablespoon gelatine
1 tablespoon Amaretto liqueur
3 tablespoons whipped cream

Peaches
4 peaches, halved, with stones carefully removed

To serve
quince jelly
strawberries
strawberry purée sweetened with a little sugar

To make the mousse

Bring the milk and cream to the boil. In a separate bowl, beat the egg yolks with the castor sugar until light and fluffy. Pour the milk mixture onto the egg mixture, stirring constantly. Return the mixture to the pan and heat, stirring constantly, until the mixture is thick and coats the back of the spoon. Do not boil. Strain through a fine sieve and set aside.

Purée the peaches in a food processor. Dissolve the gelatine in the Amaretto, add to the peach purée and stir the mixture into the custard. Place the mixture in the freezer and stir frequently to break up any ice particles that start to form (the mixture must not be allowed to freeze).

When the mixture has thickened a little, gently fold in the whipped cream.

To prepare the peaches

Dab the peaches with a paper towel to remove any excess moisture. Wrap strips of greased aluminium foil securely around the outsides of the peach halves to form a 4 cm collar above each peach half, as you would for a soufflé. Fill the collars with the Amaretto peach mousse and allow to set in the refrigerator.

To serve

Melt some quince jelly in a saucepan over low heat and allow to cool. Hull eight strawberries and cut each into thin slices. Arrange a sliced strawberry on top of each peach mousse. Spoon a little of the cooled quince jelly over the top of each mousse and return to the refrigerator until set. When ready to serve, carefully peel away the foil and serve on individual plates with some strawberry purée spooned around.

I went to Chartres market – food good and different from food I'd seen in Paris – and we visited a goat farm where I tasted the best goat's cheese I've ever had in my life. I didn't realise it then, but I guess it was because the milk wasn't pasteurised as it has to be in Australia by law.

Stayed at the Crillon in Place de la Concorde. It was absolutely beautiful, and I'd say it's my favourite hotel anywhere I've stayed, except maybe the Cipriani in Venice. Had dinner with the Taittingers, who own the hotel. It was quite amusing. We were served huge, white asparagus, which we did not get in Australia at the time. I was in a dilemma. Was I to pick it up with my fingers? I'd never eaten an asparagus as big and thick as that before, so I decided to watch and wait. Luckily I did, because everyone started eating with knives and forks. White asparagus can be hard and woody if left out of the ground too long, but this was sweet and tender and very good.

TOMATO SOUP WITH FENNEL AND BASIL BAVAROIS

Adapted from the Hotel de Crillon, Paris. When I came home from Paris, I copied this and taught it in my classes.

(Serves 8)

Fennel and basil bavarois
2 large fennel bulbs, trimmed
lemon juice
20 basil leaves
2 teaspoons gelatine
salt and pepper to taste
150 ml cream, whipped

Tomato soup
10 large, ripe red tomatoes, cored and chopped roughly
1 small onion, peeled and chopped
pinch of sugar
1 teaspoon grated lemon rind
lemon juice to taste
salt and pepper

To make the fennel and basil bavarois
Cut the fennel in pieces and cook in boiling salted water with lemon juice until tender. Drain well and allow to cool. Place the fennel in a food processor or blender, and purée. Add the basil leaves and purée again. Melt the gelatine in a little warm water and add to the mixture. Purée again, then transfer the mixture to a bowl. Add the salt and pepper and fold in the cream. Place the mixture in a glass bowl, cover and refrigerate until set.

To make the tomato soup
Place the tomatoes and onion in a food processor or blender, and purée. Add the sugar, lemon rind and juice, and salt and pepper to taste. Purée until smooth, then put through a strainer. Chill in the refrigerator.

To serve
Pour a little soup into chilled soup bowls and place a spoonful of the bavarois in the centre of each.

Dined with Henri Gault at Joël Robuchon's Restaurant Jamin. Henri ordered for me, although I probably would have preferred to order for myself, as it turned out. We had a strange cauliflower cream topped with Beluga caviar (which Neil Perry now does in his restaurant, Rockpool, and you will find the recipe in this book on page 131); then a piece of cod laced with smoked salmon, with finely julienned vegetables on top and a soy butter sauce. The main course arrived and on the plate was a tiny rack of milk-fed lamb accompanied by a small salad of baby leaves with wonderful bits of chopped up fresh truffle through it. In front of us was a small covered pot – what great delicacy was hidden there? I removed the lid and could not believe my eyes. Mashed potato! We had exactly the same lunch (minus the truffles) at my house in Sydney on the Sunday before, cooked by Annabel, my granddaughter. This was the beginning of the great mashed-potato revival and the discovery of this dish by the French.

Restaurant Jamin

FRESH CODFISH WITH AROMATIC VEGETABLES AND HERBS

This is the delicious fish dish I ate when I dined with Henri Gault at Jamin, as Joël Robuchon's was called then.

(Serves 6)

1 kg fresh cod, divided into 6 fillets
185 g smoked salmon, cut into thin strips

Vegetables
1 red capsicum, cut into fine julienne
1 green capsicum, cut into fine julienne
1 small zucchini, cut into fine julienne
6 large mushrooms, cut into fine julienne and
    tossed with juice of 1 lemon

Sauce
$3/4$ cup soy sauce
4 teaspoons tomato ketchup
5 drops Tabasco sauce
160 g butter
$1/2$ teaspoon red wine vinegar

To cook the fish
$1/3$ cup olive oil
salt and freshly ground black pepper

To serve
$1/2$ cup fresh flat-leafed parsley

Pierce the cod fillets with a sharp knife and fill the indentations with strips of smoked salmon.

To cook the vegetables

Blanch the julienne of capsicum, zucchini and mushrooms in boiling salted water for 1 to 2 minutes, then drain well and set aside. The vegetables should still be fairly crisp.

To make the sauce

In a small saucepan combine the soy sauce, tomato ketchup and Tabasco and bring to the boil. Gradually whisk in half the butter and the vinegar. Set the sauce aside and keep warm.

To cook the fish

Heat the oil in a large sauté pan and quickly sear the fish fillets on each side, cooking for about 2 minutes per side. Season each side with salt and freshly ground pepper.

To serve

Heat the remaining butter in a saucepan, add the blanched vegetables and heat through. Place the fish fillets on heated serving plates, arrange the vegetables and parsley leaves on top of each fillet and spoon over the sauce.

POTATO PURÉE

(Serves 6)

1 kg small potatoes, peeled at the last minute and left
    whole
1/4 cup coarse salt
300 g butter
3/4 cup milk
salt and freshly ground black pepper

Place the potatoes and the coarse salt in a large saucepan. Cover with cold water and bring to the boil. Reduce the heat and simmer for 35 to 40 minutes, or just until the potatoes are cooked.

Drain the potatoes and pass through a food mill or a fine mesh sieve. Place the potato purée back in a large saucepan and over low heat, stirring with a wooden spoon, let the purée dry out a little.

Stir in the butter, bit by bit, then add the milk until the purée is thick and smooth. Season to taste with salt and pepper.

Recipe from Restaurant Jamin

Dined with Peter Howard, my Australian foodie friend, at Brasserie Flo. We ate a delicious salad of baby beans with goose livers and an apple granita that I made up on my return.

Brasserie Flo

APPLE GRANITA
(Serves 8)

5 Granny Smith apples
1 cup water
1 cup sugar syrup
1 teaspoon lemon juice

To serve
Calvados

Peel and core the apples and cut into wedges. Place the apples and water in a saucepan and cook for few minutes until the apples soften. Add the sugar syrup and cook for no more than 5 minutes. Add the lemon juice.

Purée the mixture in a food processor or blender. Allow to cool, then freeze the purée in an ice-cream maker. When frozen, transfer the granita to a bowl, cover and store in the freezer to allow the granita to harden.

To serve
Spoon the apple granita into a wine glass and serve accompanied by a small glass of Calvados to pour over the granita before eating.

From Venice

Venice is gorgeous, one of my favourite places. I first went there on a trip with Marion von Adlerstein, *Vogue's* Travel Director, just after Lindsay died. We visited the church of San Giorgio; neither of us are Catholics but we lit candles for Lindsay, who would have thought it very funny. I never kept records of my visits to Venice: I was always too busy having too good a time. I remember being exhausted from walking one day, and sitting by the side of a canal while Marion consulted the map. I said to her, 'If we were in Sydney we'd just whistle, like this, and a cab would pull up'. With that, a boat taxi suddenly appeared and took us back to our hotel.

I loved every bit of Venice: the little cafés, the hidden restaurants, the bread shops, the islands. We saw everything. In Venice I learnt to make three of my favourite things: a really good carpaccio; a Bellini, a peach drink from Harry's Dolce; and a most beautiful crab and scallop pasta sauce from the Cipriani, where we stayed for a few days in great luxury.

CIPRIANI PASTA
(Serves 6)

Pasta
350 g tagliarini (I like to break my pasta into three equal
    lengths – it's easier to eat!)

Sauce
2 tablespoons butter
375 g scallops without roes, each cut in halves
    horizontally to make two thin scallops (like you get in
    Venice)
salt and freshly ground pepper to taste
250 g cooked crab meat (now available in cryovac bags
    from fish markets)
1 to 2 tablespoons brandy
1 tablespoon chopped chives
3 tablespoons freshly grated parmesan cheese
1 heaped tablespoon finely grated lemon rind
lemon juice to taste
300 ml cream

To cook the pasta
Cook the pasta in a large saucepan of boiling salted water until al dente, as instructed on the packet. Drain quickly, keeping a little of the cooking water to moisten the sauce, if necessary, and place the pasta back in the saucepan.

To make the sauce and serve the pasta
Melt the butter in a large frying pan over medium heat and quickly sauté the scallops with the salt and pepper until just cooked. Add the crab meat, brandy, chives, parmesan and lemon rind and heat through. Pour the sauce onto the pasta and cook for a few minutes, tossing with two large spoons. Add the lemon juice, cream and salt and freshly ground pepper to taste. (If the pasta is not moist enough, add a little of the pasta cooking liquid.) Serve at once in large bowls.

CARPACCIO
(Serves 6)

sirloin of beef in 1 piece, weighing 1 kg after trimming

Sauce
2 cups home-made mayonnaise
2 tablespoons Dijon mustard
2/3 cup Campbell's beef consommé
salt and freshly ground pepper

To serve
Italian bread rolls
freshly ground pepper

Ask your butcher to trim the sirloin carefully, leaving the perfect eye of the meat with no fat or membrane. Wrap tightly in plastic wrap to form a roll. Place the meat in the freezer until it is very cold and firm. (Do not let the meat freeze or it will disintegrate when sliced.)

Cut the beef in paper-thin slices and flatten each slice between two sheets of plastic wrap with the flat side of a wooden meat mallet. Arrange the slices on individual flat plates.

To make the sauce
Mix together the mayonnaise, Dijon mustard and consommé, and taste for salt and pepper.

To serve
Drizzle the sauce over the meat and serve immediately with Italian bread rolls. Pass the pepper grinder.

From Rome

In 1988 I visited Rome to do some stories for *Vogue Entertaining*. I thought it would be like Venice, but I found it airless and stifling. Went with Andrew Birley, the Australian chef I was going to do a story on, to the Campo dei Fiori where we had breakfast. Andrew was a caterer who worked with Anders Ousbäck for many years before he moved to Rome. We shopped in the market, which I loved and where we took lots of pictures. Andrew bought yellow pepper, mixed salad leaves, purple and green figs, two punnets of wild strawberries, zucchini blossoms, three tiny sweet melons, basil, a can of olive oil, a lump of parmesan and a soft farm cheese. The swordfish was very expensive. The lunch was held at the late Sydney designer Neville Marsh's apartment, a roof-top eyrie with a terrace on which was placed a big umbrella for shade. During the photo session the umbrella kept flying off across Rome in strong gusts of wind, like the Flying Nun; the men would keep rushing downstairs to collect it. Surprisingly, we got a lovely cover for the magazine from this shoot.

ANDREW BIRLEY'S BARBECUED SWORDFISH STEAKS WITH BAKED YELLOW CAPSICUM

(Serves 6)

Baked yellow capsicum
6 yellow capsicum
2 cloves garlic, peeled and crushed
1/3 cup virgin olive oil
freshly ground rock salt and pepper

Swordfish
6 swordfish steaks about 2 cm thick, with
    central backbone removed
olive oil
basil leaves
freshly ground rock salt and pepper
lemon juice

To serve
baby onions glazed in olive oil
freshly boiled green beans

To cook the capsicum
Preheat the oven to 200°C. Cut the capsicum in half lengthwise and remove the seeds and membranes. Arrange the halves in a large baking tin and scatter over the garlic. Pour over the olive oil and grind over salt and pepper. Cook in the preheated oven until the garlic browns, then reduce the heat to 150°C. Turn the capsicum halves and cook until they soften.

To cook the swordfish
Marinate the swordfish steaks in olive oil with a few crushed basil leaves for 1 hour. Just before cooking the fish steaks, grind over the salt and pepper and drizzle with lemon juice.

Cook the swordfish on a barbecue grill, turning once. Be careful not to overcook the fish or it will be dry.

To serve
Serve the swordfish steaks drizzled with more lemon juice and with the baked yellow capsicum, some glazed baby onions and green beans.

From Tuscany

Italy is my favourite country. I travelled around Tuscany with another Australian food writer, Cherry Ripe. Loved Siena, where we ate bread, cheese and prosciutto bought in a little roadside stall, along with peaches and a tomato. A simple, delicious meal. We drove to Florence on a beautiful road. In Florence, I walked until my legs wouldn't work any more. At one stage I remember we consumed a superb cake of rice and orange and almond bits with a coffee. I bought a purse at Cellini, shoes at Ferragamo and fabric at Haas for my dining-room chairs.

Drove on via San Gimignano, a fourteenth-century town bristling with towers. It was a remarkable drive up the hill, all the sunflowers with their faces to the sun. What a stunning view! I would have liked to have more legs and time to explore.

Perugia is the prettiest city, full of winding pedestrian streets, but we saw a dreadful accident. A bus seemed to have run over a small car, killing a girl. A man was hysterical. All traffic had to be diverted through the walled city.

We stayed at the Hotel Belvedere di San Leonino outside Castellana, in Chianti, amazing value for such a gracious place. I had a real view over a Tuscan farmhouse, with grape vines and olive tree, from my window. Breakfast was served with coffee or tea and rosetta rolls. We visited a fattoria nearby, Fattoria Tavernelle – in fact, we ate there frequently. They served an amazingly good antipasto, which inspired me to make my own version for *Vogue Entertaining* when I returned home. We tried anchovies wrapped in sage leaves, dipped in batter and deep-fried, served on a tiny piece of brown paper. Then ravioli filled with spinach and ricotta and a bechamel sauce with white truffle juice, tiny pieces of asparagus and shaved champignons made to look like truffles. We had gnocchi which was heart-shaped and tender: the pasta dough made from potatoes, the vegetable sauce made with chopped carrot, beans, yellow capsicum, onions and a little chilli in a tomato base. We noticed that Italian children are amazing and eat their way through every course like veterans, choosing their own antipasti and pasta.

Fattoria Tavarnelle

After I got home from my visit to Tuscany this is some of the antipasti I was inspired to make after eating in this fattoria. *How I wished we could get fresh porcini mushrooms!*

EGGPLANT WITH FRIED ZUCCHINI
500 g small eggplants, cut in half lengthwise (or
   500 g thinly sliced eggplant)
salt
freshly ground pepper
2 cloves of garlic, peeled and chopped finely
olive oil
500 g zucchini, sliced

Preheat the oven to 200°C. Spread the eggplants on a baking tray and sprinkle with salt, pepper and garlic. Drizzle with olive oil. Bake in the preheated oven for 10 minutes, turn the eggplants over and cook for a further 10 minutes. Pile in the centre of a large platter.

    Sprinkle the zucchini with salt and fry in olive oil, a little at a time, until golden-brown. Arrange around the edge of the eggplant and serve at room temperature as part of an antipasti table.

SEAFOOD SALAD
350 g cleaned calamari
250 ml white wine
250 ml water
salt
1 onion, sliced finely
handful of parsley stems
500 g scallops
1 kg mussels, cleaned
extra white wine if necessary
1 kg cooked prawns, peeled and cleaned
1 tablespoon chopped chives
2 tablespoons chopped Italian parsley
salt and freshly ground pepper
vinaigrette
juice of 1 lemon

Slice the calamari into thin rings. Place the wine, water, salt, onion, and parsley stems in a saucepan with the calamari and simmer gently until tender. Strain and reserve the liquid. Place the calamari in a large bowl and allow to cool.

    Return the reserved liquid to the saucepan and cook the scallops for a few seconds. Drain and reserve the liquid.

Pour the reserved liquid into a large pan. Add the mussels and more wine if necessary. Cook over low heat until the shells open. Remove from the pan and allow to cool. Remove the mussels from the shells and add to the other cooked seafood.

Add the prawns to the seafood and sprinkle in the chives, parsley, salt and pepper. Toss the seafood with vinaigrette and lemon juice. Cover and refrigerate for 2 hours before serving. Toss again and season to taste.

Serve as part of an antipasti table.

CELERIAC AND CELERY SALAD WITH PARMESAN CHEESE
1 bunch celery
1 celeriac root
juice of 1 to 2 lemons
salt
mayonnaise
garlic juice
lemon juice
salt and freshly ground pepper
250 g parmesan cheese, sliced in fine strips
1 kg broad beans, pods removed and the beans
    cooked and peeled

Cut the tender part of the celery in thin slices and set aside. Peel the celeriac, then slice and cut it into thin strips. Immediately place the celeriac in a stainless-steel saucepan with water and lemon juice to prevent it discolouring. Add some salt and bring to the boil. Cook for 3 to 4 minutes, then drain well and allow to cool.

Place the celery and celeriac in a bowl with enough mayonnaise to moisten. Flavour with garlic juice, lemon juice, salt and pepper and toss well. Just before serving add the parmesan and broad beans.

Serve as part of an antipasti table.

MUSHROOM AND FENNEL
350 g mushrooms, trimmed
2 bulbs fennel, sliced finely
500 g baby carrots, peeled and cooked
2 white onions, peeled and cut in rings
olive oil
salt and freshly ground pepper
2 tablespoons chopped Italian parsley
garlic-flavoured vinaigrette
250 g slivered parmesan cheese

In a bowl toss the mushrooms, fennel, carrots and onions with olive oil, salt and pepper. Allow to stand for 1 hour, then toss with the parsley and vinaigrette. Stand for another hour, then serve with parmesan slivers as part of an antipasti table.

BEANS AND TUNA

250 g dried borlotti beans
$^1/_2$ cup olive oil
4 tomatoes, seeds removed and flesh diced
2 purple onions, peeled and sliced thinly
2 x 185 g cans Italian tuna in oil, broken into pieces
salt and freshly ground pepper
garlic-flavoured vinaigrette

Soak the beans overnight and cook as instructed on the packet. Drain well, allow to cool, then add the olive oil, tomatoes, onion, tuna, salt and pepper and toss carefully with vinaigrette. Make 2 to 3 hours before serving.

Serve as part of an antipasti table.

SALAMI WITH JUNIPER BERRIES

1 kg thinly sliced Italian salami
2 tablespoons juniper berries
freshly ground black pepper
$^3/_4$ cup virgin olive oil
2 yellow capsicums

Place the salami in a large serving dish and sprinkle with juniper berries. Grind over the black pepper and pour over $^1/_2$ cup of the olive oil.

Preheat the oven to 190°C. Cut the capsicum in half, remove the seeds and membranes, and bake in the preheated oven until the skins blister. Remove the skins and cut the capsicum in strips. Arrange the capsicum strips on the salami, grind over more pepper and pour over the remaining oil.

Serve as part of an antipasti table.

One very special meal was a dinner at Antica Trattoria La Torre in the village of Castellana, in Chianti: there was dancing and music in the square to celebrate the anniversary of the Unification of Italy under Garibaldi. There was also a wedding in the square. Dinner was porcini risotto, creamy and delicious, and hutch-raised rabbit with herbs and pine nuts and olives, and a salad of radicchio, lettuce and carrot. And then the most delicious almond cake I have eaten, with a light, sweet pastry piped across the top. We finished with biscotti and vin santo.

The Locanda al Castello di Sorci at Anghiari was marvellous and I wished I'd travelled with a photographer. It was one of the most fascinating eating experiences I've had. Two women were making pasta in the cellar – tagliarini and tagliatelle – rolling it with rolling pins on a long table. We went upstairs to the restaurant to be seated next to a pile of plates, with cutlery on a paper tablecloth. The meal started with tomato, cooked with a dash of chilli, on foccacia crostini. They served chicken livers on squares of brown bread, then slices of Parma ham and salami made in the commune. Next, a large, white bowl of puréed bean soup with tagliarini – tender pasta, full of flavour. Next we had tagliarini with a good meat sauce, sprinkled liberally with parmesan cheese: nothing is wasted, there were even bits of chicken heart in the sauce. We were served a great platter of roasted meats, duck and sausage: it was coarse, salty and succulent, served with a mound of chips. We asked for red wine at this stage – they brought us a jug! Madeira cake with vin santo came next, and then, to finish, a bowl of assorted plums, including greengages, with coffee.

It was a great experience, eating the food cooked by these women in what was essentially a commune. They grew all the produce, and cooked it, and people came to eat in the restaurant.

Locanda al Castello di Sorci

ITALIAN CHICKPEA SOUP
This was the sort of soup we ate at the commune at Anghiari.

(Serves 8 to 10)

125 g pancetta (Italian bacon)
1½ cups chickpeas, soaked overnight in water
5 litres chicken stock
2 large ripe tomatoes, peeled, seeded and cut in chunks
2 cloves garlic, peeled and crushed
1 teaspoon fresh rosemary leaves
¼ cup olive oil
salt and pepper to taste
125 g noodles

Cut the pancetta in dice and put in a large boiler. Drain and wash the chickpeas and add to the boiler with the stock, tomatoes, garlic, rosemary and olive oil. Cover and cook until the chickpeas are tender. This will take about 2½ hours of slow simmering. Allow to cool and blend in a food processor or blender until you have a thick, smooth soup. Add the salt and pepper.

Cook the noodles in boiling salted water as instructed on the packet. Drain and add to the soup. Return the soup to the boil and serve.

CONVERSIONS

SOLID WEIGHT CONVERSION

Metric	Imperial
15g	$\frac{1}{2}$ oz
30g	1 oz
60g	2 oz
90g	3 oz
125g	4 oz ($\frac{1}{4}$ lb)
155g	5 oz
185g	6 oz
220g	7 oz
250g	8 oz ($\frac{1}{2}$ lb)
280g	9 oz
315g	10 oz
345g	11 oz
375g	12 oz ($\frac{3}{4}$ lb)
410g	13 oz
440g	14 oz
470g	15 oz
500g (0.5kg)	16 oz (1 lb)
750g	24 oz ($1\frac{1}{2}$ lb)
1000g (1kg)	32 oz (2 lb)

LIQUID CONVERSIONS

Metric	Imperial	US Cups
15 ml	$\frac{1}{2}$ fl oz	1 tbsp
30 ml	1 fl oz	$\frac{1}{8}$ cup
60 ml	2 fl oz	$\frac{1}{4}$ cup
125 ml	4 fl oz	$\frac{1}{2}$ cup
150 ml	5 fl oz ($\frac{1}{4}$ pint)	$\frac{2}{3}$ cup
175 ml	6 fl oz	$\frac{3}{4}$ cup
250 ml	8 fl oz	1 cup ($\frac{1}{2}$ pint)
300 ml	10 fl oz ($\frac{1}{2}$ pint)	$1\frac{1}{4}$ cups
375 ml	12 fl oz	$1\frac{1}{2}$ cups
500 ml	16 fl oz	2 cups (1 pint)
600 ml	1 pint (20 fl oz)	$2\frac{1}{2}$ cups
1.25 litres	2 pints	1 quart

STANDARDS

1 tsp = 0.2 fl oz (5 ml)
1 tbsp = 0.6 fl oz (20 ml)   US & UK = 0.5 fl oz (15 ml)
1 fl oz = 30 ml
1 ml = .035 fl oz
1 UK pint = 20 fl oz
1 US pint = 16 fl oz
1 litre = 33 fl oz (1 US quart)

Teaspoon, tablespoon and cup measurements are level, not heaped, unless indicated otherwise.

CAKE TIN SIZES

Round	Square	Springform
20cm–8 inches	12.5cm–5 inches	24cm–$9\frac{1}{2}$ inches
22.5cm–9 inches	20cm–8 inches	26cm–$10\frac{1}{2}$ inches
25cm–10 inches	30cm–12 inches	28cm–11 inches

INGREDIENTS CONVERSION GUIDE

Australia	Britain	US
baking powder	baking powder	baking soda
cream (35% fat)	single cream	light cream
thick cream (45% fat)	double cream	heavy cream
cornflour	cornflour	cornstarch
minced beef	minced beef	ground beef
plain flour	plain flour	all purpose flour
self-raising flour	self-raising flour	NA
prawns	prawns	shrimp
stock cube	stock cube	bouillon cube
castor sugar	castor sugar	superfine sugar
icing sugar	icing sugar	confectioner's sugar
tomato paste	tomato purée	tomato paste
punnet	punnet	tub
tasty cheese	cheddar	cheddar or jack cheese
sultanas	sultanas	seedless white raisins
eggplant	aubergine	eggplant
capsicum	capsicum	bell pepper
grill	grill	broil
rockmelon	rockmelon	cantaloupe
chicken Maryland	joined leg and thigh	joined leg and thigh

TEMPERATURE CONVERSION

°C

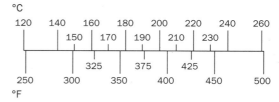

°F

TEMPERATURE DESCRIPTION – °C EQUIVALENT

	Gas	Electricity
Moderately slow	160	170
Moderate	180	200
Moderately hot	190	220
Hot	200	230
Very hot	230	250

GENERAL INDEX

A

Adlerstein, Marion von 207, 219, 229
Alcock, Margaret 148–9
Amatyakul, Chalie 201, 202, 203, 204
Arbelot, Evelyn 198
Armstrong, Mark 183, 184
Arnott, Bruce 79
Arnott, Mrs J.M. 53–4
Arnott, Sheila 26, 79
Ayrton, Mary Ellen 168

B

Bacon, Quentin 172
Bailey, Lee 55
Barton, Gordon 168
Bateman, Florence 51, 54
Bellette, Jean 87
Bendroit, Jim 92
Birley, Andrew 231, 232
Bocuse, Paul 98, 146, 201
Bragg family 44
Bray, Dr 49, 79
Bretherau, Thierry 197–8, 199
Britten, Philip 217, 218
Bugialli, Giuliano 142
Bull, Peggy 149
Buttrose, Charles 165
Buttrose, Ita 165–6, 168

C

Campbell, Joan
    acting 24, 25, 99
    American influence 18, 151, 153
    balls 88, 89–90, 149, 151
    catering 54, 123–4, 127, 128, 130–1, 141–2, 144–5, 146, 147, 148–51, 157, 166
    cook books 54, 127, 179, 216
    cooking classes 34, 36, 54, 97–9, 183
    cooking disasters 90, 99, 136, 150
    daughter Carolyn 49, 55, 84, 92, 94
    daughter Sue 49, 64, 75, 87, 88, 92, 94, 99, 130, 132, 142, 168
    etiquette 24
    father 1, 3, 4, 15, 17, 23, 26, 27, 31, 32, 33, 37, 39, 41
    grandmother Grigor 4
    grandmother Perry 1, 3
    magazines 163, 165–6, 168, 169, 170, 174, 178–9, 183

    mother 'Gar' 3, 4, 11, 15, 23–4, 25, 26, 27, 30, 31, 32, 33, 37, 41, 42, 54, 130
    picnics 84, 87
    schooldays 5, 24, 25, 28
    son Michael 49, 55, 92, 94
Campbell, Lindsay 44, 123–4, 151, 165, 166, 169, 173, 211, 229
Carroll, Sheila and Matt 87–8
Cawley, Richard 213
Charles, HRH Prince 145
Chouet, Dany 142, 143
Clerici, Tony 93
Cook, Michael 172–3, 174, 197, 198
Coolah 26, 49, 55
Coombes, Penny 97
Cox, Julie 44

D

de Cossé Brissac, Lisa 224
Dobell, Bill (Sir William) 88
Dobell, Gladys 17, 18, 21, 22, 23, 54, 70, 153
Doyle, Greg 183, 185, 186
Durdin, Peggy 153–4, 155, 156
Durdin, Tillman 153, 154

E

Ender, Val 149
England 208–22
Evans, Len 120

F

Fairfax, (Lady) Mary 132
Fairlie Cuninghame, Sue (Joan's daughter) 49, 64, 75, 87, 88, 92, 94, 99, 130, 132, 144, 168
Forell, Claude 199
France 221–9
Franks, Belinda 130, 169, 172
Fraser, Malcolm and Tamie 146

G

Gault, Henri 201, 226
Guérard, Michel 110, 146, 147, 148
Guinness, Consuelo 46, 47, 123–4, 127, 130, 141
Guinness, Perry 123–4, 145
Gygax, Carole 152

H

Heath, Di 142
Haefliger, Paul 87, 88

Hong Kong 204–7
Hotel Australia 89, 94
Howard, Peter 228

I

Irwin, William Wallace 179
Italy 229–37

J

'Joan's Sloanes' 146, 208
Johnson, Simon 157, 158, 188
Jones, Howard 172

K

Kerr, Holly 151

L

Lamb, Douglas 87
Laws, John and Caroline 174
Leser, Bernard 219
Little, Alastair 208, 209
Lockhart, Carolyn 168, 170, 172
London 208–9, 210–20
Lung, Geoffrey 172
Lusso, Adrienne 175
Lyneham, Sharyn Storrier 178

M

Mackay family 44
Mark, Willie 204
Martin, 'Uncle' Chad 84
Martin, Pat 149
McCallum, June 168, 172, 188, 197, 219
McKay, Kirsten 210, 211
McKittrick, Carolyn (Joan's daughter) 49, 55, 84, 92, 94
McNicoll, David 25
Meier, Peter 99, 120
Miegunyah 3
Moloney, Ted 124, 125, 126, 129
Moses family 44
Mosimann, Anton 9
Munroe family 44

N

Narrow Neck 33, 37
Newstead Park 4

O

O'Brien, Sally 149

Ousbäck, Anders 151, 187, 210, 231

P
Packer, Frank 92, 166
Pagan, Marjorie 141
Paris 223–9
Pavarotti, Luciano 142, 143
Pearl Beach 44
Perry, Leah 26
Perry, Neil 131, 157, 158, 226
Peter Pan Committee 132
Plisetskaya (Mayo) 144
Polese, Beppi 93
Priestley, Mona 149
Prince's restaurant 92

R
Reymond, Jacques 208
Ripe, Cherry 233
Romano's restaurant 92, 93
Rome 231–2
Russell, Patrick 172

S
Saw, Ellie 75
Schauer, Amy 12
Schmaeling, Tony 172
Schofield, Leo 98, 149, 150, 188, 211

Seper, George 172
Sherman, Millie 95, 142
Sieg, Grace M. 153
Singapore 207–8
Soles, Percy 62
Southport 31, 33, 37, 43
Stone-Herbert, Leigh 220, 221, 222
Surfers Paradise 3, 4, 31, 37, 42–3, 99, 153
Sutherland, Dame Joan 142
Svetcoff, Ivan 62

T
Tahiti 197–9
Talbragar 49–50, 51, 53–4, 55, 56, 57, 62–3, 71, 79
Taylor, Jim 145, 149
Terrigal 43–4
Thailand 199–204
Thompson family 44
Thompson, Rosemary 84, 86
Thornton, Wallace 87, 88, 89
Thumbergier, Mrs 45
Tinslay, Petrina 172
Tuscany 233–7

V
Venice 229–31
Vine, Nanny 3, 23–4

W
Wagstaff, Molly 149
Weidland, Rodney 172, 174, 207
'White Ladies' 149
White, Henry 26, 43, 49–50, 51, 55, 79, 90, 92
White, Hunter 49, 50, 55
White, Michael (Joan's son) 49, 55, 92, 93
Whitlam, Gough and Margaret 50, 157
Wilson, Charles 25
Wilson, Hamley 25
Wilson, John 45
Woodward Fisher, Emma 146, 208
Wunderlich, Danielle 87
Wynne, David 128

Y
Yeomans, Patricia 144, 157

Z
Zalapa, Carlos 124

INDEX OF RECIPES

A

Aberdeen Sausage 87
Aïoli 36
Alaphia's Chocolate Cake 217
Algerian Potatoes with Olive Oil 191–2
Alastair Little's Baby Beets and Spring Onions Stewed in Cream 209–10
Almond Cake with Chocolate Icing 27–8
almonds
   apricot torte 133
   burnt almond biscuits 30
   and chicken 89
   nut wafers 84
American Crab Cakes 40
anchovies
   with braised beef 165
   vitello tonnato 175–6
Anders Ousbäck's Roasted Garlic with Goat's Milk Feta 187
Andrew Birley's Barbecued Swordfish Steaks with Baked Yellow Capsicum 232
Angel's Food 2–3
Angel Food Cake 20–1
Angels on Horseback 2
apple
   sauce 109, 110
   tarts 82
Apple Charlotte 68
Apple Crumble 67
Apple Granita 229
Apricot Almond Torte 133
apricot and prune stuffing 160
Apricot Chutney 52–3
Armenian Lamb 176–7
artichokes
   Provençale-style Jerusalem 63
   stuffed 104
Asian Mussels 189
Asparagus with Hard-boiled Egg Sauce 63
Aunt Elsie Grigor's Frangipani Cake 85–6
Australian Fish Stew 33–4, 35

B

Baby Cheese Scones 6
Baked Fish 32
Baked Ham 20
Baked Roly Poly with Boiled Custard 6–7
Balls of Minced Pork in Golden Threads 202
bananas, caramel 10
Barley Broth 5
Basic Crêpe Recipe 99–100

Basic Orange Cake 95
basil and fennel bavarois 226
Bean and Mushroom Salad 101
bean sprouts
   and prawn salad 167
Beans and Tuna 236
beans with cream 101–2
béarnaise sauce 124, 125
béchamel sauce 44–45
beef
   Aberdeen sausage 87
   bourguignonne 156
   braised with anchovies 165
   carpaccio 230, 231
   devilled steak 5–6
   fillet with béarnaise sauce 124–5
   oxtail 59–60
   pasta sauce 152
   and pig's cheek brawn 12–13
   slow-cooked brisket 55
   steak diane 93
   steak and kidney pie 57–8
   topside roast 108–9
Beef Stroganoff 125–6
beetroot and spring onions stewed in cream 209–10
Belgian Shortbread 28
beurre blanc 114, 115
biscuits
   burnt almond 30
   chocolate walnut 28
   clifford 29
   coconut 29
   ginger 82–3
   Mrs Baxter's 29
   nut wafers 84
   pecan 83
   pecan wafers 83
   shortbread 28
Blakes Blinis 220
Blowaway Ginger Sponge 54
Boeuf Bourguignonne 156
Boiled Leg of Lamb and Caper Sauce 13
brains
   crumbed 76
   pâté 75–6
Braised Beef with Anchovies 165
Braised Fennel or Leeks 103
brawn, pig's cheek and veal or beef 12–13
bread
   garlic toast 60, 61
   rouille 36
   sauce 15
Bread and Butter Pudding 9
bugs, scallops and prawns with vermouth and prawn butter sauce 115–16
Burgundian Oxtail 59–60
Burnt Almond Biscuits 30

Bush Cake with Whisky Icing 84–5
Butter Pecan Ice-cream 141

C

cabbage, creamy 132
cakes (savoury)
   corn 19
   crab 40
cakes (sweet)
   almond with chocolate icing 27–8
   angel food 20–1
   bush, with whisky icing 84–5
   butter sponge 23, 25
   Christmas 74–5
   chocolate 217
   chocolate and raspberry 143–4
   frangipani 85–6
   ginger sponge 54
   Glad's yum yum 22
   lamingtons 79–80
   light fruit 96
   orange 95
   pavé au chocolat 134–5
   pineapple upside-down 23
   pound 95–6
   sand 27
calamari
   seafood salad 234–5
   stewed with peas 195
Cape Gooseberry Jelly 16
caper sauce 13
caponata 105
capsicums
   baked 232
   caponata 105
   ratatouille 102–3
Caramel Bananas 10
Caramel Ice-cream 139
Caramel Oranges 118
Caramel Pears 164
Caramelised Figs 66
Carolyn's Nut Wafer Biscuits 84
carpaccio 230, 231
Carrots, Parsnips and Onions 103
caviar tarts 131–2
Celeriac and Celery Salad with Parmesan Cheese 235
celery
   sauce 91–2
   Sicilian caponata 105
cheese
   casserole 151–2
   goat's cheese mousseline 210–11
   goat's milk feta with garlic 187
   parmesan with celeriac and celery salad 235
   scones 6
Cherries Jubilee 66–7
cherries with veal 65

chicken
    curry 193
    with lemon mayonnaise 145
    pink 128–9
    roasted 14–15
    salad 170
    sautéed breasts with foie gras
        sauce 112
    Southern fried 18–19
    spiced legs 164
    stock 126
    volaille au vinaigre 111–12
Chicken and Almonds 89
Chicken Kiev 92
Chicken Liver Parfait with Green
    Peppercorns 221
Chicken Pie 61–2
Chicken Salad 129–30
Chicken Satays with Panaeng Sauce
    202–3
chickpeas
    and pine nuts with couscous 192
    soup 237
chilli sauce 200
chive butter 221–2
chocolate
    cake 22, 217
    cream 143, 144
    icing 22, 27–8, 79–80,81
    pavé au chocolat 134–5
Chocolate and Raspberry Cake
    143–4
Chocolate Marquise 146–7
Chocolate Rice Pudding 70
Chocolate Torte 134
Chocolate Walnut Biscuits 28
Christmas Cake 74–5
Christmas Turkey with Walnut and
    Raisin Stuffing 71–2
chutney
    apricot 52–3
    green tomato 51–2
    mango 11
    tomato relish 51
Cipriani Pasta 230–1
Clairfontaine 198–9
Clifford Biscuits 29
Coconut Biscuits 29
Coffee and Pecan Nut Ice-cream
    138
Coffee Bean Sauce 147
Coffin Bay Scallops with Tomato
    Salsa 193–4
Cold Lemon Chicken Breasts 145
Consuelo's Ceviche 46–7
Consuelo's Escabeche of Snapper
    47
corn cakes 19
Corner of Topside Roast 108–9
Couscous with Chickpeas and Pine
    Nuts 192
crab
    cakes 40
    Cipriani pasta 230–1
    curried 206
    mud crabs 37, 39
    salad with truffle mayonnaise
        184

Creamy Rice Pudding 10
Crème Brûlée 69–70
Crème Caramel 119
Crème Glacée a la Sarrasine 140
Crème Renversée with Cumquats
    119–20
crêpes, with spinach filling 99–100
Crumbed Brains 76
cucumber
    chilli marinated 190
    spicy sauce 202
cumquats with crème renversée
    119
Currant Tart 67–8
curry
    chicken 193
    fish-head 207–8
    Thai steamed seafood 41
Curry Crab from Macau 206
custards
    baked, with Cointreau 205, 206
    baked caramel 3
    boiled 6–7
    crème brulée 69–70
    crème caramel 119

D
Damien Pignolet's Buttery
    Shortcrust 120–1
Date Torte 133
dates
    fresh, with lamb tagine 192
    sticky toffee pudding 186–7
desserts
    baked roly poly with boiled custard
        6–7
    chocolate marquise 146–7
    clairfontaine 198–9
    crème glacée à la sarrasine 140
    crème renversée with cumquats
        119–20
    lemon meringue pie 20–1
    pudim flan 205–6
    tapioca cream 50
    see also custards; ice-cream;
        individual fruits; meringue;
        mousse; puddings; souffles; tarts
        (sweet); tortes
Devilled Steak 5–6
duck liver and small greens salad
    (warm) 166–7
Duck Liver Terrine 110–11
Duck Salad 191
Duck with Oranges 181–2

E
Easy Steak and Kidney Pie 57–8
Eggplant with Fried Zucchini 234
eggs
    à la chatelaine 162
    hard-boiled egg sauce 63
    sauce 32
    son-in-law 201
Ellie Saw's Brain Pâté 75–6

F
Fabulous Cheese Casserole 151–2
fennel
    and basil bavarois 226
    braised 103
    and mushroom 235
Fennel Niçoise 64–5
Fennel Soup 181
Fernand Point's Pavé au Chocolat
    134–5
Fettuccine with a Sauce of Sun-Dried
    Tomatoes, Cream and Prawns
    194–5
Fiery Sauce 56
Fig Jam 53
figs, caramelised 66
Filet d'Agneau à la Crème de
    Ciboulette 106
Fillet of Beef with Béarnaise Sauce
    124–5
fish
    baked 32
    baked swordfish with capsicum
        232
    ceviche 46–7
    escabeche of snapper 47
    fresh cod with vegetables and
        herbs 227–8
    fried 33
    fried whole in chilli sauce 200–1
    gravlax 45–6
    machi dahiwala 215–16
    ocean trout with Moroccan spices
        189–90
    poached with egg sauce 32
    poached whiting with lobster and
        chive butter 221–2
    smoked with lentil salad 148
    smoked salmon with blinis 220
    stew 33–4, 35
    see also tuna
Fish Pie 33
Fish Stock 34
Fish with Beurre Blanc 114
Fish-Head Curry 207–8
flan, pudim 205–6
flummery, pineapple 16
foie gras sauce 112
fondant, basic recipe 30
French Onion Soup 126–7
Fresh Codfish with Aromatic
    Vegetables and Herbs 227–8
Fresh Green Pea Soup 100–1
Fricassee of Scallops 209
Fried Fish 33
Fried Whole Fish in Chilli Sauce
    200–1
fruit
    flambéed 120
    summer pudding 212–13
    see also individual fruits

G
Gar's Buttered Oysters on Toast 42
garlic
    aïoli 36

roasted with goat's milk feta 187
rouille 36
sauce 107
toast 60, 61
ginger
    fondant 30
    green, with quail 213–14
    sponge 54
Ginger Biscuits 82–3
gingered beef tongue 77–8
Gingered Pink Prawns 39
Giuliano Bugialli's Stuffed Peaches
    142–3
Glad's Yum Yum Cake 22
Goat's Cheese Mousseline 210–11
golden syrup steamed pudding
    69–70
Grandmother Perry's Baked Caramel
    Custard 3
granita, apple 229
Grapefruit Jam 12
grapes and lime with quail 113
gravy, milk 18, 19
Green Beans with Cream 101–2
Green Tomato Chutney 51–2
Green Tomato Jam 52
Greg Doyle's Cream of Scallop Soup
    with Spring Vegetables 185–6
Grilled Lobster Halves with Whisky
    Butter Sauce 223–4

H
ham, baked 20
Hard Sauce 74
Honey Ice-cream 137
Hot Strawberry Soufflés 117–18

I
ice-cream
    apple granita 229
    butter pecan 141
    caramel 139
    coffee and pecan nut 138
    crème glacée à la Sarrasine 140
    honey 137
    orange 138
    peach 137
    strawberry 139
    vanilla bean 57
icing
    chocolate 22, 27–8, 79–80, 81
    lemon 27
    orange 95
    strawberry 20, 21
    vanilla 80, 81
    whisky 85
Italian Chickpea Soup 237

J
jam
    fig 53
    grapefruit 12
    green tomato 52
    rosella 11–12
    tomato 52

jelly, Cape gooseberry 16
Julie Cox's Pearl Beach Pâté 44–5

K
kidneys
    steak and kidney pie 57–8
    veal, with madeira 78

L
lamb
    Armenian 176–7
    boiled with caper sauce 13
    filet à la crème de ciboulette 106
    in salt crust with lamb essence
        sauce 171–2
    navarin 60–1
    noisettes on onion soubise
        177–8
    tian d'agneau Niçoise 107–8
Lamb Loins with Garlic Sauce
    106–7
Lamb Tagine with Fresh Dates 192
Lamingtons 79–80
Lasagne Imbottite 152–3
leeks
    braised 103
    and truffle tarts 158
Leg of Lamb in a Salt Crust with
    Lamb Essence Sauce 171–2
lemon
    butter 135, 136
    cheese 82
    and grapes with quail 113
    icing 27
    meringue pie 20–1
    tart 218
Lemon Cheese Tarts 81–2
Lemon Mayonnaise 146
Lemon Mousse 17
Lemon Rice 216
Lemon Syrup 53
lentil salad 148
Leo Schofield's Tomato Salad 150
Light Fruit Cake 96
lime and grapes with quail 113
Lisa de Cossé Brissac's Amaretto
    Peaches 224–5
lobster
    and poached whiting with chive
        butter 221–2
    and vegetable terrine 168–9
    with whisky butter sauce 223,
        224
Lygon Arms Sticky Toffee Pudding
    186–7

M
Machi Dahiwala 215–16
Malaysian Chicken Curry 193
Mark Armstrong's Crab Salad with
    Truffle Mayonnaise 184
mayonnaise
    truffle 159, 184
    lemon 146
meringue

with lemon butter 135–6
    lemon meringue pie 20–1
    passionfruit snow eggs 161
mint butter 177, 178
Miss Amy Schauer's Good Pig's
    Cheek and Veal or Beef Brawn
    12–13
mousse
    lemon 17
    peach 224–5
    strawberry 117
mousselines, goat's cheese
    210–11
Mrs Baxter's Biscuits 29
Mrs Dobell's Lemon Meringue Pie
    21–2
Mrs Dobell's Pineapple Upside-Down
    Cake 23
Mrs Dobell's Southern Fried Chicken
    with Milk Gravy and Corn Cakes
    18–19
Mrs Thumbergier's Gravlax 45–6
mud crabs 37, 39
mushroom
    and bean salad 101
    ragout 179–80
Mushroom and Fennel 235
mussels
    Asian 189
    seafood salad 234–5
My Mother's Oyster Cocktail Sauce
    42
My Mother's Plain Butter Sponge 25
My Mother's Rose, Ginger,
    Peppermint and Coffee Fondants
    30

N
Navarin of Lamb 60–1
Neenish Tarts 80–1
Neil Perry's Caviar Tarts 131–2
Noisettes of Lamb Served on Onion
    Soubise with Melting Mint Butter
    177–8

O
Ocean Trout with Moroccan Spices
    189–90
Oeufs à la Chatelaine 162
Olive, Crème Fraîche and Thyme Tart
    214–15
onions
    caponata 105
    with carrots and parsnips 103
    French onion soup 126–7
    ratatouille 102–3
    soubise 177, 178
orange
    cake 95
    caramel 118
    with duck 181–2
    icing 95
Orange Ice-cream 138
Oven Potatoes 103
Oyster Soup 42
oysters

angels on horseback 2
  buttered on toast 42
  cocktail sauce 42
Oysters with Beurre Blanc and
  Julienne of Mixed Vegetables 115

P

Paillard alla Milanese 109
Panaeng sauce 203
parsnips, carrots and onions 103
Passionfruit Snow Eggs 161
pasta
  Cipriani's 230–1
  fettuccine with sun-dried tomato,
    cream and prawn sauce 194–5
  lasagne imbottite 152–3
pastry
  pasta frolla 214–15
  pie 20
  shortcrust 120–1
  sweet 218
  tarts 80, 81–2, 131
pâté
  brain 75–6
  chicken liver 86
  Pearl Beach 44–5
Peach Dumpling 70–1
Peach Ice-cream 137
peaches
  Amaretto mousse 224–5
  pickled 10–11
  poached 136
  stuffed 142–3
pears, caramel 164
peas, green
  piselli 104
  soup 100–1
  with stewed calamari 195
pecan
  and coffee ice-cream 138
  ice-cream 141
Pecan Biscuits 83
Pecan Wafers 83
Peggy Durdin's Chinese Mixed
  Vegetables 155
Peggy Durdin's Chinese-Style Thrice-
  cooked Pork 154
peppermint fondant 30
Peter Meier's Flambéed Fruits 120
Peter Rowland's Vegetable Tarts
  219
Philip Britten's Lemon Tart 218
Pickled Peaches 10–11
pies (savoury)
  chicken 61–2
  fish 33
  steak and kidney 57–8
pies (sweet)
  lemon meringue 20–1
pilaf 177
pine nuts and chickpeas with
  couscous 192
Pineapple Flummery 16
Pineapple Rice Pudding 165
pineapple upside-down cake 23
Pink Chicken 128–9
Pipi Soup 43

Piselli 104
Plum Pudding 73–4
Poached Fillets of Whiting on
  Noodles with Lobster and Chive
  Butter 221–2
Poached Fish with Egg Sauce 32
Poached Peaches 136
pork
  balls in golden threads 202
  Chinese-style thrice-cooked 154
  stuffed with apricots and prunes
    160–1
Pork Neck with Apple Sauce and
  Potatoes 109–10
Potato Purée 228
potatoes
  with olive oil 191–2
  oven cooked 103
  with pork neck and apple sauce
    109–10
  and truffle salad 159
Prawn and Bean Sprout Salad 167
Prawn Bisque 37–8
Prawn Cocktail 93
Prawn Risotto 182
Prawn Rolls 203–4
Prawn Soup 36–7
prawns
  butter 115, 116
  gingered pink 39
  scallops and bugs with vermouth
    and prawn butter sauce 115–16
  seafood salad 234–5
  sun-dried tomatoes and cream
    sauce 194–5
  Thai salad 38
Prawns with Mustard 158–9
Provençale-style Jerusalem
  Artichokes 63
prune and apricot stuffing 160
puddings
  bread and butter 9
  chocolate rice 70
  creamy rice 10
  pineapple rice 165
  plum 73–4
  rice 183
  sago plum 7–8
  steamed golden syrup 69
  sticky toffee 186–7
  summer 212–13
  tapioca cream 50
Pudim Flan 205–6

Q

Quail Salad with Soy and Chilli
  Marinated Cucumber 190
quail with green ginger 213–14
Quail with Lime or Lemon and
  Grapes 113
Queen's Soufflé 8–9
Queen Victoria's Favourite Rice
  Pudding 183
Quiche Lorraine 127–8

R

ragout, mushroom 179–80

raspberry
  and chocolate cake 143–4
  summer pudding 212–13
Ratatouille 102–3
rémoulade, tomato 40
rice
  chocolate rice pudding 70
  lemon 216
  pineapple rice pudding 165
  prawn risotto 182
  pudding 10, 183
Rice Pilaf 177
Richard Cawley's Quail with Green
  Ginger 213–14
risotto, prawn 182
Rolled Turkey Breast 113–14
Rosella Jam 11–12
Rosemary Thompson's Chicken Liver
  Pâté 86
Rouille 36

S

Sago Plum Pudding 7–8
salads
  bean and mushroom 101
  celeriac and celery 235
  chicken 129–30, 170
  crab 184
  duck 191
  lentil 148
  prawn and bean sprout 167
  quail 190
  seafood 234–5
  small greens and duck liver
    (warm) 166–7
  Thai prawn 38
  Thai seafood 188
  tomato 150
  truffle and potato 159
Salami with Juniper Berries 236
salsa, tomato 194
Sand Cake 27
sandwiches, truffle 157–8
satays, chicken 202–3
sauces (savoury)
  béarnaise 124, 125
  béchemel 44, 45
  beurre blanc 114, 115
  bread 15
  caper 13
  celery 91–2
  chilli 200
  chive butter 221, 222
  ciboulette 106
  egg 32
  fiery 56
  foie gras 112
  garlic 107
  hard 74
  hard-boiled egg 63
  lamb essence 171
  oyster cocktail 42
  panaeng 203
  prawn butter 115, 116
  spicy cucumber 202
  sun-dried tomato, cream and
    prawns 194–5

tomato 77, 168, 169
tomato rémoulade 40
vinaigrette 88
whisky butter 223
sauces (sweet)
apple 109, 110
coffee bean 147
Sautéed Chicken Breasts with a Foie
Gras Sauce 112
scallops
Cipriani pasta 230–1
cream soup with spring vegetables
185–6
fricassee 209
seafood salad 234–5
seared on creamy cabbage 132
with tomato salsa 193–4
Scallops, Prawns and Bugs with
Vermouth and Prawn Butter Sauce
115–16
scones, cheese 6
seafood
Asian mussels 189
caviar tarts 131–2
Cipriani pasta 230–1
pipi soup 43
stewed calamari with peas 195
Thai salad 188
Thai steamed seafood curry 41
see also calamari; crab; fish;
lobster; oysters; prawns; scallops
Seafood Salad 234–5
Seared Scallops on Creamy Cabbage
132
Sheila Carroll's Vinaigrette 88
shortbread 28
Sicilian Caponata 105
Slow-Cooked Brisket 55
Small Meringues with Lemon Butter
135–6
Smoked Fish with Michel Guerard's
Lentil Salad 148
Son-in-Law Eggs 201
soufflés
hot strawberry 117–18
queen's 8–9
sweet potato 72–3
soup
barley broth 5
chickpea 237
cream of scallop with spring
vegetables 185–6
fennel 181
French onion 126–7
fresh green pea 100–1
oyster 42
pipi 43
prawn 36–7
prawn bisque 37–8
summer tomato 127
tomato 226
spice paste 41
Spiced Chicken Legs 164
Spicy Cucumber Sauce 202
Spinach Filling for Crêpes 100
spring onions and baby beets
stewed in cream 209–10

Steak Diane 93
Steamed Golden Syrup Pudding 69
Stewed Calamari with Peas 195
strawberries
hot soufflé 117–18
icing 20, 21
summer pudding 212–13
Strawberry Ice-cream 139
Strawberry Mousse 117
Stuffed Artichokes 104
Stuffed Loin of Pork with Apricots
and Prunes 160–1
Sue's Baked Tomatoes 64
Summer Pudding 212–13
Summer Tomato Soup, adapted from
Robert Carrier 127
Sunday Roast Chicken with Bread
Sauce and Gravy 14–15
Sweet Potato Soufflé 72–3
Sweet Potato Timbales 102

T
Tapioca Cream 50
Tartlets with Mushroom Ragout
179–80
tarts (savoury)
cases 131
caviar 131–2
olive, crème fraîche and thyme
214–15
seared scallops on creamy
cabbage 132
truffle and leek 158
vegetable 219
tarts (sweet)
apple 82
cases 80, 81
currant 67–8
lemon 218
lemon cheese 81–2
neenish 80–1
Terrine of Little Vegetables with
Lobster 168–9
terrine, duck liver 110–11
Thai Prawn Salad 38
Thai Seafood Salad 188
Thai Steamed Seafood Curry 41
Tian d'Agneau Niçoise 107–8
Tiny Tarts 131
Tomato Jam 52
Tomato Relish 51
Tomato Rémoulade 40
Tomato Soup with Fennel and Basil
Bavarois 226
tomatoes
baked 64
green tomato chutney 51–2
green tomato jam 52
ratatouille 102–3
salad 150
sauce 77, 180–1, 194
summer soup 127
sundried tomatoes, cream and
prawn sauce 194–5
tongue, gingered beef 77–8

Tonno con Salsa di Pomodoro
180–1
tortes
apricot almond 133
chocolate 134
date 133
Trippa alla Romana 76–7
Truffle and Leek Tarts 158
Truffle and Potato Salad 159
truffle mayonnaise 159, 184
Truffle Sandwiches 157–8
tuna
and beans 236
con salsa di pomodoro 180–1
vitello tonnato 175–6
turkey
boiled 90–2
rolled breast 113–14
with walnut and raisin stuffing
71–2

V
Vanilla Bavarois 173
Vanilla Bean Ice-cream 57
vanilla icing 80
veal
paillard alla Milanese 109
and pig's cheek brawn 12–13
vitello tonnato 175–6
Veal Kidneys with Madeira 78
Veal with Cherries 65
vegetables
Chinese mixed 155
with cream of scallop soup
185–6
and herbs with fresh cod 227–8
julienne with oysters and beurre
blanc 115
and lobster terrine 168–9
ratatouille 102–3
tarts 219
see also individual vegetables
Victorian Boiled Turkey 90–2
vinaigrette 88
Vitello Tonnato 175–6
Vogue Boardroom Chicken Salad
170
Volaille au Vinaigre 111–12

W
walnut
and chocolate biscuits 28
and raisin stuffing 71–2
Warm Salad of Small Greens and
Duck Liver 166–7
Washington Currant Pound Cake
95–6
whisky butter sauce 223

Z
zucchini
fried with eggplant 234
ratatouille 102–3